STRATEGIC
HEALTH MANAGEMENT

JEFFREY S. HARRIS, M.D., M.B.A.

STRATEGIC
HEALTH MANAGEMENT

A Guide for Employers, Employees, and Policy Makers

Jossey-Bass Publishers · San Francisco

Substantial discounts on bulk quantities of Jossey-Bass books are available to corporations, professional associations, and other organizations. For details and discount information, contact the special sales department at Jossey-Bass Inc., Publishers. (415) 433-1740; Fax (415) 433-0499.

For sales outside the United States, contact Maxwell Macmillan International Publishing Group, 866 Third Avenue, New York, New York 10022.

Manufactured in the United States of America. Nearly all Jossey-Bass books and jackets are printed on recycled paper that contains at least 50 percent recycled waste, including 10 percent postconsumer waste. Many of our materials are also printed with vegetable-based ink; during the printing process these inks emit fewer volatile organic compounds (VOCs) than petroleum-based inks. VOCs contribute to the formation of smog.

Library of Congress Cataloging-in-Publication Data

Harris, Jeffrey S.
   Strategic health management : a guide for employers, employees, and policy makers / Jeffrey S. Harris.
     p. cm. — (A joint publication in the Jossey-Bass health series and the Jossey-Bass management series)
   Includes bibliographical references and index.
   ISBN 1-55542-655-7
   1. Medical care — United States.   2. Medical policy — United States.
3. Insurance, Health — United States.   I. Title.   II. Series: Jossey-Bass health series.   III. Series: Jossey-Bass management series.
RA395.A3H378   1994
362.1'0973 — dc20   93-47964
                                                          CIP

FIRST EDITION
HB Printing   10 9 8 7 6 5 4 3 2 1   *Code 9450*

A JOINT PUBLICATION IN

The Jossey-Bass
Health Series

AND

The Jossey-Bass
Management Series

Contents

ix

Figures and Tables

Figures

Tables

Preface

As most Americans are aware of by now, the medical care industry accounted for over 14 percent of the gross domestic product in 1993, and the share increases each year. Government expenditures on medical care have climbed each year since 1966 as well. Devoting a certain percentage of a country's output to a specific sector may or may not be an issue. But there are bound to be effects on the rest of the economy.

By some estimates, employers' expenditures for medical care now equal their collective profits and may erase them in the next few decades. The use of funds for medical care may affect jobs; wage levels; international, interregional, or interemployer competitiveness; and the ability to maintain our infrastructure and educate our children. However, there is a rising demand for medical care insurance as the prices of medical services become so high that they threaten families' financial stability.

Through their benefits programs, employers fund the majority of medical care for the under-sixty-five population of the United States. However, employees' satisfaction with these benefits, which were initially offered as ways of competing for valued employees in the labor market and bonding employees to the organization, has dropped significantly in the last few years. A key satisfier is in danger of becoming a double-headed dissatisfier: a negative if retained and a greater negative if cut back.

Many American employers are still reacting to their suppliers of care rather than proactively managing this large, growing, sensitive, and politically charged purchase. Why have employers not taken charge of this massive flow of funds? Possible answers range from financial to human resource to strategic issues, including the following:

- Lack of economic power relative to suppliers in the medical care industry
- The large number of suppliers they must deal with
- A desire to avoid negative employee feedback when payment is not made for unnecessary or uncovered expenses
- Lack of understanding of the dynamics of the medical industry, the precursors of illness and injury, and the demand for services
- A hope that the government will solve the problem or take the blame for necessary changes or cutbacks
- Lack of a long-range, effective strategic plan for managing *health,* as opposed to short-term efforts to contain costs

As more and more funds are transferred to the medical sector, employers, employees, and policy makers are finally asking questions that need to be asked about both the quality and the value of medical (not to be confused with health) care: Are the prices they are paying fair? Are medical procedures appropriate and necessary? What are the alternatives? Is expensive care of acute and chronic illnesses more cost effective than preventing those illnesses and injuries? Is expensive palliative care of the terminally ill worth more than ensuring that children are healthy? Are wages being held down because of the costs of medical benefits?

Background of This Book

My twenty-year involvement with the development of medical delivery systems and decade-long efforts to document, understand, and manage health and medical care costs on behalf of employers have convinced me that while medical care *is* different, it can be managed like any other business expenditure if the right perspectives, strategies, and tools are applied. Furthermore, many medical expenditures can be prevented with the right focus and tactics for wise use, self-care, disease prevention, and health promotion. The strategic approach has simply not been effectively or comprehensively applied by enough purchasers (or providers) to make a discernible difference in the overall curve.

It is true that health promotion and medical care are relatively complex, requiring a number of skills to effectively orchestrate and deliver them. Yet many employers still use people from a single discipline to attempt to analyze data, administer the benefits program, design strategy, and manage vendors. Multidisciplinary teams have been quite effective in understanding and managing health and medical care. It is hard to do otherwise. But this cross-disciplinary approach requires a knowledge of all the perspectives and skills — another reason to write this book.

Need for This Book

The argument can be made that employers are not in the business of managing or providing medical care: that is not their core business. This argument is true, but unless active steps are taken to manage price, volume, quality, and technology and product mix, the cost curve that has existed for the last twenty years and that is approaching the hyperbolic will continue to soar. Medical care costs have reached center stage, and a new approach to their management is needed now.

Strategic Health Management: A Guide for Employers, Employees, and Policy Makers explains that approach from a perspective synthesizing medical, human resources, operations management, and political information and skills. Most other books in this area have focused on short-term "cost containment" or have lacked a unifying framework. I would argue that short of a radical and far-reaching political solution, these costs cannot be contained; they must be managed, and managed exceptionally well, to avoid further erosion of wages and profits. Without these two key economic ingredients, there is little reason for business to exist.

As a businessperson and a student of the processes and delivery of health care, it seems to me that strategic management of the financing and provision of medical benefits and health care is long overdue. This longer-range, organization- and environment-wide view would have anticipated and managed the steep rises in costs and the eroding value of these services.

This book attempts to explain and make usable the application of strategic management to the management of health. Strategic health management implies active management or comanagement of medical care. It goes beyond forecasting short-term cost increases and entails working with suppliers to improve the value of care. It will require a considerable amount of knowledge and skill to structure benefits plans that meet the needs of both employees and employers in a reasonable manner. It will also require a larger skill set to negotiate with financing organizations, claims payers, and providers of care about the price, volume, technical intensity, quality, and value of care. It is not clear that the medical industry, with its present management, paradigms, and players, could transform itself in the necessary way to provide more efficient and effective services and care. It will in all likelihood need help, guidance, and, above all, clear definitions of what its customers want. Even so, changing the infrastructure of the medical industry will not deal with consumer education and involvement, prevention of increasingly costly illness and injury, or the human resource issues associated with medical benefits, as long as they are provided through employers.

Purpose and Audience

Accomplishing this comprehensive and yet more effective approach requires a multidisciplinary team empowered by senior management. This book is intended for those senior executives and the entire strategic health management team as a guide to the process and use of the recommended strategies. The strategic health management team might include experts in corporate finance, benefits design, medical care, communications, and organizational effectiveness. Each of these disciplines can make a significant contribution. Finance experts can help in the handling of large amounts of paid or retained funds, and benefits managers can provide information on the probable causes, costs, and effects of benefits plan changes. Medical professionals are necessary to deal directly with utilization management and provider organizations and to analyze data on the type and quality of care being received by employees. Communications practitioners are needed to work with employees about their needs and preferences for coverage and service, and organizational effectiveness consultants are required to facilitate the strategic health management and quality improvement teams. Joint employee and management teams should take a leading role in shaping what can be done with increasingly limited funds for total compensation.

Background on the structure of the medical care system, both from a delivery and a financing standpoint, is presented to provide a common ground and vocabulary for the different members of the team. The perspective this book takes is fundamentally a business one, although informed by considerable prevention, clinical, and medical management experience.

The strategies discussed are synergistic and interlocking. I do not intend employers to select one or two strategies but to use employee involvement and health promotion in combination with a progression of strategies to finance or deliver medical care, alone or in concert with other employers or purchasing organizations. Only with all the pieces in place can the team, or a consortium of teams, achieve the maximum effect.

Overview of the Contents

In the following pages, I describe the strategic health management process in detail, discuss the medical industry and how it developed, look at quality and value, and then outline tested strategies to manage health. Several strategies are needed, ranging from efforts to prevent illness and injury, to modifying demand, to considering a total compensation approach, to contracting with selected providers, to continually improving the value of care paid for.

Strategic Health Management: A Guide for Employers, Employees, and Policy Makers is divided into two parts. The first part describes the current quandary that employers are caught in — financing benefits to bond employees to the organization yet paying for what is becoming a major *dis*satisfier — and the mechanics and incentives of the medical industry that are creating the bind through greatly increasing costs. The second part discusses a series of interlocking strategies that employers would do well to pursue with or without "national health reform," unless it is particularly well thought out, comprehensive, effective, and immediately implemented. The history of American politics makes achievement of that criteria list unlikely in the near term, as much as it is to be hoped for.

Chapter One describes the drivers of cost and value in the medical care industry and the evolution of our longstanding health care crisis. Chapter Two delineates the reasons employers and employees demand medical care financing and further describes the mechanics of the nonsystem/industry, showing the incongruence between the three parties in interest (providers, employers/financers, and employees/end users). Chapter Three explores quality as the basis for comparing the value received for medical care dollars. Chapter Four further describes the various segments of the medical industry, so that purchasers can understand their business dynamics and points of leverage. Chapter Five details the strategic health management process that should be used to map a coherent, long-range strategy for managing employee and dependent health, not just short-term costs.

In Part Two, strategies are outlined to prevent disease, promote health, modify consumer demands, and better manage care as an integrated system for each employer's "microenvironment" of health needs and care. A number of specific strategies are known to be effective to manage health care costs, quality, and value. These include promoting health, preventing injury and disease, value and expectation management, a partnership with employees, intelligent purchasing, possible partnerships with medical care suppliers, and continuous improvement in all aspects of health management.

Chapter Six takes the bull by the horns and discusses what many employers have been waiting for: salvation from Washington that will prevent them from having to solve the health management puzzle. Chapter Seven analyzes the successes and failures of conventional benefits plans. Chapter Eight explores the need for greater employee involvement in designing the options for total compensation and in wiser use of the medical system. Employee partnership is important to manage the growing dissatisfaction with medical benefits. Techniques of involvement range from employee sensing (through surveys and focus groups) in the design phase, to involvement in communication design and testing, to constant feedback about satisfaction with the benefits plans, the providers in the plans, and other health management efforts.

Chapter Nine describes a key component of any *health* management strategy: health promotion and disease prevention. Chapter Ten details the total compensation approach for increasing individual utility, which can increase satisfaction and reduce unnecessary services and insurance. Chapter Eleven characterizes various types of managed care and discusses their effectiveness in regulating costs and quality.

Chapter Twelve outlines a newer strategy for better managing quality and value: contracting directly with a limited number of suppliers and working with them closely and continuously to assure delivery of high-quality contracted services. Supplier partnership is the precursor of continuous improvement in customer service, medical service quality, appropriateness, and health management. Chapter Thirteen takes direct management of health one step further, outlining a strategy for internal organizations or cooperatives that can be used to provide integrated services ranging from wellness programming to rehabilitation. Chapter Fourteen outlines an integrated health management strategy for individual employers or groups of employers and discusses barriers and opportunities for its implementation. Finally, an appendix brings together information on the medical care systems in other major industrialized countries.

Most of the positions and action in the recent debate on "national health care reform" have come from politicians, financing intermediaries, and providers. Many employers have yet to join the debate, remaining curiously quiet about their preferred solutions. Some are quietly moving ahead on their own, others are taking a wait-and-see attitude, and still others have stopped the evolution of their medical benefits programs. The small-business lobby has made it clear that it is not in favor of actions that will increase out-of-pocket labor costs. Powerful interests are mobilizing to ensure that their financial and professional interests are not compromised: in short, that political change will be incremental at best. I therefore see a key role for employers in both the reform process and in managing health for the foreseeable future.

I hope this book will prove useful for employers and employees as they manage their collective health and the costs associated with the current failure of health management. Some elements of the solution are known. Production of the evidence for others can be required contractually or legislatively. The issues are how to implement known solutions and how to start on the road to those we think will work while constantly improving quality of execution.

Acknowledgments

I would like to express my gratitude to my wife, Mary Anderson, an astute health care attorney, for many helpful suggestions as well as for driving while I typed, and to my children — Sarah, Noah, Susannah, Howard, and Dominic — for putting up with this time-consuming and diverting pursuit, even during ball games and visits to the beach.

I thank my colleagues and the members of the Alexander & Alexander Health Care Advisory Council for review of the manuscript and for many helpful suggestions. Michael McGarvey, M.D., managing director of health strategies for the Alexander & Alexander Consulting Group; Armand Bengle III, managing director of Alexander & Alexander Consulting Group's San Francisco office; and James Stark, western division managing director, provided enthusiastic support and helpful critiques. The advisory council includes Alan Hillman, M.D. (associate professor of medicine and health care management, University of Pennsylvania School of Medicine, and director, Center for Health Policy at the Leonard Davis Institute of Health Economics and the Wharton School of Business and School of Medicine, University of Pennsylvania); Harold Luft, Ph.D. (professor of health economics and acting director, Institute for Health Policy Studies, School of Medicine, University of California, San Francisco); Barbara McNeil, M.D. (Ridley Watts Professor and chair of the Department of Health Care Policy, Harvard Medical School); Steven Schoenbaum, M.D. (associate professor of medicine, Harvard Medical School, and medical director, Harvard Community Health Plan of New England); and Donald M. Steinwachs, Ph.D. (professor of health policy and management, School of Hygiene and Public Health, and director of the Health Services Research and Development Center, both at Johns Hopkins University). Harold Luft in particular helped hone the accuracy and perspective of the project, despite the untimely demise of his red pen halfway through the manuscript.

Special thanks go to Rebecca McGovern, editor of the Jossey-Bass health series, for her patience, sage advice, listening skills, and support. Thanks also to Xenia Lisanevich and the others who worked on the manuscript in production. Any remaining errors and omissions are my responsibility, and the point of view of the book is my own.

San Francisco, California   Jeffrey S. Harris
February 1994

The Author

Jeffrey S. Harris is western regional practice leader for health strategies at Alexander & Alexander Consulting Group (A&ACG) in San Francisco and president of Harris Associates in Mill Valley, California. He received his B.S. degree (1971) in molecular biochemistry and biophysics at Yale University, his M.D. degree (1975) at the University of New Mexico in Albuquerque, his M.P.H. degree (1982) in medical care organization at the University of Michigan, and his Executive M.B.A. degree (1988) in general management at Vanderbilt University, where he received the Dean's Award for Academic Excellence.

Harris's career interests have focused on the efficient and effective delivery of community and population-based health care, the prevention of illness and injury, and the promotion of health and well-being. His interests in healthy workplaces, business systems, and evaluation and improvement have come together in an active involvement in team-based health care quality improvement. He has published articles and book chapters on health care policy and reform, strategic management of medical care and workers' compensation, physician behavior, medical care quality improvement, health promotion, and epidemiology. He is coeditor of *Managing Employee Health Care Costs: Assuring Quality and Value* (with H. D. Belk and L. W. Wood, 1992) and *Health Promotion in the Workplace* (with M. P. O'Donnell, 2nd ed., 1993). He is coauthor of *The OEM Manual of Occupational Health and Safety* (with D. V. DiBennedetto and R. J. McCunney, 1992). He is currently at work on a manuscript tentatively titled "Reengineering Medicine."

Harris is a member of the board of directors and a Fellow of the American College of Occupational and Environmental Medicine and chair of the college's committee on health care quality and cost management. He is also a Fellow of the American Academy of Family Practice, the American College of Medical Quality, and the American College of Preventive Medicine. He is board certified in emergency medicine as well. Harris is a member of the editorial board of the *American Journal of Health Promotion* (for case studies) and the *OEM Report* and is an editorial reviewer for the *Journal of the American Medical Association,* the *Journal of Occupational Medicine,* and the *American Journal of Public Health.* He holds a key from the Beta Gamma Sigma Business Honor Society.

Before joining A&ACG, Harris was medical director of the Aetna Health Plan in Nashville, Tennessee. Previously, he served as president of HDM, Inc. (a management consulting firm), as director of health care management for Northern Telecom, Inc., and as assistant to the commissioner and director of health promotion for the Tennessee Department of Health and Environment. Prior to those management positions, Harris was in clinical practice of family and emergency medicine in Alaska, where he also helped develop emergency care and native health care systems.

STRATEGIC
HEALTH MANAGEMENT

PART ONE

The Current Quandary

We are now undergoing the fourth wave of financial and organizational upheaval in American medical care (Starr, 1982). The current concerns about the financing, accessibility, orientation, and quality of medical care therefore have important historical precedents that should offer lessons and direction for public policy, private financing mechanisms, and health plan and delivery system design. Some of the structures, financial incentives, and attitudes and beliefs created during these periods of change arguably must be revised or modified. Many observers feel that if the mechanics and dynamics of the "system" are not changed or improved, national health care reform could repeat the mistakes of the past and make cost and quality problems worse rather than better (Angell, 1993). Universal access, by itself, echoes the introduction of Medicare and Medicaid in the mid 1960s, which set off the current cost spiral. A more comprehensive approach by both the public and private sectors is needed to ensure efficient, effective care that satisfies the demands of all customers of the medical industry.

CHAPTER ONE

The Evolution
of the Health Care Crisis

The current health care "crisis" has been in evolution for over a hundred years. Technological change, financial incentives, and beliefs about what medical care could and could not do have driven major shifts of funds to the medical care sector. The first major change in medical technology and service delivery occurred before the turn of the century. Then, as now, new technology changed the product offered by physicians and facilities, changed the delivery system, and set off an unintended price spiral. When antisepsis and modern surgical techniques began to make surgery more beneficial than risky, there was a rapid growth of proprietary hospitals and an equally rapid movement of care from the home setting to the hospital. A sharp increase in the price of services then threatened the financial stability of some middle-class families. In response, a number of employers began to offer defined benefit hospitalization insurance, mainly through casualty insurers.

The second major change resulted from an economic downturn. The foundation for modern insurance coverage was laid during the Depression, when Blue Cross and Blue Shield plans were started to accept a fixed monthly payment for coverage from various labor groups. The plans in turn paid scheduled fees to hospitals and physicians, initially to ensure the solvency of hospitals, which were regarded as a quasi-public resource.

During and following World War II, when wage and price freezes were in effect, organized labor and employers were allowed to offer benefits on a pre-tax basis as a substitute for wage increases. As a result, coverage for hospital care grew rapidly and surgical coverage was added. Before the insurance system developed, health care was typically paid for last out of the family budget. With the development of private insurance, money for medical care was taken out of employees' paychecks. As a result, payment was assured, making growth of for-profit health care entities more attractive (Starr, 1982). The nonprofit Blues were eventually eclipsed by commercial insurers, who were able to "experience rate," segmenting the market and offering lower rates to selected employed groups that tended to be healthier than the general population. Private insurance also added to the market power of physicians. Insurance companies used doctors as gatekeepers to benefits and excluded payment to other practitioners such as midwives, chiropractors, and a variety of others who were commonplace in the 1930s and 1940s. That approach may now have backfired, given the evidence that physicians may not always ensure the most cost-effective care.

The third change mirrored the first. The watershed for this latest transition occurred in the mid 1960s. Repeated attempts to enact a program of national health insurance since before the turn of the century had failed. Opposition came from medical care professionals and facilities managers who were satisfied with the prevailing system. Despite massive initial opposition from the American Medical Association, President Lyndon B. Johnson succeeded in shepherding through the passage of Medicare for the elderly and disabled and Medicaid for poor women and children and some other individuals in 1965 (Iglehart, 1992c, 1992d). Typical of American health politics, these were narrow attempts at national health insurance for a specifically targeted group. Also typical of American politics, there were trade-offs. In exchange for the passage of these pieces of social legislation, the AMA was given statistically based, fee-for-service reimbursement, and hospitals were to be paid on a cost-plus basis.

Medicare and Medicaid, and the expansion of commercial insurance benefits that followed them, proved a bonanza for providers. They ensured payment for services in a manner that had no relation to value or to other goods and services (Fuchs, 1968). These pricing mechanisms ultimately proved uncontrollable, especially when price increases unique to the medical sector were added to general inflation. The rate of growth of costs more than doubled, from 3.2 percent a year in the seven years before Medicare to 7.9 percent during the five years afterward. Hospital costs, which had risen an average of 8 percent annually, jumped after 1965 to annual increases of more than 14 percent (Levit, Lasenby, Cowan, and Letsch, 1991; Iglehart, 1992d). The compound annual growth rate for medical care costs was 11.8 percent from 1965 to 1990, compared to a compound annual growth rate of 8.5 percent for the gross national product. Interestingly, providers seemed to have lost this perspective in their ongoing antagonism toward externally imposed management of the price or volume of medical care.

At virtually the same time, large amounts of funds were channeled to the National Institutes of Health and through them to medical schools, expanding the pool of available medical technologies. Simultaneously, funds were made available to medical schools to sharply increase enrollment, expanding the supply of physicians, and to build more facilities, expanding the supply of high-tech equipment and hospital beds. At the time, it was thought that there was a serious shortage of physicians and that prices would rise if the shortage was not alleviated. In retrospect, the forecasts were far off the mark (Wennberg, Goodman, Nease, and Keller, 1993) for reasons that are not entirely clear but may have included an apparent need for physicians to use new technology and obvious shortages in rural and inner-city areas (which persist today, but not because there is an inadequate supply of physicians). Most of the new physicians were higher-cost, procedurally oriented specialists who were more apt to use technology (Freimann, 1985) and facilities and practice in higher-income urban or suburban areas. A technology spiral, which underlies the price spiral, resulted (Ginzberg, 1990).

Function Follows Form:
Financing Breeds Entrepreneurialism

The medical care industry is now doing exactly what one would expect given its structure. There is 20 to 60 percent oversupply of physicians overall, with an undersupply of primary care physicians and a significant oversupply in surgical as well as radiology, anesthesia, and pathology (RAP) and medical subspecialties (Wennberg, Goodman, Nease, and Keller, 1993). Because there is a large and growing body of technology for specialists to use and they are guaranteed reimbursement for the use of that technology, it is used. In the typical path of diffusion of these technologies, they are introduced for a specific indication and then are applied for wider and wider indications, which may or may not be backed by research. The benefit-to-cost ratio drops as these peripheral applications occur. An excellent example is coronary bypass surgery which was originally introduced for two specific anatomic lesions but has come to be used for practically any type of coronary artery lesion at degrees of obstruction much lower than originally dealt with by the research. Similarly, imaging studies are used for indications for which they were not originally intended, greatly increasing their total costs. Using MRI studies for nonspecific low-back pain, without a trial of conservative therapy, is one particularly egregious example. Since about half the adult male population over forty has some disc abnormality but few have directly referable symptoms, these studies act as an invitation to unnecessary and potentially harmful surgery (Borenstein and Wiesel, 1989).

This "diffusion of indications" is also true of pharmaceuticals. Typically they are introduced for very specific reasons and then become used for marginal indications for which practitioners speculate they may be effective. Use may also increase due to patient demand. Good examples are tranquilizers and antiulcer medications, which are prescribed out of proportion to the actual prevalence of treatable disorders in the population or for much longer periods than originally intended. Few limits are placed on these expenditures because providers and suppliers are able to be reimbursed through the insurance system at excellent profit margins.

Medical care prices are also distorted by a variety of provisions in current reimbursement schemes. Prices continually increase under mechanisms where statistical averaging such as "usual, customary, and reasonable" (UCR) fee screens are used. As individual physicians raise their fees, the average goes up inexorably. Fees can be raised because there is little price sensitivity; employee-consumers "see" only their copayments and other contributions. Following these waves of price inflation, managed care organizations have the potential to "shadow price," or price just slightly lower than competing indemnity plans rather than at a price more reflective of their actual or potential cost structure. Thus UCR is inflationary in and of itself and has provided cover for managed care organizations to potentially increase profit. They have not increased profit chiefly because, sheltered from true price competition by UCR, managed care organizations have not fully explored all opportunities to increase efficiency and effectiveness. If they show slower growth rates or some savings compared to an indemnity plan, they appear to be a good deal. But given tighter medical management and better process management, managed care could be priced significantly lower than indemnity care.

Providers are also able to increase prices to private payers to compensate for any deficit they incur in payments from public payers such as Medicare and Medicaid and county indigent funds. This removes any financial incentive to improve cost-effectiveness and efficiency.

This entire cycle is fueled by a continuously growing supply of specialists, pharmaceuticals, and procedures that should replace older procedures but in fact merely supplement them in most cases (Eisenberg and others, 1989). Until buyers start to demand proof of cost-effectiveness for new therapies, negotiate prices closer to actual or potential costs, and manage utilization (or contract with medical groups that will), this situation is likely to persist. Again, this is not a mystery. It is a rational economic response to existing supply, demand, and financial incentives.

Employers Have a Dilemma

American employers have now painted themselves into a corner. Over time, they have incrementally increased the medical care benefits offered to their employees. The federal government, one of the largest employers in the country, led the way in expanding employee medical benefits in the mid 1960s, so that it went from paying very little for employee benefits to making a major contribution (Levit and Cowan, 1991). This resulted in the creation of a de facto policy of employment-based medical financing. Two hundred and eleven million Americans were covered by employment-based insurance as of 1992 (Health Insurance Association of America, 1992). The employed public now expects medical care to be financed through employment. In one recent study, 80 percent of employees stated that employers should be required to provide health insurance for full-time employees, even if the benefits were taxable (Taylor and Leitman, 1991a).

Increases in benefits changed the sources of funds for care. If only insurance premiums are considered, while households paid for 41 percent of insurance premiums in 1965, they paid about half that in 1989. Private business's share increased from 54 to 64.5 percent and the government as an employer increased its share from virtually nothing to 12.7 percent, partially by offering very comprehensive plans. So in the aggregate, employers paid over three-quarters of medical insurance premiums by 1989 (Levit and Cowan, 1991).

Employers now also pay a larger percentage of total medical costs. In 1965, business paid for 17 percent of *all* medical care outlays. That number almost doubled by 1989 to 30.6 percent. The distribution of expenditures is of some interest. Of the $173 billion spent by business in 1989, 42.2 percent was used for hospital care. In addition, 28.1 percent was spent on physician care, 3.5 percent on drugs, and 13.4 percent on administrative costs, significantly more than the proportion spent in the public sector. The cost for drugs is the fastest-growing component in private insurance outlays.

These numbers differ significantly from the numbers seen for total national expenditures, reflecting differences in coverages. For example, Medicare paid 62 percent of its outlays for hospital bills and 27.5 percent for physician care. Less than 2 percent was spent on drugs, which are not covered; 2.5 percent went for administrative costs (Levit, Lasenby, Cowan, and Letsch, 1991; Iglehart, 1992d).

The financing of this system has fueled a cost spiral that

seriously limits the funds available for total compensation of employees (V. R. Fuchs, 1993; Service Employees International Union, 1992). At the point where employees resist cost shifting or coverage limitations, labor unrest results. Because employees have come to expect these benefits and now feel threatened by rising medical care costs, attempts to limit coverage cause a strong reaction and even negate the labor relations advantages of offering benefits. Yet the cost of the total compensation package can threaten budgets or the ability to compete.

Employers may have been the victims of a conjunction of circumstances. But they were also willing participants. At the least, they can be seen as shortsighted, failing to plan and manage the future of their compensation packages. In this chapter, we will review the way this situation developed as a basis for strategic health management efforts that may be more successful. We will consider costs, the demand for medical services, the need for better information to improve health management, and employers' responsibility for improving the health care situation.

Costs and Their Consequences

Medical benefits costs now amount to just under $4,000 per employee in the United States, according to unpublished data from Blue Cross and Blue Shield of Rochester. These figures agree with those obtained in nonrandom surveys of larger employers (A. Foster Higgins, 1992). The per employee cost varies widely, depending on coverage and the industry involved, ranging from $4,758 in 1991 for energy and petroleum to about $1,000 for department stores (Geisel, 1993). (These figures, of course, are not corrected for the number of dependents employees have. One might suspect that in department stores there are a large number of single employees.) More than a doubling of the per peron cost was projected between 1990 and 2000, from $2,585 to $5,712 (Sonnefeld, Waldo, Lemieux, and McKusick, 1991). By some estimates, the cost per employee will exceed the average wage by 2030.

The magnitude of medical care costs, their distribution,

and their rate of increase are important for several reasons. First, benefits costs compete with or limit cash wages as part of what an employer can afford as total compensation (see Figure 1.1). As benefits costs increase in excess of employers' ability to raise prices or increase productivity, wage increases are constrained, lowering workers' standards of living (V. R. Fuchs, 1993; Service Employees International Union, 1992).

Second, because medical benefits were installed as a competitive edge in the labor market for needed workers, some companies will find it more difficult to find necessary skilled labor as benefits are scaled back. This would be particularly true in industries that have traditionally used benefits in a competitive manner, such as transportation, equipment, chemicals, metal fabrication, and high technology.

Third, the industries with the highest benefits costs tend to be highly organized. One can anticipate significantly more labor conflicts as benefits costs threaten the available pool of money for wages and then begin to threaten the viability of the enterprise itself. In fact, according to the Service Employees International Union, disputes over medical care coverage already account for most labor unrest.

Fourth, unanticipated increases in medical benefits costs can force limitation or changes in other areas of an organization's budget (Brailler and Van Horn, 1993). On a higher level, the configuration of the economy is changed as more and more of the GNP or GDP are devoted to the medical sector.

Fifth, in those industries that have foreign competition and a significant labor component to their cost structure, increases in total compensation can adversely affect price competitiveness (though perhaps not competitiveness with respect to features or quality). The United States has the highest and fastest-growing outlays for medical care for employees. Canada is less by a significant margin, and some of our competitors such as Germany and Japan are between a third and half of our costs (Schieber, Poullier, and Greenwald, 1993). The relative costs in developing countries such as Korea, Singapore, Malaysia, China, Mexico, and Brazil are even lower. Some of this difference is due to more efficient medical care systems in developed

Figure 1.1. Average Nonsupervisory Hourly Wages, Private Sector, in 1992 Dollars.

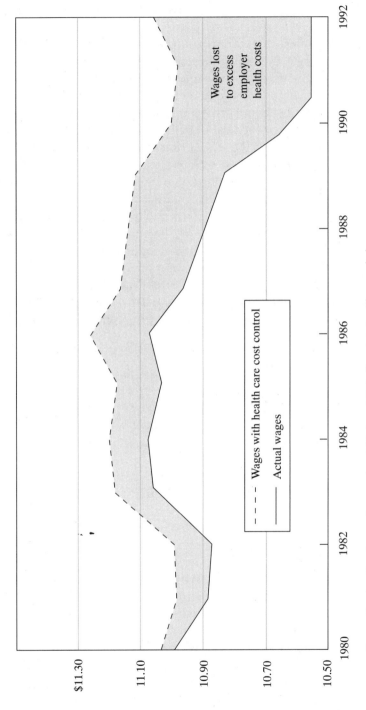

Source: Service Employees International Union, 1992. Reprinted with permission.

nations, some is due to more comprehensive public health systems emphasizing prevention, and some is due to other demand factors.

To the extent that wages must be added to benefits and benefits have not been managed, the costs for total compensation may not be competitive internationally. The net effect of increasing costs for medical benefits in the United States is anticompetitive only to the extent that labor market pressure keeps total compensation higher than it otherwise would be. Otherwise, wages and the standard of living simply fall (V. R. Fuchs, 1993; Service Employees International Union, 1992). Within the United States, as the growth in benefits exceeds the growth in wages, some employers may become less competitive with smaller organizations that do not offer benefits.

This comparative discussion of costs lays the foundation for a discussion of value: Are we getting all we could from our medical care dollars, or are there gains in appropriateness, efficiency, and effectiveness that could moderate or reverse cost escalation? (See Chapter Three.)

Impact of Costs on Profits

There are a number of ways of analyzing employer-paid medical benefits costs, none of them particularly encouraging. Looking at the impact on the bottom line, medical care costs are rapidly overtaking profits. Employer payments for health care, including health-related payroll taxes, amounted to 14 percent of aggregate after-tax profits in 1965. Today they exceed the amount of after-tax profits (Levit and Cowan, 1991).

It is projected that medical benefits expenditures will consume earnings entirely some time between the years 2000 and 2030. Clearly, at the point at which this category of expenditures exceeds profits, any rational employer would ask what it is in business for (Lichtenstein and others, 1993). This is not a viable situation.

Costs to the Economy as a Whole

A look at total costs paints a picture of the impact on the economy as a whole (the macroenvironment in which employers function). The total cost of medical care in 1992 was $838.5 billion, or over 14 percent of the gross domestic product (GDP). The most recent projections for total health care costs, including Medicare costs, is that they will continue to increase at an almost 10 percent annual rate. Expenditures are expected to exceed $1.6 trillion by the year 2000. This estimate may be conservative. Given the recent increases and the percentage of the GDP consumed, the curve could be considerably accelerated and we could have a $2 trillion bill by the year 2000.

This cost curve raises a question and suggests a key point. The question is, What is wrong with putting more resources into the "health" sector? The key point is that if the curve continues on its present trajectory, the entire gross national product will be devoted to medical care by about 2030 (Lichtenstein and others, 1993). Clearly this is unlikely, and unlimited growth is impossible — but what are the bounds, and what would the impact be at that boundary? Do we want to attempt management first, or wait for a worsening situation?

Employers, not employees, have absorbed most of these cost increases. Comparing private employers' outlays for medical care to personal income macroindicators such as the gross domestic private product (GDPP) demonstrates this shift in funding. Private employers' outlays for medical benefits rose from 1 percent of the GDPP in 1965 to 4.2 percent in 1989 — a fourfold increase. By contrast, the proportion of a similar indicator for private income, the Adjusted Personal Income Index, increased less than a percentage point, from 4.2 percent in 1965 to 5.1 percent in 1989 (Levit and Cowan, 1991).

American spending on medical care was the highest among all industrialized countries in both 1980 and 1990 in terms of absolute per capita spending in U.S. dollars. The United States also had the highest rate of growth in expenditures. The U.S. per capita outlay of $1,064 in 1980 was 24 percent higher than in Germany, 38 percent higher than in Canada, 45 percent higher than in France, 97 percent higher than in Japan, and 124 percent higher than in the United Kingdom. By 1990, U.S. spending of $2,566 exceeded that of Canada by 45 percent, Japan by 119 percent, Germany by 73 percent, and the United Kingdom by 164 percent. The 9.2 percent average annual rate of growth of medical care costs per person in the United States significantly exceeded the 8.6 percent in Canada, 8.1 percent in Japan, 7.6 percent in France, 7.4 percent in the United Kingdom, and 5.7 percent in Germany. In 1980, the U.S. rate was 57 percent above the average for the other five countries. By 1990, it was 85 percent above that. Similar figures result if comparisons are adjusted for per capita GDP (Schieber, Poullier, and Greenwald, 1993). Even with these very large expenditures, the United States is the only industrialized country other than South Africa that does not provide coverage for its entire population. Is this good value?

Impact of Costs on Individuals

The impact on the individual employee is considerable as well. The percentage of personal consumption expenditures spent on medical care has risen from 10.7 percent in 1980 to 14.7 percent in 1990 (Levit and Cowan, 1991). Of the $215.6 billion spent by individuals, 10.2 percent was paid for hospital cost, 18 percent was spent on physicians, and 25.9 percent was spent on drugs. The remainder was spent for various personal health care products, nursing home care, and other generally non-covered items (Levit, Lasenby, Letsch, and Cowan, 1991).

    Even as medical care costs rise, they disproportionately affect those who can least afford them. While medical care spending increases with income, it tends to be regressive. In other words, the persons with income in the lowest 10 percent of the population devote nearly 20 percent of cash income to financing their own health care compared with about 8 percent of cash income for people in the highest 10 percent (Holahan and Zedlusky, 1992).

    Employer outlays for health insurance as a percentage of total compensation rose from 0.3 percent in 1948 to 1.1 percent in 1960, 2.1 percent in 1970, 4.4 percent in 1980, and 6.3 percent in 1990 (Piacentini and Foley, 1992). Health care benefits accounted for 23 percent of total benefits in 1970, but by 1988 they accounted for 34 percent of all benefits. The numbers are now estimated to exceed 10 percent of total compensation in many firms (Feldstein, 1988). These costs constitute a direct threat to the compensation management of both public and private employers and to the standard of living of employees.

Retiree Cost Liability

In addition to experiencing a cost burden to pay for current employees, employers are now suffering massive financial shocks to handle the accrued liability of future medical care of retirees. Because those over fifty-five consume several times more medical care than younger individuals and tend to rely on high-technology care if their health fails, their medical cost curve over time is likely to be considerably steeper. Employers are required under Financial Accounting Standards Board (FASB) Rule no. 106 to recognize these future liabilities. General Motors, for example, recently took a write-off amounting to a quarter of a billion dollars to fund retiree health care, which had previously been accrued only off the books. The problem will only get worse without health promotion. Further, a new FASB regulation, no. 112, will require companies to accrue funds for future workers' compensation payouts on the books.

Countervailing Influences

Countervailing influences to attempts at medical cost management include factors such as employee demand for benefits, concerns about costs, satisfaction with benefits, and opinions about cost management.

Employee Demand for Benefits

While the costs of medical benefits are exerting a number of adverse effects on employers, the unilateral options for constraining them have negative consequences as well. Employees in many industries have come to consider benefits a critical part of their total compensation package. In one study, sixty-one percent of employees rated health benefits as their most important benefit (Piacentini and Anzick, 1991). Employees paid for almost all medical care prior to the mid 1960s (hospitalization insurance was reasonably common but covered only uncommon events). However, there is little collective memory of this situation. Employees now become very upset, at least initially, if there is talk of changing the benefits package.

Benefits are clearly important to employees in choosing jobs. According to a survey by the Employee Benefits Research Institute, nearly three out of five employees said they consider benefits very important when deciding whether to accept or reject a job. An additional quarter of employees said benefits were important (Employee Benefits Research Institute and the Gallup Organization, Inc., 1990). A majority of those interviewed said they would not accept a job if it did not provide them with health insurance. Health benefits were mentioned as the most important employee benefit by far.

Employees seem to realize that benefits have significant value, although the results do not always reflect the actual amount spent. In a recent Gallup poll, employees stated that employers would have to pay them $4,219 to give up their current medical benefits (Employee Benefits Research Institute and the Gallup Organization, Inc., 1990). Slightly more than half of employees would choose health insurance rather than an equivalent amount of pretax cash. Employees seem to recognize that employers obtain better health care deals because of their market power. Sixty-six percent of employees in that survey noted that they would have to pay more if they had to pay for the insurance themselves.

Concerns About Costs

People are clearly worried about health care costs. In one poll, as many as 50 percent of those interviewed were very worried about paying for their own health care. The percentage increased the lower the respondent's income was (Clements, 1992). In another survey, 62 percent of Americans were worried that health insurance might become so expensive that they would not be able to afford it, 50 percent were worried that they might have very expensive bills that were not covered, and slightly less than half (48 percent) were worried that they would not be able to get health care they needed when they were very ill. The same percentage was worried that benefits would be cut back substantially, and some respondents (39 percent) were worried that if they had large medical bills, their health insurance plan would refuse to insure them. In each case, the percentage worried about the issue increased the lower a person's income was (Henry J. Kaiser Family Foundation and Louis Harris and Associates, 1992b).

We should note that these polls were done without any sort of discussion or interaction to increase respondents' understanding of the cost impact of medical care on total compensation or on the competitiveness of business or industry. In the studies cited above, only 31 percent were worried that health care costs would constrain wage increases and only 26 percent were worried that their employer would stop providing health insurance. Those with higher incomes were more concerned, possibly because they tended to be members of middle or upper management and were more knowledgeable about the wage-benefit trade-off. Half of those were as worried about health care as they were about maintaining their standard of living (two factors that are closely related). It is entirely likely that if employees had more information and were more intimately involved in the benefits planning process, the results might be significantly different, particularly if explicit trade-offs were discussed (see Chapter Seven).

Satisfaction with Benefits

One of the key reasons that employers offer medical insurance is to provide what employees perceive as a valuable benefit in order to compete in the labor market and to enhance employer-employee relations. However, satisfaction with medical benefits had dropped substantially in the last decade. In 1982, 87 percent of employees rated their hospital and medical insurance as very good or good. By 1990, this percentage had dropped to 45 percent (International Survey Research Corporation, 1991). This drop in benefits satisfaction has paralleled a drop in morale. Further, the percentage of those satisfied with the medical care they had received in the last few years (paid for by the benefits plan) has dropped from 84 to 71 percent between

1987 and 1992 (Henry J. Kaiser Family Foundation and Louis Harris and Associates, 1992b). More tellingly, the percentage who are dissatisfied has doubled — from 13 to 26 percent — in the same time period.

Opinions About Cost Management

Potential problems for those attempting to manage costs and quality more effectively surface when employees and physicians are asked about the acceptability of a number of techniques that might reduce cost escalation or result in better-quality care. Neither group is particularly supportive of measures generally accepted by employers as effectively containing health care costs. Physicians' opinions are important here, because they would need to accept cost or quality management measures and because they tend to have strong opinions about insurance plans.

In a Harris and Associates poll of Americans in 1991 (Taylor and Leitman, 1991a), the most acceptable solution to the medical care cost problem was thought to be accepting limits on the right to sue for malpractice (61 percent). Obtaining prior approval for emergency care garnered only 57 percent support, and being a member of an exclusive provider organization that excludes non-cost-effective providers gathered 42 percent. Queuing and being a member of a plan that does not cover some expensive procedures and treatments gathered only 36 percent support, and having to pay substantially higher out-of-pocket costs (the most popular option among benefits managers) received only 22 percent support (Taylor and Leitman, 1991a).

About 90 percent of consumers oppose restriction of choice of physicians, which, if structured correctly, could reduce variance in care and raise the overall level of quality. Yet people do not actually seem to shop for medical care. Only 30 percent report ever having compared the price of a specific medical procedure between two or more different physicians (Peter D. Hart, 1992). This is not surprising, since with many forms of insurance coverage, price does not matter.

While consumers evidently do wish to be able to shop for quality, most of them do not have the information to do that effectively. In addition, there is a serious lack of information about plans where there may be some limitation of access, presumably in exchange for lower cost or better quality. For example, many consumers do not know about the relative cost of managed care plans such as HMOs, whether they get a choice of doctor, and whether they get more preventive care. Even fewer understand PPOs (Employee Benefits Research Institute and the Gallup Organization, Inc., 1990).

The public (and again, by extension, employees) does not feel personally responsible for today's health care problems (Roper Center for Public Opinion Research, 1991). The consumer blames physicians and hospitals for high costs and the health insurance industry and government for the lack of access (Taylor and Leitman, 1991a; Kohut, Toth, and Bowman, 1993). However, physicians have a markedly different point of view. Fifty-three percent of them report that their patients make unrealistic demands (Harvey and Shubat, 1989). Likewise, almost the same percentage of physicians surveyed by the American Medical Association believe that patients generally demand too many services such as laboratory tests, x-rays, and drugs (Harvey, 1991). Nearly half of practicing physicians blame patient behavior, specifically demand for unnecessary care, for increasing health care costs. Lack of incentives for patients to use their health care efficiently is said to contribute as well. It is not clear why physicians feel unable to say no to inappropriate demands.

The leading factors named by physicians as causes of medical inflation were malpractice insurance and defensive medicine (86 percent), as well as the increased availability of expensive new medical technology (36 percent). Almost half of doctors believe that drug companies cause substantial cost problems by setting high prices. However, less than a quarter of physicians believe that price setting by doctors and hospitals is responsible for cost problems.

What doctors *do* think should be done is also interesting. Consistent with their belief that patients are the cause of many problems, 54 percent of physicians think that requiring consumers to pay more out of pocket for their care should be a high priority. Almost half favored price controls for prescription drugs. Very few (15 percent) indicated that putting doctors at financial risk is needed to get cost under control. Very small numbers believed that it was acceptable to have preauthorization or a fixed budget or to be required to follow practice guidelines or obtain approval of a primary care gatekeeper. Almost no physicians found capitation acceptable. (Either the sample was drawn from among those who still are paid strictly on a fee-for-service basis — a vanishing breed — or covert dissatisfaction is greater than is apparent.) Five percent felt it was acceptable to be compensated on some basis of patient satisfaction. Four percent found capitation acceptable, and 5 percent found salaried payment acceptable (Taylor and Leitman, 1990).

Newer surveys show somewhat more flexibility. In a 1993 poll, over half of physicians were favorably disposed toward managed care, and over 40 percent were in favor of a single-payer system. Nearly two-thirds of physicians agree that regional plans to reduce duplication of high-tech hospital services and expensive equipment should be a high priority. They also favor lower-tech medicine (Kohut, Toth, and Bowman, 1993).

The divergence between physicians' opinions on the causes and solutions of health care crises and the views of employers and consumers poses a problem for several reasons. First, as noted, physicians are not shy about expressing their dissatisfaction with the insurance system. Second, physicians make decisions that affect about 80 percent of medical care expenditures, although they are directly paid for only 20 percent of total payouts (Eisenberg, 1986). Third, physicians have raised prices consistently for the last twenty-five years, accounting for a substantial amount of the inflation in the cost of their services. In addition, physicians have in past polls been categorically opposed to most strategies for reducing costs other than increasing cost shifting to patients, which is unacceptable to employees. Since many doctors do not appear to regard themselves as responsible for increases in medical care costs, it has been difficult to negotiate or have them become involved in more efficient systems of care.

These perceptions have also contributed to the gridlock over both public efforts for reform and employers' efforts to redesign benefits plans. However, the situation appears to be changing (Kohut, Toth, and Bowman, 1993) and will continue to evolve during the ongoing debate on health care reform.

Need for Better Information

One difficulty that employers have had in designing both health and benefits management structures is that little research exists on what works and what does not in plan design, medical management, and clinical medicine. (We will cover the research that exists on plan design, utilization management, and managed care in Chapters Seven and Eleven.) For example, it is not clear at what level copayments and deductibles have any effect on consumption in the ranges that they are typically used. There is evidence from the RAND Health Insurance Experiment that copayments much more substantial than those currently used do have a significant effect on consumption if used at the point of service (see Chapter Seven). What is known suggests that managed care would be an effective option, and that commonly used indemnity insurance funding mechanisms have created more problems than they have solved. As an example of the former, closed managed care organizations such as staff-model HMOs are up to 40 percent more effective in managing utilization with concurrent decrease in costs (Luft, 1981). In the latter instance, fee schedules seem to be much more manageable than statistical average payment techniques. Per diem payments to hospitals may have reversed the incentives involved in a charge-base payment system. Payments per episode or per person may be even more effective than payments per day.

Given the availability of empirical evidence, it is not necessary for employers to wait for academic institutions to conduct this type of research. If employers or employer groups collected and managed information from their providers more effectively, they could (if enough covered lives were available) evaluate changes among groups and over time as different medical and financial management techniques were introduced or fine-tuned. It is possible to statistically adjust for changes in the employee and dependent population, the benefits design, and the underlying inflation rate to determine which design and health management changes are actually effective. In other arenas, this type of periodic or ongoing "due diligence" would be expected to make sure that expenditures are worth making and well managed. Further, such analyses form the basis for the continuous improvement of design and management.

It is also unfortunately true that little information is available on the relative effectiveness and cost-effectiveness of various treatments and procedures for common illnesses. A science of optimal treatment patterns is emerging that should be linked to "outcomes research" to determine what works best. Again, employers could put in place data systems that collect information on diagnoses, treatment provided, and outcome (McEachern, Makens, Buchanan, and Schiff, 1992). Outcome can be measured in a variety of ways, including length of disability (which is collected by some employers), patients' opinion of their increase in function, and decreased use of medical resources to obtain the same outcome. A combination of survey research and claims payment analysis can be used to answer these questions. If the employer is too small to do this kind of analysis, it would be worthwhile to join a pool of similar employers to collect and analyze data to guide what it is doing. Paradoxically, while a certain amount of "follow-the-leader" behavior seems to exist in the designs of benefits plans — particularly in the introduction of the "latest" devices for benefits management — there is poor or little information exchanged about what others are doing and how effective it is.

Finally, surprisingly enough, many employers are not aware of what they specifically spend their claims dollars on. Part of the problem is that the analyses done in the past were financial and actuarial. These analyses dealt with total cost and claim lags. Plan sponsors have only recently begun to understand that one should measure *rates* of cost or service use rather than absolute numbers (the cost per employee or per dependent). Analysis has been hampered to some extent by lack of "positive enrollment," or registration of dependents so that an accurate age and gender profile is available to compute and compare rates and costs. Employers are generally aware of the number, age, and gender of employees but not of dependents. Without this information, they are simply speculating about the number of individuals covered and their probable health service use. While financial and actuarial analyses are necessary for plan funding purposes in a reactive and projective sense, they do not give information about what was actually purchased and whether those services were clinically appropriate.

What is needed, particularly to set the stage for strategic planning for the benefits program and for health management in general, would be an analysis of the medical services used for each diagnosis, the frequency of surgeries and other procedures, pharmaceutical use rates, and other similar types of analysis per person. These *rates* can then be compared to a variety of benchmarks, ranging from averages in the region of the country where the employer is located to "best achievable" utilization rates as proven by well-run managed care organizations. While providing financial protection and medical care is an admirable goal, it is not in anyone's interest to provide unnecessary care that could have serious side effects and a low benefit-cost ratio. The differences between actual values — adjusted for age, gender, and case mix — and benchmarks provides targets of opportunity for improved financial and medical management. Adjustments for age and gender are proxies for health risk and severity of illness. The accuracy of most analyses could be improved by adding these adjustments.

Because of the state of claims tapes and the sometimes minimal information collected by managed care organizations, it is often difficult for employers to conduct the type of analysis I have just described. Claims administrators often collect incomplete data and collect them in a "flat-file" format from which it is difficult to retrieve information. Despite the availability of relational data base technology, which allows quick and easy comparison of different groups and situations, very little data is stored in that way. It is also important to agree on key management indicators to follow so that data can be collected, retrieved, analyzed, and used for active management of health and medical care (Harris and Theriault, 1993).

In addition, medical expertise is needed to understand the reason for differences between benchmarks and observed practices. Medical professionals with expertise in population and preventive medicine should be active participants on the health management team, either as employees or consultants. Thus, better data collection and the expertise to analyze an improved data base are both needed.

A particularly valuable analysis is that of variance in practice patterns among geographic areas, physicians, and major diagnostic categories. Variance is generally accepted as an indicator of poor quality. In addition, those areas with the lowest adjusted utilization or costs could, after determining that the health of the population was not compromised, provide benchmarks to work toward. This mode of thinking is based on progressive reductions of hospital bed days in the last two decades—from over 600 to less than 150 in managed care organizations—with no apparent effect on health (Doyle, 1990).

Another key area of data analysis is predicting future expenditures based on health risks in the population. These data are obtainable from Health Risk Appraisals or employee surveys and can be correlated with current expenditures and used in projective analyses of future expenditures. A number of studies have shown that those with higher health risks consume more resources and could well benefit from a variety of preventive services (see Chapter Nine).

Employers' Responsibility

In 1969, President Nixon declared a crisis in medical care and predicted a breakdown in two years (Falkson, 1980). *Business Week* ran a cover story on the "$60 billion crisis" in 1970 (cited in Starr, 1992), and the same month the editors of *Fortune,* in a special issue on Medicare, stated that American medicine "stood on the brink of chaos." They indicted American medical care as being inferior in quality, wastefully distributed, and inequitably financed ("It's Time to Operate," 1970). *Business Week* and *U.S. News and World Report* had published similar articles. Both the 1970 and 1992 issues concluded that it was time for a radical change. The costs of medical care were categorized in both instances as "skyrocketing." Is this a crisis? Of what proportions? Will the system collapse under its own weight?

What is so curious about this situation is that employers (and policy makers) have not taken many steps that are known to be effective in managing medical costs, even in the absence of changes in public policy such as changes in reimbursement for Medicare (which would substantially affect cost shifting) or some attempt at managing the supply of providers or facilities (which would reduce the tendency for overtreatment).

Plan Design Changes

Plan designs have remained relatively unchanged for the last twenty years. Copayments and deductibles have risen only slightly and at a much slower rate than overall medical cost increases. However, benefits packages have been consistently expanded. There has been no change in the indemnity model, such as a return to defined contributions, which might increase cost sensitivity (Bureau of Labor Statistics, U.S. Department of Labor, 1990, 1991).

One wonders why more changes have not been made, given that less than half of employers responding to a recent survey felt that their costs were under control (Taylor and Leitman, 1989). Only a third of benefits managers said that their costs were under control; most employers felt that they will not get costs back under control in the near future. Ninety percent anticipated their costs would rise dramatically over the next five years despite their best efforts. Seventy-six percent felt that their employees will be paying much more out of pocket as well.

However, even with this pervasive sense that the system is broken and costs are out of control, cost management is not at the top of managers' "to do" list. Forty-seven percent said that making sure their employee can get the health services they need is their highest priority, whereas 37 percent cited keeping the cost of care down. (Never mind that there is substantial overuse of medical resources in many plans—see Chapter Three.) Only 15 percent want to improve the quality of health service as their first priority. Similarly, while 56 percent of employers say that health benefits costs are very important, the quality of products and of the work force is more important than either wages or benefits (Taylor and Leitman, 1989). Furthermore, 45 percent of executives feel that human resources and employee benefits are just more costs that have to be managed effectively.

It is clear that the cost-sharing and medical management options employers have been willing to use are not powerful enough to make the system more market sensitive and managed. Copayments and deductibles are not high enough to substantially affect purchasing decisions. Typically, when employers introduce plans that vary in effectiveness, the price differential of contributions is not enough to cause a substantial shift into the more effective plans — although there are significant exceptions to this. Out-of-pocket maximums typically blunt the effect of copayments and deductibles.

While managed care plans have been available for over thirty years, they are still not widespread, with only 15 percent of the population enrolled in HMOs of some sort and only 5 percent enrolled in group-model HMOs (Camerlo, Giffin, Hodges, and Palsbo, 1992).

Pressure to Act (or Not)

The pressure to take action is increasing but is still not as great as one would expect it to be. In 1987, some fifteen years after President Nixon first declared the health care crisis, only 19 percent of benefits managers felt they were under a great deal of pressure from top management to contain cost. The number who felt they were under great pressure had risen to 26 percent by 1989, and the proportion under some pressure rose to 46 percent. Those under a great deal of pressure had risen to 42 percent by 1992, and 45 percent felt that they were under some degree of pressure (Taylor and Leitman, 1989). This is still less than half the total of midsize to large employers.

Large employers show little interest in adopting tough corporate costs containment policies, according to a study done by a group at Harvard University (Blendon, Edwards, and Hyams, 1992). There is also little interest in changing the many health care options available to employees, even though multiple plans are difficult to manage and vary tremendously in quality. In addition, employers are not particularly interested at the moment in using gatekeepers, who might well be required under a total replacement of multiple benefits plans by managed care. They also show little commitment to rationing high-cost technologies. This is not a particularly realistic reaction to what appears to be a crisis.

Sharing Responsibility

A key problem has been the failure to involve employees in plan design and awareness of payouts for health care. They are truly "out of the loop." Employers in general have taken the paternalistic attitude of designing plans and making them available but really not checking with employees to find out what they believe they need and discussing what they and the organization can afford. Because employees are making individual purchase decisions at the point of use, and because they appear to have little understanding of either the total cost of care or its effectiveness, it is critically important to involve them in many of these decisions and to provide information to them on the relative cost effectiveness of various tests and types of treatment (Barge and Carlson, 1993).

Employers have rarely taken the longer-term view or looked at management of health comprehensively. There has been much incremental change and following of trend factors, but few long-range strategic plans and few corporate or public sector programs that comprehensively address reduction of health risks, wise use of the medical care system, long-range financial targets, and employee satisfaction with both the plan and the treatment received.

A cardinal problem is that the objectives of the benefits plan are often not clearly enunciated. Employers know that they must stay competitive in labor markets and want to satisfy employees or at least avoid antagonizing them, but management and employees rarely sit down and overtly decide on the mission, goals, and objectives of the benefits or health management programs.

Now, however, the rapidly escalating debate on national health care reform indicates a rising level of concern and perception of financial threat. The advocacy of a number of policy changes by large employers suggests either that they believe the problem is systemic and must be addressed across all public and private sectors or that they would rather someone else accept the task of restructuring the medical care system and its financing.

In fact, large and small employers are not at all in agreement about preferred solutions. The small-business lobby has defeated several reform attempts because the reform attempts were focused on increasing access and forcing all employers to offer insurance. Small businesses evidently perceive that this initiative would pose an economic threat to their survival if they were forced to provide the coverage rather than have it come out of a tax-supported pool or be paid for by employees under changed taxing mechanisms.

Advocates of changes in the current levels of resource use, control, and decision making have been opposed by powerful lobbies in the medical, hospital, pharmaceutical, and other sectors of the medical care industry. They have fielded their own proposals stressing increased access (see Chapter Six). That situation and the long history in American politics of slow incremental change make it unlikely that government action will save employers from unmanageable cost increases.

Each employer has a series of decisions to make:

- Whether to use conventional reimbursement techniques that are subject to price increases without notice or to use fixed terms that can be negotiated
- Whether to passively manage dollars or to actively manage care
- Whether to involve employees or dictate to them

These decisions will shape private sector strategic health management programs. As we will see, making them overtly rather than passively will make it possible to manage costs, care, and health.

Conclusion

Employers have become enmeshed in the consequences of a series of political and human resource decisions that made a large volume of funds available to the medical industry. That industry, including medical schools, research institutions, hospitals, and suppliers of medical supplies and services, responded as one would expect — by developing many new technologies and the specialists to deliver those high-margin acute services and extended chronic medical management. This cycle fueled the development of what is now the largest dollar sector of the U.S. economy. Unfortunately, resources are moving disproportionately from all other sectors to the medical sector. The main result is to reduce the standard of living of employees. Employees are at least partially aware of the increasingly difficult balancing act between cost management and offering a balanced wage and benefit package, because their satisfaction with benefits has fallen precipitously.

Employers, as independent actors and as agents for their employees, can continue to buy what the medical industry presents to them, or they can start to carefully manage those purchases. This is no longer a simple undertaking, since well-insured employees are not anxious to move to a situation that might cost them more without necessarily leading to an improvement in value.

The first step in the process just described is data collection and analysis to understand price comparisons, the appropriateness and necessity of purchased medical services, prevention alternatives, and employee needs and wants. Once the current situation is clearly understood, a strategic plan can be formed and consistently followed to achieve greater value for each employer or group of employers (see Chapter Five).

CHAPTER TWO

Square Pegs and Round Holes: Matching Health Care Needs with Realities of the System

Until relatively recently, the reasons employers offered medical benefits as part of their compensation package were generally assumed rather than explicitly stated. The benefit expected to be derived for each unit of cost was not typically quantified. As a competitive measure in labor markets, employers simply matched or bettered what those in similar companies were offering. Benefits packages tended to vary by industry but to be reasonably similar within industries. There was a certain amount of inertia in changing the package, particularly if it meant reducing benefits. Cost management was primarily an exercise in predicting and budgeting for trend increases.

Under pressure from increasing costs, employee dissatisfaction, and questions about value, matching and trending will no longer suffice. In rationalizing alternative expenditures, finding the best use of funds, and determining the optimal outlay, one should be clear about what one is doing and why. It is a particularly important exercise when one considers taking potentially unpopular actions to deal with a fiscal problem. In this chapter, we will examine more carefully the intersection between employer intent, financial constraints, employee demands and needs, and how the medical care "system" actually operates. The gap between employer and consumer needs and demands and the way medical care works should set the stage for strategic planning to create a better alternative.

Why Employers Offer Benefits

It is constructive to review historical and current reasons why employers offer benefits programs. These reasons and needs could easily be translated into key quality characteristics or "things which delight the customer" (Makens and McEachern, 1992) to then govern and evaluate purchase decisions and supplier improvement efforts. At the least, they will provide guidance in determining whether the program is accomplishing its objectives. Reasons generally cited in human resource texts (Milkovich and Glueck, 1985) and in discussions with benefits officers and human resource executives include the following.

To be competitive in specific labor markets. As noted in the section on costs in Chapter One, some industries have much higher benefits costs than others. Some of this has to do with the age structure of the work force. For example, the average age for those engaged in skilled crafts tends to be higher than that for other occupations, as do their costs. Another reason has to do with collective bargaining agreements, which are typically dominant in public entities and skilled crafts. Much of the reason for industry differentials, however, has to do with a need to compete for key skilled workers. Reaching agreement with labor organizations is part of this. This was an original reason for offering benefits and will become more and more critical as the work force changes with the trend toward fewer skilled workers and a lower average educational level, leading to a shortage in key occupations. It will not be such an issue in unskilled and part-time occupations such as fast food restaurants and retail operations.

Employers have almost reached the limits of expanding benefits coverage. Virtually universal coverage now exists among the employed, including insurance for hospitalization, surgeries regardless of setting, physician visits, diagnostic testing, x-rays, dental care, laboratory tests, prescription drugs, mental health benefits, and in-home nursing visits (Bureau of Labor Statistics, U.S. Department of Labor, 1990, 1991).

Larger companies are more likely to offer specialized services than smaller companies. About the only option left is long-term care. Some 40 percent of employers say their company may add that as a flexible benefits option over the next five years (Taylor and Leitman, 1989).

To protect employees from major financial losses. Many employers have taken the somewhat paternalistic attitude that they should protect their employees from catastrophic loss. This is an admirable social goal but should be carefully structured financially. It was one of the original reasons for offering benefits and for the growth of the insurance industry.

To maintain the health of the work force. This was the original motivator for offering company-provided medical care around the turn of the century. With the general improvement in the health of the American population and better access to care, it is a less prevalent issue but is still a factor with low-birthweight infants, immigrant populations, low-income populations without adequate access to health care, and in certain other situations. This is also an admirable social goal.

To bond the employee to the employer. Retention as well as recruiting are desirable goals that can be achieved in part through benefits packages. Of course, there is a mirror image to this. Ill employees who might otherwise leave the work force in force-reduction situations may be reluctant to leave because they would lose benefits or be unable to obtain insurance from other sources at a reasonable cost.

Constraints and Needs

While employers offer benefits for the reasons just cited, they also operate under a series of constraints. These constraints initially had to do with the rising costs of medical care but now increasingly have to do with access, quality, and value.

To offer benefits that cost less in net than wages. Under the present tax structure, it is less expensive in net dollars to offer a certain face value of benefits than it is to pay that same amount in wages. Benefits are pretax, so that employers avoid paying federal income tax on that amount, as do employees. In addition, however, they also avoid paying unemployment, social security, and state and local taxes that would have been paid on the wages. If benefits were replaced by cash wages, employers would have to pay these additional amounts to make employees whole (Enthoven, 1985). In situations where workers' compensation premiums are set at a percentage of wages, they are also reduced to the extent that benefits are substituted for wages.

To manage the cost of employee benefits. For some employers, the costs of maintaining the same or expanded benefits package can rise as fast as 40 percent a year because of cost shifting and adverse selection in some indemnity or self-insured plans. Because most businesses are economic enterprises, cost management is clearly a top priority. However, there are strategies other than cutbacks or cost shifting to employees that can affect the cost structure of a benefits plan and improve the value of what is being delivered.

To maintain competitiveness in product and labor markets. One underlying issue behind managing the costs of the total compensation package, given their large size at this point, is maintaining a competitive market position, employee standard of living, or profitability. As noted, as soon as medical care costs equal the net income from operations otherwise, one would logically question why one would be in business. If this is a nonprofit or public sector institution, these costs would prevent management from meeting their fixed budget.

To prevent illness and injury. A less well enunciated or understood but clearly important issue is preventing illness and injury. When a significant proportion of medical problems are due to life-style or environmental situations and the costs are as high as they are, it is clearly important to do all that one can to prevent illness or injury (as long as there is a positive benefit-cost ratio). Thus, preventive services should be covered, and the strategic health management plan should include health promotion and disease prevention.

To reduce overhead costs. In an industry that has attracted as many entrants as medical care financing and delivery, nonprice competition, or competition on features and perception, has become the norm. To make one's company or practice heard in the marketplace, significant amounts of money must be expended on prospecting, marketing, and selling. Nowhere is this better seen than in the pharmaceutical industry, where $6,000 to $10,000 per doctor may be spent each year on "detailing," a sophisticated form of selling in the guise of information transmission.

At the same time, financing organizations such as insurance companies and health plans have ventured into the active management of medical care. Organizing these plans, conducting enrollment, ensuring customer service, and managing care adds several layers of administration and significant amounts of overhead. These costs have been magnified by the relatively primitive information systems that are used. A concerted effort to reduce layers of management, increase administrative efficiencies, integrate information systems, and otherwise reduce overhead cost structures is a key to improving the value of medical services. Although it is not the primary responsibility of the employer, it is certainly a factor to be considered in the purchasing decision.

To increase the efficiency and effectiveness of care. It has been estimated that 30 to 70 percent of the steps in the process of care may be unnecessary (Berwick, Godfrey, and Roessner, 1990). These observations form the basis for the quality improvement initiative in medical care. Convoluted processes are more characteristic of care in large organizations such as medical centers but are also present in medical groups and even individual physicians' offices or small imaging centers. An unsophisticated use of information systems contributes to this, but there are many unnecessary or missequenced steps in the process of care. This is an area that has not been well studied but may yield tremendous cost savings. Once again, this may not be a primary responsibility of employers, but it certainly is something to be sought in the purchasing decision or to be pursued in joint improvement projects after a plan is selected.

To reduce malpractice costs. Medical professionals commonly believe that a threat of malpractice is causing large increases in their costs of diagnosis and treatments since they now order more tests and possibly even conduct more treatments than they would otherwise. The economic literature on this point is not at all clear, and some studies show that the effects are actually small (Harvard Medical Practice Study, 1990). In any event, it is not clear that the threat of malpractice action has improved the quality of care substantially or driven out marginal providers.

To manage workers' compensation costs and care. Workers' compensation costs have risen dramatically in the last decade, driven primarily by the costs of medical care. The patterns of practice in the medical care of the worker injured on the job are very different for no apparently good reason from those for the same disorders that occur off the job. One suggestion that makes sense but has a number of administrative impediments is unifying coverage or medical care on the theory that the techniques of managed care could be brought to bear and that practice patterns would become similar. Some issues that have not been dealt with include the need to create parallel insurance plans for disability wage replacement and revision of the legal system that has grown up around workers' compensation. Nonetheless, workers' compensation medical care is becoming a key target for many employers.

To make employees better consumers of medical care. Physicians and a number of employers feel that employees and dependents demand far more medical care than is needed to maintain their health (American Medical Association, 1992). Studies show that there is a significant amount of inappropriate care. It is clear that if employees developed better understanding of what medicine can and cannot do and better skills to deal with the medical care system, some of this unnecessary care would not take place and some of the complications that result from it would not happen. But there is no obvious vehicle for people to obtain this information and skill building at present. Since employers have (albeit somewhat unwittingly) taken on the role of financing medical care, they have an incentive to also finance services that reduce inappropriate demand and restore an equal balance of power between patients and physicians or buyers and sellers.

To purchase the best value. Value is quality obtained per unit cost. While quality has not been a major perceived issue among employers until the last year or so, knowledge from their core businesses should tell them higher quality costs less per unit. Though it may initially be difficult to agree on a definition of medical quality, it makes great sense to move beyond quality assurance (or inspection for bad apples) to quality improvement. In cooperative arrangements with vendors of medical services, unit cost can be continuously reduced in real terms.

What Employees Want in
Benefits and Health Programs

Employees have approached medical benefits with mindsets and demands that sometimes parallel those of employers but often diverge. Again, these could be translated into key quality characteristics. These can in turn be operationalized into criteria to guide benefits and health programs and vendor proposals. The following are commonly noted employee opinions, attitudes, and preferences.

Entitlement to medical care. Probably because of the widespread availability of medical benefits through employment and because the vast majority of adult Americans are employed, a mentality has grown up that benefits are an entitlement. Perhaps a more accurate statement would be that access to medical care may be a social right, as it is in almost all other countries. This attitude leads to employee or labor relations problems and workplace disruption when benefits are reduced or removed and affects employment choices.

Maximizing benefits received. Another preference that employees have is to maximize benefits or coverage and reduce out-of-pocket costs. This is the mirror image of cost management. This desire clearly conflicts with attempts to shift costs or even keep pace with cost increases.

Portable benefits. Another employee preference — in this case, related to fears of not being able to obtain insurance — is portability of benefits packages. Even with the knowledge of the relationship of life-style and environment to illness and injury, it is still unpredictable who will develop an illness or suffer an injury and when this might occur (with the exception of some fairly obvious cases, such as drunk driving or heavy smoking). If serious illness seems to develop at random, the fear of losing coverage when changing jobs or in economic downturns is a significant issue.

Freedom of choice. There is clearly preference for freedom of choice in some form. Initially, this was expressed as the wish to be able to choose providers and facilities. More recently, as employers have become aware that unlimited free choice is associated with increased costs, some have begun to express a preference for a choice of benefits plans and options about the way they spend their money instead. This is also true for those who have healthy life-styles and are aware that they are subsidizing those who do not.

Better information to make medically related decisions. Today's employees have expressed a serious interest in information to better understand their choices in prevention, diagnosis, and treatment (Reiser, 1992).

Communicative and helpful providers. This is tied to the preference for information. Interpersonal skills are key to providing better information and relieving anxiety.

A wish to assume more responsibility for medical care. Paradoxically, given the almost total control that patients have given to health professionals in this society, the consumer activism of the last several decades has created a serious interest in regaining some measure of control and joint governance of medical decisions. This may be more true for routine services than those needed in a crisis.

Access and direction to quality medical care. This is generally implied rather than actively sought.

Preventive services. Another outcome of the health promotion movement is a demand for preventive services and health promotion programs and information. While these are not widely offered by medical benefits plans, the question is frequently raised, particularly when employees are confronted by increasing contribution rates, copayments, and deductibles. Prevention is high on many employees' lists as a way of feeling better, maintaining function, and avoiding costs and disability.

Reduced paperwork and administrative details. Bureaucracy is a major reason cited for moving to HMOs and other prepaid or preplanned services.

A number of other preferences translate into key quality characteristics for benefits, programs, and delivery systems. Many of these are derived from surveys of employees, interviews, and focus groups. They are generally characteristics of any purchase that apply particularly to health and medical services and, in fact, are the mirror image of the system today.

- Excellent customer service
- Rapid access and turnaround
- Reduction of undue risk
- Affordability

Current Situation

It is sobering to contrast the above demands, needs, and preferences with the way the American medical industry really functions and the demands employees place on providers.

As described briefly in Chapter One, the American medical industry and the cost escalation with which it is involved
are the product of a unique confluence of circumstances that
started in the post–World War II period and accelerated and
changed in the mid 1960s. There are a number of relatively well-
known reasons why costs have begun to increase at a rapid rate.
It is not entirely clear which of them are most salient or which
came first, although a cycle can be defined involving availability of technology, specialization, and increasing supplies of
providers, as shown in Figure 2.1.

We will identify and briefly discuss each of these primarily so that strategic health managers can be aware of the
forces acting in and on the system. These forces can produce
price and volume effects on medical care programs that could
interfere with the attainment of goals or lead to employee dissatisfaction.

*There is a significant and expanding oversupply of technology and
specialists.* In the mid 1960s, as a result of a series of studies al-
leging that there was a significant shortage of medical care
providers in this country, federal programs were put into place
that provided grants-in-aid to medical schools through capitation and other means to significantly increase the number of
graduates. There was a similar program for nursing schools and
some other professional education programs. At the same time,
support was increased for residency programs and graduate
training through Medicare reimbursement of hospitals and
grants for construction of medical schools and hospitals. The
result was an exploding supply of providers (Starr, 1982).

Because they were trained in specialty-oriented institutions, these new providers tended to be specialists, a trend that
continues. In fact, the physician work force in the United States
is now approximately two-thirds specialists and one-third generalists, which is the inverse of the ratio in most other countries.

Figure 2.1. Supply Growth Spiral.

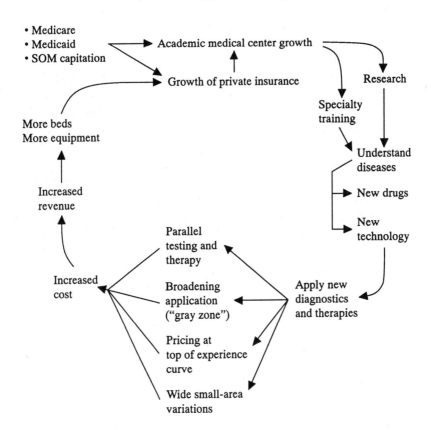

This emphasis on specialists produces narrow but deep diagnostic pursuits and a tendency to use complex therapies and
procedural interventions when they might not be appropriate
(Freimann, 1985). Using a collection of specialists rather than
a primary care provider as an organizing point for care means
that no one understands the total person and the life context
of illness and wellness (Rakel, 1993).

In Canada, at least 53 percent of the physicians are pri-
mary care physicians. There are more physicians per capita in
Canada than in the United States, but many fewer are specialists.
This may be one explanation for the higher intensity of resource

use in the United States. Further, the average Canadian specialist has a full-time workload, while the average American specialist does not (Fuchs and Hahn, 1990).

At virtually the same time, there was a great increase in the resources available to these specialists. The individual National Institutes of Health multiplied rapidly and a good deal of private and public money flowed into medical schools and other research institutions, often on a disease-specific basis. It is interesting to note that a great deal of NIH funding was "extramural" or contracted to medical schools. This rapidly expanded the supply of new pharmaceuticals, new diagnostic techniques, and new interventions that specialists could use (Ginzberg, 1990). Even with the introduction of the less technologically focused Resource Based Relative Value Scale (RBRVS), procedurally oriented specialists are paid more than twice the median salary of generalists, and the ratio of the revenue they generate to their compensation is much higher; generalists generate about twice their compensation, while procedural specialists bill over three times their base compensation (Hammett and others, 1993). Medicare expenditures, for example, have grown rapidly due to the adoption of new technologies (Holahan, Dor, and Zuckerman, 1990).

The effects of supply expansion in the context of unrestricted funding is clearly illustrated by the case of imaging equipment. There are many fewer MRI and CT scanners in Canada, which results in much less downtime or inefficient use of the machinery. There is also a much higher per capita use of magnetic residence imaging, cardiac catheterization, and open heart surgery in the United States (Rubie, 1989). This appears to be a corollary of Roemer's law ("a built bed is a filled bed") — that is, "a present MRI is a used MRI."

There was also an increase in funding to Veterans Administration medical centers, including funding of residency programs. Many VA hospitals affiliated with medical schools, partly to strengthen their staff, but in the process reinforced the growth of specialist residencies. Because public programs like the VA tended not to have obvious financial constraints, they fostered styles of practice that did not focus to any great extent on the economics of the situation.

Pharmaceutical research accelerated at this time, partly as a private initiative and partly because of the availability of funds through Medicare and private insurance. Whether a number of the new techniques and drugs that were introduced confer any superior benefit-cost ratio is a matter of debate.

It could be argued that there is an excessive number of pharmaceuticals. For example, of the 223 new pharmaceuticals introduced in the last eight years, only fourteen attained Class 1A status. Class 1A is the designation for a pharmaceutical with a unique action and a significant therapeutic advance over other available preparations. New drugs are priced at the top of the curve because of patent protection and then are vigorously marketed. Many of them have garnered significant market share. This causes inflation in total price, because much less expensive drugs could accomplish the same effect.

There also appears to be a significant oversupply of insurers and plan administrators. This industry is clearly lucrative, since it now includes over 1,500 insurers and probably several times as many plan administrators. The presence of so many competitors and the slow pace of change in plans drive up total cost. While there does seem to be some price sensitivity for insurance plans and administration, the significant amount of marketing investment being made accounts for a substantial amount of overhead. Exactly how much overhead is consumed in these marketing activities is not clear, but a tremendous amount of time and energy seems to be consumed in meetings and relationship building that is not directly related to the price or quality of the product.

For comparison purposes, because of its single payer system, administrative costs in Canada represent 4 percent of the total health budget. This compares with 12 percent when multiple payers were previously involved and with about 29 percent in the United States (Fuchs and Hahn, 1990; Lundberg, 1993).

Technology is often inappropriately applied. Another interesting result of the expansion of technology is known as the *gray-zone phenomenon*. A good example is coronary bypass surgery. Techniques are generally introduced for fairly narrow indications. However, practitioners have typically tended to use them for unapproved applications or have used surgical procedures — such as bypasses — for legions of patients for which they were not initially tested and for which the benefit versus the risk is not clearly known. Hysterectomy, which is arguably one of the most widely abused surgical procedures in this country, is another example. The gray zone expands the range of uses of technology for specialists and therefore is inflationary as well as potentially detrimental to the patient.

The pricing framework for services and supplies is irrational and not market driven. A number of pricing mechanisms are used in medical care. Most are completely detached from market forces. The first of these is the "usual, customary, and reasonable" statistical pricing system used for physician and other professional reimbursement. This system had its origins in the mid 1960s when Medicare and Medicaid were introduced. Statistical profiles of charges were set up throughout the country. Unfortunately, these profiles included a large number of newly graduated specialists who arbitrarily set prices at levels relatively higher than existing generalists and some specialists. Thereafter, physicians have been reimbursed at a "percentile" of the profiles. Because many insurers and plans reimburse at the 80th or 90th percentile, virtually all bills are paid. (This is a percentile ranking rather than a percentage of a submitted charge.) As providers raise their prices on a semiannual or annual basis, the floor rises and reimbursements increase. There is no negotiation in the mechanism. As a result of this type of reimbursement, doctors' incomes have risen in nominal terms for years and have even risen faster in real terms than wages and salaries for other professionals.

Another mechanism that was solidified at the installation of Medicare and Medicaid was cost-based reimbursement for hospitals. This had been followed by Blue Cross and Blue Shield plans but became institutionalized in the mid 1960s. The theory was that hospitals are quasi-public utilities and therefore should only be paid their cost structure plus some reasonable profit or surplus for future development. This reimbursement method provides absolutely no incentive to increase efficiency if all costs are guaranteed to be paid. In the case of Medicare and Medicaid, a very complex accounting formula is used to determine cost. It is possible that costs can be moved around to different parts of the organization to maximize reimbursement under the formula. Because hospital accounting is relatively arcane, there is no clear and comparable way to determine what costs are attributed to which parts of the organization.

Pricing for new technology is an interesting issue. It appears that as new technologies and new procedures are introduced, they are priced at the top of the price curve as innovations. However, two things then happen. One is that the innovations do not entirely (or even partially, in some cases) replace the old technology they were designed to improve on. As a result, more procedures and tests are performed. Second, even if the prices are set to pay off the equipment relatively quickly rather than amortizing it over a longer period of time, once it is paid for, prices do not drop. They also do not appear to drop when competition is introduced. They appear to be somewhat arbitrary and related to the bargaining power (or lack thereof) of the owning institution.

Hospitals and other providers have adapted to restricted reimbursement from government and managed care organizations by raising prices to other payers, particularly unmanaged indemnity plans and workers' compensation. Medicare reimbursement increases have been capped for a number of years at approximately 3 percent a year. HMOs and other managed care organizations have extracted significant discounts from providers, as have Blue Cross and Blue Shield. Because some buyers will pay full charges for facility care and even practitioners' services, cost shifting is used rather than any improvement in efficiency.

Retroactive discounting creates another distortion in payment between payers. Pharmaceutical manufacturers have started giving large discounts to managed care organizations based on the number of prescriptions consumed for a year at the end of the year. This is an incentive to influence whose medications wind up in their formularies. Widely varying prices are charged to different buyers, depending on their market power. It is not clear whether cost shifting occurs in this context, but it may.

Many insurance plans have simply passed through higher costs, blunting any incentive that suppliers to the hospital and practitioner industries might have to restrain their costs, although some multihospital systems and large group practices have begun to aggressively attempt to negotiate price.

Plan prices seen are unrelated to costs. In addition to the prices paid by health care plans to providers, the pricing of the plans themselves is often divorced from their costs. Prices vary widely for the same apparent benefits package between plans, depending on whether they are attempting to "buy" market share. This accounts for the insurance cycle to some extent.

If benefits managers assertively reject initial large increases in prices, plan sponsors will often return with significantly lower bids. This raises the question of what the actual cost structure is and whether this discounting is sustainable or fair. It also suggests that there is more elasticity in the pricing of health care plans than one would originally be led to believe.

Another plan pricing issue has to do with what is known as *shadow pricing* for managed care organizations. A number of these organizations simply track indemnity costs and then price some small amount lower than that to have a price advantage. In fact, if they realize the economies inherent in managed care both in price contracting and utilization management, plans should be able to price significantly lower even with their additional overhead for management functions. This change has finally begun (Winslow, 1993).

The only way to really expose shadow pricing is to demand a cost audit or to negotiate aggressively for prices and see what the outcome is. A further way might be to analyze utilization data and correlate them with proxy market prices to see what the actual cost of production is. This may well be one of the reasons why managed care organizations have assertively resisted providing utilization data until very recently. One other reason given by these organizations for not providing the data is that they simply did not collect it, since they were basically operating on a fixed budget and the activities within that were not relevant to consumers. That is a debatable proposition that such organizations are beginning to change.

Health insurance creates perverse incentives and economic effects.
In our current health care system, payment for services is not
made at the time of the decision to purchase medical services,
and most of the cost is borne by someone other than the patient. In prepaid plans and in most insurance plans (when the
provider accepts insurance rather than billing the patient), the
only price visible to the patient is a relatively small copayment.
The apparent price to the consumer is much lower than the actual price, reducing any sort of price sensitivity, which in other
markets would restrain purchase of unnecessary services or at
least equate utility with purchasing levels. Some plans require
larger copayments for hospital care. If copayments are requested
at the time of service, they do create some price awareness, but
they are still not a reflection of the full price of care (Employee
Benefits Research Institute, 1992).

The current practice of paying a substantial percentage
of prevailing physician and ancillary charges has reduced the
relative effects of copayments. Under this "usual, customary,
and reasonable" scheme, prices rise as providers raise their
charges, but copayments and other costs paid by employees
do not do so proportionately. As a result, the proportion of
the real price paid by the ultimate consumer — the employee —
has dropped considerably since this mechanism was introduced
in the mid 1960s. Previous insurance schemes were basically
defined benefit plans, which used fixed fee schedules or fixed
benefits levels to pay only for specific treatments and procedures
at a fixed price. Indemnity insurance essentially replaced defined
benefit plans in the 1960s, contributing significantly to the cost
spiral by changing the pricing mechanism (Starr, 1982; Iglehart, 1992e).

Taxation policy encourages over insurance. Because benefits are
less expensive than wages in net, due to their tax deductibility,
employees and employers have tended to overinsure. Overinsurance blunts price effects, since it covers most if not all costs
of service. For example, if two-job couples both purchase insurance, the second insurance policy will typically pay any
copayments or deductibles through what is known as *coordina-*
tion of benefits. The price to the consumer is then essentially zero,

creating unbounded demand limited only by discomfort, time sensitivity, and good sense (Enthoven, 1985).

Another flaw in taxation policy has been to encourage the expansion of benefits. Since benefits are relatively less expensive than wages, and as the financial threat from rising prices for medical care has increased, employers (presumably abetted by employees) have added more and more coverage (Enthoven, 1985). In some sense, they were following the lead of the federal government, which has added benefits to its employee programs and to some extent to public programs. Insurance policies initially covered hospitalization only. In the 1950s, surgical coverage was added. Coverage for ambulatory care, imaging, and laboratory testing was then added, followed by maternity care (which was formerly viewed as discretionary), payment for prescription drugs, and vision and dental care (Starr, 1982). Each time there has been an expansion of benefits, a surge in expenditures for that particular service has occurred. Apparently that which is paid for is that which is ordered.

An interesting sidelight to this situation is that another unintended incentive was created. The initial presumption was that hospital care must be medically necessary since it occurred in the hospital. Therefore, it was reimbursed at 100 percent. The assumption that it was medically necessary has turned out not to be the case, but the copayments designed into ambulatory care insurance to discourage unnecessary use have been left intact. In an era in which care is being shifted to the outpatient arena since it has lower overhead and lower service intensity as well as lower risk of hospital-acquired infections and other errors, paying for inpatient care at a greater rate than outpatient care makes no sense. This tendency has also encouraged providers to attempt to unnecessarily hospitalize patients to minimize their out-of-pocket expenses (Eisenberg, 1986). Of course, this also decreases price sensitivity, inflates costs, and exposes patients to unnecessary risk.

The system is institutionally based and capital intensive. Hospitals have acquired a financial momentum of their own. Each hospital is a medium- to large-sized business, and chains, nonprofit HMO groups, and some large medical centers are among the largest corporations in the world. Very large amounts of cash flow through these institutions, and total return remains high, although much if not all of the return is return on investments rather than operations (Blendon and Edwards, 1991). In this sense, hospitals operate much like banking, insurance, or credit card companies.

As new vertically integrated systems take shape, therefore, they are dominated by hospitals, which have the surplus cash and in many cases tax-free bonding capacity to buy physicians' practices, new equipment, and facilities. In part, this ability to expand is due to the fact that capital reimbursements were not included in the Prospective Payment System (sometimes known as the DRG system) installed for Medicare in 1984. As a result, investment in plant and equipment has continued apace, although it has dropped a bit in recent years (Blanchfield, 1992).

Hospitals have managed to generate significant pools of excess cash and have continued to expand and construct new facilities and buy new equipment. They have then built medical office buildings and offered various concessions to physicians to use the expensive new equipment. This intensifies the trend toward specialization and toward high-tech medicine. The United States is one of the few countries that has a hospital-based system without vertical integration, although this appears to be changing, in part due to the perceived direction of national health care reform.

The momentum is sustained further because hospitals have become major employers, particularly of lower-income individuals. Reducing their financial impact on communities then becomes difficult because of their central economic role and political power base.

The growth of self-insurance has undermined fully insured plans. Self-insurance plans have expanded at a rapid rate, particularly during the 1970s and 1980s. Many companies have chosen to assume risk for their benefits coverage to reduce their substantial state premium taxes and avoid state-mandated benefits. Under the Employee Retirement Income Security Act (ERISA) of 1984 for self-insured plans, federal law preempts state mandates. Such employers also avoid paying marketing and other overhead expenses involved with fully insured products. As more and more employers become self-insured, there is typically adverse selection against fully insured pools of people who may hold individual policies or small-group policies. Characteristically, these populations are less healthy and have higher premiums for that reason as well. This creates inflationary pressure as well.

Demand has expanded to reduce uncertainty. The increasing medical sophistication of most employees has led to an increased demand for both financial protection — which tends to reinforce overinsurance — and more medical care. People now want to have more diagnostic certainty and therefore will often ask for additional tests that physicians otherwise might not suggest (Eisenberg, 1986; Wennberg, 1985; Fuchs, 1968). If one couples an increased knowledge of medical care with diminishing relative out-of-pocket expenses, a premium on time (particularly time when one is feeling reasonably well), and the "medicalization" of a number of situations that are really social problems or emotional issues, demand has certainly increased. Physicians blame patients for excessive demand. In some cases, that appears to be the situation.

A paradox: The delegation of decision making. Despite the increasing sophistication of the consumer, patients have delegated almost all their authority for decision making about their own medical treatment to physicians in this society (Vickery, 1991). This may be partly a function of the increased complexity of medicine and partly the result of a tendency to delegate to specialists by people who work in specialized organizations. What we mean here is not that people should become medical specialists, but that there are different risks, side effects, and consequences to different courses of action. Since each individual's utility, or personal preferences, for functionality, side effects, and potential morbidity and mortality differ (Donabedian, 1992; Mulley, 1992; Reiser, 1992), they should be at least fully informed and at best fully involved in the decision.

More delegation of auto and appliance repair now occurs than in the past, and this may be an example of the same phenomenon. Neither of those decisions entails much personal risk. There seems to be no real consideration of the personal utility of the benefit-to-risk trade-off and pain and lost time involved in some medical treatment. This delegation of authority may act synergistically with the observed increase in demand.

Conclusion

Employers offer benefits as a competitive tool in labor markets, because they have agreed to in collective bargaining agreements, in order to bond employees to the organization and to provide financial protection to them. Employees demand benefits as an alternative or complement to cash wages, and increasingly, to provide protection against financial catastrophe. These factors would be in general agreement were it not for constraints imposed by the rising costs and questionable value of some medical care and somewhat unrealistic demands made of the medical industry for cure for all symptoms and diseases.

The medical industry, meanwhile, has responded to the availability of high and essentially guaranteed levels of funding by continually expanding its supply of technology, facilities, and specialists. This infrastructure then demands more patients and illnesses to support it. So far there has been little actual competition on price in medical care, presumably on the grounds that quality corresponds to price. There is no proof that this is true. There is good evidence that medical care is inefficient and in some cases ineffective, suggesting that price and quality are not necessarily correlated.

The incongruity of employer reasons for offering medical care financing (and prevention and care in some cases), employee demands for medical care, and the behavior of the medical industry under the current financing and organizational models leads to conflict, dissatisfaction, and, again, questions about value—this time from both employers and employees. And again, the solution is active management of this important and expensive purchase.

CHAPTER THREE

Buying Health Care:
Quality and Value
in Medical Care

The debate about medical care costs is shifting from apprehensiveness about costs to concerns about quality. This is a critical change, because without considering the dimension of quality, one cannot compare the relative value of diagnostic approaches and alternative therapies on the individual level or the aggregate value of what is being purchased with multimillion-dollar benefits budgets. Value is increasingly important in a time when both the amount and appropriateness of care are increasingly questioned.

Employers should have no desire to purchase unnecessary, inefficient, ineffective, or inappropriate care. Public programs could probably cover all un- or underinsured Americans within their existing budgets if care were more efficient and effective.

Employers who are familiar with the quality improvement process and the links between resource use, customer satisfaction, and freedom from defects or errors (which is an endpoint accepted by medical care) could be very helpful in working with medical care providers to understand this viewpoint and to adopt the well-accepted techniques of quality improvement to reduce unwanted variation and adverse outcomes and resource use as well as to increase positive outcomes (Laffel and Blumenthal, 1989; Berwick, 1989). The knowledge and resources for quality improvement reside in the very industries that are contracting with medical care providers for services. It would be to employers' advantage to work with their medical care suppliers to convey the principles of quality improvement and to coach them so that quality improvement could become a key part of medical care. Because of a deficit of knowledge about outcomes of medical care, standardizing protocols for testing various processes to treat disease or improve health makes eminent sense.

In this chapter, we review definitions of quality and then discuss some of the evidence that suggests that significant value improvement in medicine is possible and in fact imperative. To frame this discussion of quality and value improvement, we begin by considering definitions of medical quality.

Defining Quality

In older medical paradigms, quality of care was assumed. This assumption underlies the frequently heard assertion that American medical care is the best in the world (in fact, cross-national studies are rare to nonexistent). It also used to be assumed that more medical care was better care and that expensive care was necessarily good care. Patients, physicians, and administrators have tended to view technological sophistication as an indication of high-quality care, though no necessary correlation exists between the availability of technology, the quality of the results it produces, and the appropriateness with which it is used (Warner, 1978).

Providers find it difficult to define quality of medical care. At least five definitions have been proposed by health professionals. Quality has been characterized as a "professionally defined optimum," or that amount of medical care that results in the greatest improvement in health (Donabedian, 1992). This definition acknowledges the benefit-cost relationship but can lead to provision of less and less *cost-beneficial* care at the margin. That is, the benefit-cost curve yields less and less benefit per unit cost as more and more care is provided, until the benefit becomes negative as the risks and side effects of testing and treatment outweigh the benefits. One would want to determine how much benefit is needed to continue to pursue unlikely diagnoses, use less sensitive and specific tests, and add marginally helpful treatments. This definition does not specifically address the measurement of health status, which presumably is the desired outcome.

The second and third definitions are taken from industrial definitions of quality. The second is "conformance to specifications." The definition makes intrinsic sense if one is concerned with quality control. It does beg the question of who determines the specifications (the individual provider, an organization, the patient, or "expert" professionals). It also forces us to decide whether we know enough to identify specifications, and how they should be defined. These latter points would force providers to find "best processes" without necessarily having researched the correlation between process and outcome, since little has been done in many areas. They also raise the question of how to quantitatively measure process and outcome.

The third way quality has been defined is "fitness for use" (Juran, 1988). In this latter definition, therapies, courses of therapy, or processes of care that cause iatrogenic (physician/provider-induced) disease or yield little benefit would be considered unfit for use.

Another definition that is useful in a number of other contexts is the "best match with consumer preferences." Recent research has shown that on average patients are well aware of the technical quality of medical care and that their judgments as nonexperts correlate fairly well with expert judgments of quality (Nelson, Caldwell, Quinn, Rose, 1991; Nelson and others, 1992). In addition, patient judgments about "nasty surprises" strongly influence the decision to use a provider again, so it would be in providers' interest to minimize untoward outcomes or undesirable processes and to prepare patients for the consequences of treatments (Nelson and Larson, 1993).

Agreement must be reached on who decides on the highest level of effectiveness. Candidates might include the practitioners who have superior knowledge of the hazards or benefits of care (although some surveys demonstrate an alarming ignorance in this area). Employees are also candidates to determine effectiveness as measured against the quality of life they seek. It is critically important to determine the ultimate value of purchased care to those who might use it. For example, in one study of options for treatment of lung cancer, many people selected radiation therapy, which has a lower hazard of immediate death but also a lower rate of long-term survival over surgery (Mc-Neil, Weichselbaum, and Pauker, 1978). A similar study of trade-offs between speech and survival in laryngeal cancer again demonstrated that patients' attitudes toward certain procedures may be different from those of practitioners, since they chose therapies that would conserve speech but reduce survival (McNeil, Weichselbaum, and Pauker, 1981). More recent experience with interactive video education about alternatives for prostate disease has confirmed that many patients prefer non-surgical interventions when fully informed (Mulley, 1992; Darby, 1993b). On a more mundane level, it is also important to have a cooperative agreement with patients before embarking on diagnostic testing or treatment in order to avoid committing what could be construed in a later lawsuit as assault or battery.

One should also be aware that patients may have preferences for surgery for cosmetic or psychological reasons or may prefer psychotropic drugs. Prescribing these "therapies" may not be considered best professional judgment. On occasion patients will also express preferences for avoidance of care, which—from a certain standpoint—it would be professionally irresponsible to condone.

Purchasers are also customers in this context. Benefits managers' methods and criteria for evaluating quality have changed in the last few years. In 1990, quality was not considered a measure of managed care success. But in 1992, 76 percent of benefits executives ranked quality very important, whereas 66 percent emphasized dollars saved and 61 percent employee satisfaction (Blendon and Edwards, 1991b; Blendon, Edwards, and Hyams, 1992). Employer priorities have changed as well. They have also changed the way they view and assess quality. Employers' criteria have become more quantitative and less anecdotal (see Table 3.1). In 1989, key employer priorities were as follows: making sure employees get the health care they need, 47 percent; keeping costs down, 37 percent; and improving quality, only 15 percent (Taylor and Leitman, 1989). Employers have now recognized that access is not the issue for many employed Americans.

Table 3.1. How Employers Judge Quality of Care.

	Percentage of employers judging measures as important	
	1988	1992
Employee feedback	87	74
Reputation of providers	83	56
High price	80	N/A
Recommendations of consultants	68	48
Statistical measures of quality	16	45

Source: Blendon and Edwards, 1991b; and Blendon, Edwards, and Hyams, 1992.

The final definition of quality — a definition used in industrial statistical quality improvement — is to minimize variance. This presupposes that the process for a particular course of care has been well defined. One would then want to stabilize the process and reduce the variance around the mean or some other measurement of central tendency (Berwick, 1989). In many contexts, variance for other than what is known as "special causes" is considered an a priori sign of poor quality (Executive Learning, 1993).

Advances in medical care, which have taken it from an art to a science, have been based on the application of population and statistical techniques to determine whether or not a test is accurate or cost effective, and whether a treatment is effective or not compared to control groups or untreated populations. In other words, if the effects are seen in some people and not others, for a net effect that is no greater than random, the test or treatment is not considered effective. A corollary to this initial determination of effectiveness is that the test or treatment should be applied the same way in the same circumstances, or its use lies outside that which was intended and will most likely be less effective than intended. But these approaches are often lost in the transition from the laboratory or test site to the community practice of medicine (Chassin, 1992). In fact, the longer physicians have been out of school and away from an organized practice setting, the greater the divergence from standard practice.

To restore the scientific approach to medical care and dramatically increase cost effectiveness, the statistical techniques used in quality improvement, which are somewhat similar to those used in medical-effectiveness research, should have wide application in medicine as it is practiced. *Variance* is a sign that care is not being delivered the same way for similar problems. In other words, the process of care is not stable and, therefore, less than optimally effective (within the limitations of the current process). Of course, genetic variation and patient condition could account for some variation, so these factors should be adjusted for statistically. After that is done, variance can be determined and reduced on a routine basis.

Reducing variance is a key quality-improvement technique. It is important whether "best practices" are defined as those supported by well-designed studies in the scientific literature or whether professional consensus is used because the evidence is incomplete. One must stabilize the process of care before outcomes research can be done in a meaningful way to provide the basis for improving the current version of best practices.

Bridging Medical and Business Approaches

In other industries, and in some instances in medical care, improvements in quality have led to lower costs by reductions in rework (correction of errors or complications) and removal of unnecessary steps (Laffel and Blumenthal, 1989; Walton, 1990; Berwick, Godfrey, and Roessner, 1990). To achieve these results, process and outcome variance, relative resource use, and customer satisfaction have been employed as key measures of quality. These concepts are not yet as well accepted in medical care, for a variety of reasons. Exactly what quality is in medical care has been a hotly debated topic. This is slowly changing, as it is recognized that inappropriate use of resources constitutes inefficiency or rework and that variance is not a matter of the "art of medicine" but of inefficient and ineffective practice (Blumenthal, 1993b).

Variance may be observed in a number of dimensions in medical care, from variance in performing a certain step in a process to variance in rates of preventive services, surgery, complications, and so on. If equally good care were provided by all providers at all times, with adjustment for health status and health risks and comorbidity, there should be little variance in process or outcome variables. The process of care for a given entity would be performed the same way most of the time, with adjustments for genetic and psychosocial variation, and outcomes would be similar (Brook, 1989).

Efficient resource use may not be accepted as a measure of quality because of a belief that no stone should be left unturned in the effort to alleviate suffering or preserve life. Unfortunately, resources are indeed finite. In addition, most medical treatments have adverse effects; carrying them out when the cost outweighs the benefit causes a decrease in health rather than an improvement. As Donabedian (1992, p. 14) says, "The practice of efficient care is the hallmark of virtuosity in the craft of health care. It is twice blessed: first in reducing waste and second in averting harm."

Customer satisfaction is not fully accepted because of a belief that professionals are repositories of knowledge about quality. There are two difficulties with this mindset. First, evidence would suggest that patients and their relatives understand more about the process of medical care than previously appreciated. Second, there are many customers of the medical process, including physicians and other medical care professionals, ancillary staff, and purchasers of care. Their opinions are all relevant. When medical care providers understand the linkage between customer satisfaction, resource use, variance, and improvement in outcomes, there will be common ground for discussions about quality improvement between employers who pay for care and those who provide it.

A common ground between health professionals and payers may be quality improvement. A profession could be defined as an occupation that is self-perpetuating through control of a special body of knowledge, that polices itself, and that attempts to do the best job at all times (Friedson, 1970; Mirvis, 1993). Mutual discussions of ways to improve quality should be a nonthreatening or neutral way of approaching the efficiency with which care is provided.

Quality Assurance, Control, and Improvement

Understanding the basic differences between quality assurance, quality control, and quality improvement presupposes an understanding of the different definitions of quality. Important distinctions exist (Table 3.2), but they are not widely appreciated in the medical and benefits communities. As one example, when we ask utilization management and managed care vendors to describe their quality improvement programs, what they discuss in proposals and marketing materials is usually a weak form of quality assurance. There seems to be little understanding of quality improvement, although this understanding is increasing. Part of the difficulty may be that health care has been

Table 3.2. Quality Paradigms.

	Quality assurance	Quality control	Quality improvement
Timing	Retrospective	End of process	Prospective or concurrent
Inspection	Yes	Yes	No
Evaluation framework	Implicit	Explicit	Explicit, consensus
Data based	No	Yes	Yes, changing
Data ownership	"Profession"	Quality engineering	Workers
Explicit specifications present	Sometimes	Yes	Yes
Source of specifications	Reviewer's experience or government or review body standards	Designed	Derived
Content of specifications	Adverse events	Physical measurement	Process outcome
Focus	Individual	Output	Process
Consequence	"Corrective action"	Reject output	Improve process

so centered on individual performance and the alleged individuality of patient reactions that the concepts of process, statistical control, and teamwork are foreign to many professionals.

Quality Assurance

Quality assurance is a time-honored but not particularly effective technique often used in health care institutions but long since abandoned in many industries. Health care presently is results oriented or inspection based (Makens and McEachern, 1992). This approach tends to involve overall statistical inspection or sometimes random record review in an effort to find relatively rare adverse events such as returns to the operating room, readmissions within thirty days, deaths, or acquired infections. While the federal Health Care Financing Administration (HCFA), defines these parameters as basic "quality" parameters, they are in fact indicators of the absence of quality. Some of these events are not rare in themselves but occur rarely for individual physicians unless egregiously bad quality exists.

Quality assurance as an approach entails a number of problems. Its capacity to detect poor process quality is relatively low. It is conducted as a review of records, not a review of measurements of process statistics or observations of the processes of care. It can be quite inaccurate because of the typically inadequate state of medical records (Winslow, 1992). It increases overhead because of the need to hire inspectors (or quality assurance coordinators), it is inherently adversarial, and it focuses on the individual rather than on modifying the process so errors cannot occur.

The remedy normally recommended for problems in medical care detected in quality assurance inspections is to subject the offender to more education. This really sidesteps the key issue of how the process of care can be structured in such a manner that errors cannot occur. It also does not square with the notion of health care or health management as continuous processes. And it may or may not work, if the defective process remains in place. In that case, knowledge or intelligence may be used to attempt to overpower the process, a less-than-optimal solution.

A classic example of the inspection paradigm in the health care field was the framework used until recently by the Joint Commission on the Accreditation of Healthcare Organizations (JCAHO) in its audits. These audits focused on structural issues such as the age of buildings, available technology, and the presence of some procedures such as sterilization or surface disinfection. Structural issues about providers included licensure and board certification (the conventional credentialing process). The audits also looked for rare adverse outcomes, but there was little focus on correlating process and outcome. Recently, the JCAHO added a key requirement that institutions have quality improvement programs in place. However, there has been much sound and fury but little meaningful activity in the understanding and installation of effective quality improvement programs. As a transitional step, quality improvement can use the data gathered in quality assurance to identify problems, which can then be rank ordered and subject to process analysis and improvement. And risk-adjusted outcomes can be used to highlight problems on which to focus quality improvement efforts. In this way, the quality assurance process can be used as a front end for quality improvement and as a detector and a continuous feedback loop (Harris, 1992a).

Quality Control

Quality control is also inspection based, but it is concerned with adherence to standards or specifications of each item or service as it is produced. The problems here are similar to those problems with quality assurance. Quality control is labor intensive because of the number of inspectors involved in the quality control effort. The standards tend to be internally derived rather than benchmarked and may reflect only the judgment of one set of customers of the process. They also tend to be static over time rather than continually improving.

Quality Improvement

Quality improvement, on the other hand, returns the responsibility for high quality to those performing the actual work.

Standards are derived from the expectations of the customers of a process. A major effort should be made to determine aspects of the product or service that customers value, perhaps among a group of employers or purchasers, and then to identify factors that cause deviation from these characteristics. Makens and McEachern (1992, p. 25) have described the quality management paradigm as evolving into "delivering the best value to the customer that the producer could afford at a price the customer is willing to pay through the use of total quality management." In medical care, "customers" include patients, physicians, payers, and a host of other intermediate customers.

A key principle of quality improvement is that many services and manufacturing techniques are processes that can be defined and stabilized, have the variance around them reduced, and then be improved in a continuous cycle. Another characteristic of quality improvement is that there is continuous statistical, as well as customer, feedback.

It is difficult to keep a process under control without constant feedback. For example, a number of experiments have demonstrated that when information feedback is provided to physicians, practice variation decreases. But as soon as the information loop is severed, practice variance and costs increase again (Eisenberg, 1986; Berwick and Coltin, 1986; Barton and Schoenbaum, 1990). Unfortunately, mechanisms for meaningful information feedback are not part of most health care delivery systems.

To solve many of the efficiency problems that might be identified during quality improvement efforts, it is important to work across boundaries in organizations and between disciplines (Ferguson, Howell, and Batalden, 1992). Medical and health care have been segmented into smaller pieces, among differently trained professionals and staff, and have evolved different paradigms and languages. Thus the use of teams, accountable and responsible both for their actions and for the improvement of health care processes, would be necessary. It simply is not possible for individuals to provide all services or to effectively control a process, because no one individual has the knowledge of how each aspect of the process works.

A good deal of discussion about multidisciplinary teams in health care has occurred. However, while there are many "teams" of physicians, nurses, and others, in most cases medical care delivery is hierarchical and not based on true participatory teamwork. In addition, there are parallel hierarchies within medical care institutions: a physician hierarchy, the administrative hierarchy, and sometimes a separate nursing hierarchy. These groups typically have experienced friction and have not worked well as an integrated team. Some serious team building, role redefinition, and paradigm change will be needed for these efforts to succeed. In today's medical care climate, it is imperative that they not fail.

Quality and Cost

Because efficiency and effectiveness "move together" (Donabedian, 1992), continuous improvement in quality should by definition result in improvement in cost-effectiveness. One reason that efficiency and effectiveness are highly correlated is that any medical treatment modality contains an element of risk. Provision of ineffective or unnecessary services decreases the net benefit for the patient on an individual level. Provision of high-risk or low-net-benefit services is also "socially inefficient" at the level of a group or society. For example, providing liver transplants for alcoholics who are not firmly in recovery probably has little net benefit for the individual as well as a low efficiency in the social allocation of resources. Therefore, the "pursuit of efficiency" in practice and in overall resource allocation becomes an imperative rather than a choice. Donabedian recommends that health care professions "see to it that effective and efficient care is taught in practice in all settings by creating a new science of parsimonious care" (p. 17).

Donabedian and his co-workers have noted that three kinds of efficiency in medical care exist. The first is *production efficiency,* which has to do with the cost of producing goods or services. This is generally thought to include the functions in medical care that do not involve a direct-judgment clinical component, including the relative efficiency of facilities as a function of scheduling, appropriate or excess capacity, useful or redundant administrative steps, amount of information available, and other related service tasks. *Clinical efficiency* is the cost per unit of improvement in health. The third type of efficiency is not labeled but is caused by a failure of the science of medical technology itself or the absence of research on the relative cost-effectiveness of alternative courses of care (Donabedian, Wheeler, and Wyszewianski, 1982).

Production efficiency can be improved by studying the flow of service processes and improving them, and by reducing excess capacity. Clinical efficiency can be improved by studying alternative flows of clinical decision making and determining the most effective process to use, with branches for differing genetics history and clinical states. With improvement in clinical efficiency, the relative effectiveness of treatment increases as well. Failures of knowledge, judgment, attention, or skill contribute to ineffective care by causing rework. But it should be noted that these problems can be engineered out through the use of carefully designed processes. Focusing on the individual practitioner or employee rather than the process creates antagonism and is not ultimately effective.

Practitioners frequently complain that a focus on the average or usual process would lead to "cookbook medicine." This reaction and the possible reasons for it bear careful thought and analysis. Physicians may be concerned with the many variations in psychosocial factors and the bell-shaped continuum or subtypes of biological response to factors causing disease and to treatment. I would simply point out that the entire science of medicine is based on determining best practices for the "average" case. The contents of any medical school course or standard textbook do precisely that, yet they are not regarded as cookbook medicine. The process of a diagnostic or surgical procedure can be honed and improved, and the process of clinical inquiry can be made more efficient through the use of clearly articulated branching inquiry rather than random application of knowledge. Both inter- and intrapractitioner variation have been observed to be common. Both are inefficient as well as less than optimally effective.

Medical care lends itself well to quality improvement since in fact it is process oriented, and ongoing debate already exists about the best way to do many things (Berwick, 1992; Blumenthal, 1993b). Because outcomes have not been tested for many diagnostic and treatment alternatives, focusing on processes might well be a good starting place, since testing many alternatives at once is insupportable by most research designs. The initial issue is understanding and defining the process. It can then be tested or several alternatives can be compared. One could then correlate a standardized process (or processes) rather than a somewhat random one with specific outcomes. Random processes do not lead to reproducible results.

Another important advantage of the quality improvement process is that it involves workers in the process of health care (Ferguson, Howell, and Batalden, 1992). Since delivering high-quality care has always been an ideal of health care professionals, the quality improvement process has the potential to reengage many disaffected health care workers in the process of care itself. For example that there are several hundred thousand nurses, technicians, and others who have withdrawn from the medical labor force. Two reasons appear to be dissatisfaction with their lack of intellectual involvement in the process of care and their unequal status and treatment. Some observers believe that the current nursing, therapist, and technician shortages would not exist if these highly skilled workers returned to the labor force. It is a waste to society and to the industry to ignore the creativity and commitment of any members of the health care team. The loss in this area has not been quantified, but it is undoubtedly large.

Deming (1986) and others have noted that quality improvement often requires cultural transformation. The following list includes some of Deming's famous "Fourteen Points" that are particularly salient to health care (Makens and McEachern, 1992, pp. 28–29).

- Cease dependence on inspection [that is, quality assurance and utilization management] to achieve quality.

- Improve constantly and forever the system of
  production and service, to improve quality and
  productivity and thus decrease cost.
- Institute more and different training on the job.
- Institute leadership.
- Drive out fear.
- Break down barriers between departments.
- Eliminate work standard "quotas" [such as the
  reimbursement system in health care].
- Remove barriers that rob people of their pride
  in workmanship [that is, empower people and
  change the traditional hierarchy].
- Institute a vigorous program of education and
  self-improvement.
- Put everyone in the company [institution, prac-
  tice] to work to achieve the transformation.

A cultural transformation is clearly needed to place the focus
on efficiency and effectiveness rather than on creating more
redundant facilities, turf battles between various types of health
care professionals, pursuit of target incomes, insistence that patients and payers are not able to judge quality, and inappropriate use of medical resources.

The quality improvement process is remarkably similar
to the strategic management process recommended to manage
health. In this view, there are three levels of total quality: strategic, managerial, and operational (Snee, 1990). At the *strategic
level,* visioning activities indicate when and where to put resources
into action to achieve total quality. The strategic level requires
management leadership, understanding of product quality and
customers, an emphasis on teamwork, and constancy of purpose, or an unfailing determination that the organization will
constantly improve and innovate. Systems are implemented at
the *managerial level* to align the organization's activities with a
strategic direction. At the *operational level,* a series of activities
(Scholtes, 1988; Executive Learning, Inc., 1993) then prioritize,
characterize, standardize, reduce variance around, and improve
the processes.

Need for Quality Improvement in Medical Care

Recent health service research has demonstrated a number of findings that, in light of quality improvement principles, indicate substantial opportunities for improving the quality and cost structure of medical care.

Variance

The wide variation in hospitalization rates observed among medical care plans and benefits options implies that at least the upper end of the curve is not optimal resource use. As recently as 1990, there were over 500 bed days per 1,000 persons under age sixty-five for fee-for-service patients (Camerlo, Giffin, Hodges, and Palsbo, 1992), as opposed to figures as low as 110–150 bed days per 1,000 for the most efficient managed care organizations (Doyle, 1990; A. M. Wiesenthal, personal communication, 1993). There may be some differences in the underlying populations of the managed care organizations versus the Group Health Association of America figures, which apply to the population as a whole, but room for improvement clearly exists. The situation is similar for ambulatory care.

There is considerable variance in the appropriateness and frequency of the use of surgery and medical therapies and procedures among small areas, counties, states, and regions within the United States and among countries (Chassin and others, 1987; Connell, Blide, and Hanken, 1984; Connell, Day, and LoGerfo, 1981; Leape and others, 1990; Wennberg, Freeman, Shelton, and Bubolz, 1989). This variance cannot be explained on a "medical-necessity" basis. There is even significant "intraphysician" variance among courses of action taken by the same practitioner for the same disorder at different times. This variance may either be random, in which case it is undesirable, or it may be related to unmeasured factors such as differences in patient situation. It could be an intuitive interaction between the practitioner and the patient and his or her environment and previous behavior. The variance has been observed to be large, suggesting at least some element of the first possibility. It deserves careful consideration and study in the near future (Wennberg, 1991).

In one series of studies, there were fourfold variations in the rates of hysterectomies and prostatectomies and a sixfold variance in the rates of tonsillectomies and adenoidectomies among small areas of New England (Wennberg and Gittelsohn, 1973; Wennberg, Barnes, and Zubkoff, 1982). Wide variations in surgical rates have been noted among England, Wales, Canada, and Norway, with the United States having much higher rates of almost all kinds of surgery but essentially no difference in health status (McPherson, Strong, Epstein, and Jones, 1981).

In a more recent study of coronary bypass surgery volume and prices in Massachusetts for one of this country's largest corporations, a substantial variation was found in both the price and the amount of surgery. The same group has also demonstrated wide variations in the Caesarean section rate and in the rates of cardiac catheterization, colonoscopy, tonsillectomy, and hysterectomy in the Northeastern United States (Caper, 1992).

Documentation from utilization management and managed care organizations has clearly shown that there is a wide variation in the intensity of service rendered to patients with similar diagnoses and apparent clinical severity in different geographic areas and among physicians. The admission rate and length of stay for similar diagnoses is highly variable as well (Harris, 1988b; Harris, 1991; Harris, 1992e; Connell, Day, and LoGerfo, 1981; Wennberg, Freeman, Shelton, and Bubolz, 1989).

Overuse

A good deal of the care rendered in this country makes no measurable or detectable difference to health status. Despite massive increases in inputs of medical care, the evidence is not clear that there has been much improvement of our population's health. The sharply increased use of medical services after the enactment of Medicare and Medicaid did not result in fewer symptoms or disability days or higher perceived health status (Benham and Benham, 1975). Similarly, the increasing use of health services, which has been related to income, does not improve health, at least according to one major study (Grossman, 1972). In fact, the marginal gain for increases in medical expenditures in this country is only 1 to 10. In other words, a 10 percent increase in medical expenditures leads to a 1 percent improvement in mortality. While other endpoints such as morbidity and the quality of life should certainly be considered as well, the finding raises the question of whether this is the most efficient use of these funds (Fuchs, 1974).

On a smaller population level, in the RAND Health Insurance Experiment, in which patients were randomly assigned to several insurance and managed care plans (see also Chapter Seven), markedly increasing the copayment caused physician visits to drop by 40 percent, hospital admissions to decrease by 21 percent, and total cost to drop by 19 percent. Similar figures were obtained for ambulatory care, mental health services for the outpatient setting (which demonstrated a 57 percent drop) (Manning, Wells, and Benjamin, 1986), dental care, prescription drug use (43 percent decrease), and emergency department use (Newhouse, 1985). When care was free, 33 percent of hospital days were judged to be medically inappropriate and 17 percent of the admissions could have been taken care of on an outpatient basis for surgical procedures (Siu and others, 1986). However, with the exception of small changes in blood pressure and corrected distance vision in low-income patients, there were essentially no differences in health status among the groups with high and low utilization. These observations validated the results of a previous study conducted in the 1970s in the San Francisco Bay Area (Scitovisky and Snyder, 1972).

When procedures are overused (or are used for inappropriate indications), a significant downside is likely to exist. For example, in the RAND study of carotid endarterectomy, 10.8 percent of patients who underwent their procedure for inappropriate indications either died within thirty days of surgery or suffered an intraoperative stroke. However, the clinical literature suggests that this procedure ought to be performed with a major complication rate of 3 or 4 percent (Chassin and others, 1989).

A specific example of clinical inefficiency is the excessive use of Caesarean sections. Caesarean section rates vary significantly internationally. The rate is 6 percent in Ireland and 10.5 percent in England and Wales, with no difference in morbidity or mortality. In the United States, the rate was 5.5 percent of deliveries in the 1960s and now exceeds 40 percent in some geographic areas. A National Institutes of Health study in 1980 concluded that the rate was too high (at that point, the rate was 17 percent) (Gleicher, 1984; Kanouse, Winkler, and Kosekoff, 1989; National Institutes of Health, 1981). Studies have not demonstrated any correlation between the Caesarean section rate and improved outcomes. In some academic medical centers and a few community settings — one in Chicago in particular — the rate has been reduced from a level just below 30 percent to below 12 percent with no adverse effect on outcome but a significant savings in morbidity, mortality, and cost (Gould, Davey, and Stafford, 1989; Gleicher, 1984; Goyert, Bottoms, Treadwell, and Nehra, 1989; Myers and Gleicher, 1988; O'Driscoll and Foley, 1983; Stafford, 1990). The only reasonable conclusion is that a large number of these surgeries are performed for inappropriate reasons (Chassin and others, 1989).

Misuse

A number of studies from the RAND Corporation demonstrated significant inappropriate use of medical and surgical procedures (Chassin and others, 1989; Greenspan and others, 1988; Chassin and others, 1987b; Kahn and others, 1988). Other studies have demonstrated that drugs are frequently used inappropriately — that is, used without a clear indication for which therapeutic efficacy has been demonstrated (Wells, Goldberg, and Brook, 1988; Helling, Norwood, and Donnor, 1982; Schaffner, Ray, and Federspiel, 1983; Avorn and Soumerai, 1983).

A number of procedures have been used for indications far beyond those proven effective by the original clinical trials. For example, the Swan-Ganz catheter, which is used to measure blood flow in the heart, was introduced for very specific reasons. However, it is complicated and requires training for proper use. In one study, a large number of injuries and deaths were attributed to its overuse without accepted clinical trial evidence that the benefits of the catheter exceeded the risk except in cases of overt heart failure following myocardial infarction (Jennings and Robins, 1985).

Process Safety: A Clue to Process Efficiency

There is now a body of literature documenting the high rate of medical misadventures. At first glance, a number of processes in medical care appear to be unsafe. However, the real issue is more likely that the processes are not stabilized or well adhered to. The typical medical response to this has been that a problem existed with practitioner training or confidence. However, there are several impressive experiments which demonstrate that if the process were standardized, these supposed human factors would be much less likely to occur.

For example, it was estimated in 1985 that 10,000 people per year died from anesthesia administration (Pierce, 1985). The professional consensus was that 80 percent of these were "human errors." Other negative consequences of anesthesia can range from loss of life or a major organ through functional impairment to pain, nausea, and vomiting. When the spectrum is expanded in this way, the number of cases which are potentially suboptimal expands enormously. In another study, human error in dispensing anesthetics was listed as a primary reason for a wide variation in the risk of heart attack among adult, child, and emergency patients (Keenan and Boyan, 1985). The anesthesiology profession went on record as stating that this did not constitute reasonable care (Hamilton, 1979; Cooper, Newbauer, and Kiz, 1984).

The series of potential causes for anesthesia deaths and other adverse consequences can be indicated in a "fishbone" or cause-and-effect diagram — a diagnostic tool commonly used in quality improvement (Figure 3.1). When a standardized process for anesthesia was introduced by the Massachusetts Medical Society and was accompanied by a prospective reduction in malpractice premiums when physicians agreed to abide by

Figure 3.1. Root Causes of Anesthesia-Associated Injury.

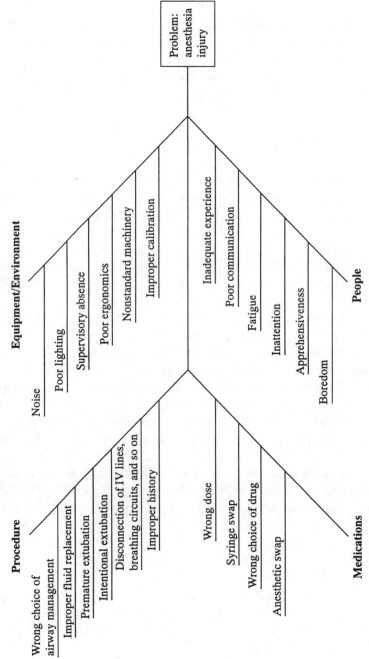

Source: Adapted from Cooper, Newbauer, and Kiz, 1984.

the guidelines, there was a 40 percent drop in anesthesia deaths and at least that much of a decrease in malpractice premiums in the first year (Eichorn and Eichorn, 1989).

Another example of the lack of standard procedures can be seen in the use of defibrillators. In one study, at least half the operators were not completely aware of how the machine worked, were not properly trained, and did not perform in a standard way (McGergan, 1984). Problems in this case may range from incomprehensible technical manuals to lack of training to lack of practice. These are all process variables rather than individual problems. Often sales personnel are used to train medical personnel how to use equipment, but they may not be familiar with the equipment or have the right technical background. And most nursing school curricula do not include a basic introduction to instrumentation.

One additional example may make the point clear. Failure to make a correct diagnosis is apparently common in medical care. Some studies have shown that the incidence of diagnostic error among medical students, residents, and interns is 40 percent or more, with a *commission* rate of about 7 percent and an *omission* rate of 25–35 percent (Wray and Freedlander, 1986). The list of errors sounds like a brainstorming session to build a cause-and-effect diagram during a quality improvement study, implying that the issue is indeed standardization and then improvement of the core process of taking a history and performing a physical examination (Figure 3.2).

The high incidence of errors of commission and omission is not confined to physicians in training, and one might suspect again that it is probably due to the lack of a systematic approach. For example, in one study only, 53 percent of heart attacks were discovered clinically (Zarling, Sexton, and Milnor, 1983). Autopsy studies at Washington University revealed that one in two pulmonary emboli, one in two cases of peritonitis, and four in ten pulmonary abscesses were also overlooked. Similar results were found at the Brigham and Women's Hospital and Harvard Medical School, some of our foremost medical institutions. In another study, the mistake rate of reading x-rays compared to autopsy results was put at 20 to 40 percent (Berlin, 1977).

Figure 3.2. Root Causes of Diagnostic Errors.

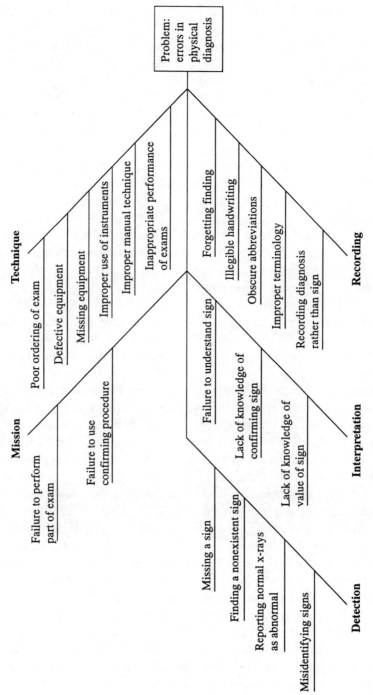

Source: Adapted from Wray and Freedlander, 1986.

One would suspect that a more systematic approach to diagnosis and treatment would reduce these rates. It certainly would not hurt to try quality improvement techniques, since the economic and personal consequences of this level of sensitivity and specificity are significant in an employed population.

The point of this review is not to attack the medical profession but to demonstrate that the great variation in the way problems are approached is a symptom of process variation and inefficiency. By studying process flow, alternative routes to the same endpoint can be identified (Wennberg, 1985). Typically, the most parsimonious approaches save tremendous amounts of money with no change in the outcome. For example, when the conditions under which x-rays were really needed for injuries at Yale New Haven Hospital were identified, significant savings resulted that were projected to save hundreds of millions of dollars annually if implemented on a national basis (Brand, 1984). Similar conclusions have been reached about the use of percutaneous transluminal angioplasty for peripheral vascular disease (Doubilet and Abrams, 1984), Caesarean sections (McEachern, Hallum, and Schiff, 1992), hysterectomies (Bernstein and others, 1993), and a wide variety of other procedures.

There appears to be a J-shaped curve in which risk decreases with conservative management of many conditions (for example, watchful waiting). In other words, with watchful waiting, the risk-benefit ratio drops and then after a certain point begins to rise again (Neutra, 1977). Documentation and implementation of best practices, including a more conservative approach to procedural intervention, would result in reduction in variation. That in turn would lead to significant savings in time, expense, morbidity, and mortality (Chassin, 1992; Schoenbaum, 1991).

Usefulness of Information Feedback

Wennberg, Eisenberg, and other long-time observers of the medical care system feel that a good deal of practice pattern variation results from physicians' lack of feedback about their practice patterns and the consequences of them (Wennberg, Blowers,

Parker, and Gittelsohn, 1977). Many physicians have asked for concise directives (or practice guidelines) to give them guidance on standard procedures (Kanouse, Winkler, and Kosekoff, 1989). There are a number of demonstrations of the effectiveness of peer or professional information transfer in changing behavior such as prescribing patterns (Schaffner, Ray, and Federspiel, 1983; Avorn and Soumerai, 1983), length of stay (Eagle and others, 1990), and test use (Berwick and Coltin, 1986; Long, Cummings, and Frisoff, 1983). (Also see Chapter One.) However, Eddy (1992) has noted that practice guidelines and treatment protocols are not effective unless they are coupled with communitywide dissemination of practice pattern information.

Need for Better Record Keeping

Medical records are one of the major "products" of medical care and the foundation for information feedback loops. Improving medical record keeping is a major opportunity for improvement; it has ramifications both for the process itself and for the ability to obtain data, analyze them, use them for a feedback mechanism, and improve other processes. According to a recent study by the Institute of Medicine (1991), medical record keeping is a major activity in medical care that is often poorly or redundantly executed. In its present state, it engenders a tremendous amount of rework. Poor record keeping also leads to erroneous or dangerous treatment.

According to a compilation of studies by the *Wall Street Journal* (Winslow, 1992), 38 percent of physicians' time and 50 percent of nurses' time is spent dealing with or producing medical records of various types. In 27 percent of records, however, physicians failed to note the chief complaint. Forty percent of records had no diagnosis recorded. Seventy percent of patients' paper records were incomplete. Thirty percent of the time, physicians could not get access to a record during an office visit; in 11 percent of the charts examined, laboratory results were not recorded and the tests had to be reordered.

Several industrial engineering studies have shown that there are multiple computer systems in hospitals that cannot interact and from which it is difficult to access and retrieve data. Further, these systems typically do not collect clinical data, so that the correlation between the process, resources used, costs, and condition of the patient is difficult to assess.

Conclusion

Both employers and employees are increasingly concerned about the value of medical care. Is the quality received worth the cost? There is still considerable debate about the definition and measurement of quality in medicine, but it has become clear that a number of dimensions are important: efficiency, effectiveness, customer satisfaction, and provider satisfaction. Efficiency is in turn the product of clinical efficiency and production efficiency. Clinical efficiency is affected by overuse, misuse, and (rarely, except for preventive services and risk reduction therapy) underuse. Generally used measures of "quality" such as adverse events and missed diagnoses are in fact metrics of poor quality, or the mirror image of quality.

Quality improvement holds the promise of dramatically increasing the value of medical care while decreasing medical misadventures. Effective quality improvement probably will require a culture and paradigm shift in medicine, which could be aided by "technology transfer" from employers. The savings from better production and clinical practice are projected to provide more than enough funds to cover the uninsured or to markedly reduce expenditures or both (Starr, 1992).

CHAPTER FOUR

Supplying Health Care: The Dynamics of the Medical Care Industry

It is important to keep in mind that the United States has a large, profitable, and growing medical care industry rather than a "health care system." In planning strategies to provide medical care for employees and dependents, employers should understand who they or their benefits plans buy services from. The way the industries are organized, what services are actually provided, the way each group of companies or providers looks at the world, how financing is arranged, the extent of competitiveness, and how various "systems" are put together dictate constraints and possible advantages for buyers.

This knowledge is also important in the context of the debate on "national health care reform." That debate has mainly been framed as a matter of access to health services, implying that we have a "medical care system" in the United States. *Systems* characteristically have central or regional planning, budgeting, and control. In most other industrialized countries, the medical care "system" is run in a government framework, with central planning and some control. None of these characteristics applies to the medical care industry in the United States.

The U.S. medical industry does not involve "health care" but medical care. A small fraction of total outlay or attention is devoted to disease prevention or health promotion, at least within the conventional system (Leaf, 1993). (See Chapter Nine.) A good deal of evidence suggests that socioeconomic programs probably have greater overall effect on health than medical care, which is invoked only after people become ill. These socioeconomic needs range from housing and nutrition to education to jobs to individual and group life-style or health promotion activities (Lundberg, 1992). Unfortunately, those programs have lost funds in recent years, in part because burgeoning government medical expenditures have taken a disproportionate share of the budget, and in part due to the ideological bent of the past two administrations.

The medical care industry is the largest employer in the United States (Francis, 1993). It is a major and expanding source of employment in many communities, as well as a major cost to most employers. Payers should understand the business structure of each sector, to understand the nature of competition (if any), the oversupply or shortage of each factor, one's ability to negotiate, and alternatives as these affect access and cost. The relative profitability of each sector, in the context of reimbursement and level of supply, may provide one basis for negotiations on price. Because the current reimbursement system may introduce serious distortions in motivation to negotiate, the payment mechanism in use must be kept in mind as well.

Industry Overview

It is useful to divide the medical care industry (or "sector") into three general categories (or "segments"): (1) the "delivery system" or "retail" segment, which provides services directly to patients; (2) the "intermediate supplier" segment or group of companies and organizations, which supply the delivery system (including manufacturers of imaging equipment, durable medical equipment, laboratory supply companies, and so on; and (3) the financing system — the group of companies that provide financing for medical care. Although the distinction between the delivery system and the financing system has become increasingly blurred, it is important to understand both segments.

As a generalization, each segment of the medical care industry is highly fragmented, without clear market leaders or groups that have a large market share. Physicians and hospitals also compete, with a few exceptions, only in local or regional rather than state or national markets. The exceptions may be supply and equipment manufacturers. There are many com-

petitors and constant market entry (for example, off-site laboratories, imaging centers, home health care agencies, ambulatory
facilities, and mobile procedures suites).

This analysis can be confusing, because some suppliers
may have many customers, and some relationships work in both
ways (Garvin, 1988). Hospitals are good examples of a two-
way relationship. Hospitals are a "workshop" for doctors, and
they also provide facilities and services for patients. Doctors,
on the other hand, provide patients to the hospitals, so they are
both customers and suppliers. In the pharmaceutical industry,
about half of sales are made to the delivery system and half
directly to the public.

We will briefly discuss each segment and groups within
those segments to clearly delineate how the industry is organized
and how it might best be dealt with. This is a business view,
rather than the typical medical/sociological view taken in most
descriptions of the American health care "system." While the
ability to function as a system is important for continuity of care,
access, and social reasons, our concern here is to enable the strategic health management team to understand how best to work
with providers. This knowledge can be merged with knowledge
of the financial mechanics and other dynamics of the present
"system," so that the economic behavior of the industry can be
understood as well. Economic behavior in this context would
include motivators to provide more or less service, reasons why
providers might increase or reduce prices, and the likelihood
that they would be interested in contracting with employers or
their surrogate financing organizations.

The Largest Sector in the U.S. Economy

Employment in the medical care sector increased from 6.8 million people in 1987 to over 10 million by the end of 1992 (Francis, 1993). That represents an annual increase of more than 6
percent, even as the rest of the economy was in a recession and
many other sectors were shrinking. The Commerce Department
has predicted that the medical care industry will employ about
10 percent of the U.S. labor force by the year 2000 (Mosbacher

and others, 1991). That prediction may well be conservative if the economy continues to grow at a slower-than-predicted rate. Because medical care is one of the main underpinnings of the economy of many communities, benefits managers and executives face the paradoxical situation of possibly affecting employment in other industries in an attempt to make sure that theirs survives (Greene, 1991).

There is a debate among economists about whether medical care creates new or real wealth for two reasons. First, medical care is basically a service rather than a producer of goods (although the supplier side of the industry certainly does produce goods, and whether services produce new wealth is a subject of some debate). Second, because there is marked inefficiency within the industry, it is not clear if any wealth has been created in net, even if the argument that services do not create wealth is rejected (V. R. Fuchs, 1993).

A solution must be found to these problems in order to ensure a balanced economy in many areas ("As Outpatient Care . . . ," 1993). It is possible that, through joint quality improvement efforts, some resources currently used for acute medical care may be redeployed and the industry might become more efficient. As a political and tactical matter, it might make sense for communitywide organizations of employers and medical care providers to make plans for workers who might be displaced from the medical care sector if efficiency were increased or demand were decreased. Many of these employees are at the low end of the wage scale, and termination of their employment might well have an impact on public sector spending for welfare and other types of social outlays.

Retail/Delivery System

Employers will most likely have contact with the "retail" side of the industry if they build their own delivery systems or attempt to improve an existing one (see Chapter Twelve). We will therefore briefly survey the supply of these resources, their organization, and their relative profitability to provide an overview of pricing structure and possible negotiating positions. At the retail or delivery system level, there is most often nonprice competition (amenities, reputation, customer service, and so on), since the reimbursement ensures payment at some level, be it charges, reimbursement profiles, or cost plus some margin.

Physician Services

Physician groups or physician practices have been a cottage industry, with solo or small group practices. This is changing rapidly as physicians choose personal life-style over long hours of service and as groups expand for a variety of reasons, including direct interfaces with employers, greater use of contracting with paying organizations, and the ability to provide administrative services to physicians who can then concentrate on practicing medicine (De La Fuente, 1993c, 1993d). Physicians have been joining group practices, which provide an organizing framework (see Chapter Eleven), at an increasing rate. The proportion of physicians in private practice in groups of three or more has increased from 10.6 percent in 1965 to 32.6 percent in 1991 (Havlicek, Eiler, and Neblett, 1993). A number of these organizations are also structured to assume large debts that individual practitioners have incurred for equipment and facilities.

In 1992, physicians' services accounted for 18.7 percent of the total outlays for medical care (Francis, 1993). This is predicted to increase slightly to 22 percent by the year 2000 (Sonnefeld, Waldo, Lemieux, and McKusick, 1991). Physicians generate over half a million dollars of annual expense each, so every additional doctor drives costs up further (Eisenberg, 1986).

Supply and Employment. The "physician" segment of the retail sector of medical care includes both doctors and nonhospital support personnel. Both groups are growing. The supply of physicians has increased rapidly since 1960, rising from just over 250,000 in 1960 to over 615,000 by 1990. Over 400,000 are in active patient care (Roback, Randolph, and Seidman, 1992). The American Medical Association has projected that the total supply of active physicians in the United States will increase to over 760,000 by 2010, with most of the growth occurring in the surgical subspecialties (Rodgers, 1992). In 1960, there were 148 doctors for each 100,000 people in the United States; by 1990, there were 245 per 100,000.

The specialist physician surplus is now estimated to be equal to as much as 50 percent of the number actually needed. That is, the current supply is 50 percent over capacity in many specialties, and up to 200 percent over capacity in some specialties such as neurosurgery (Kronick, Goodman, Wennberg, and Wagner, 1993; Wennberg, Goodman, Nease, and Keller, 1993). Another recent study using staffing patterns at seven large, closed-panel HMOs in 1983 as a benchmark demonstrated that the true "need" might be as few as 111 physicians per 100,000 Americans, or less than half the current supply (Mulhausen and McGee, 1989). These estimates assumed that there would not be an increase in the use of mid-level practitioners. The use of mid-level practitioners has been constrained by a variety of economic and political factors. However, there is consensus that they could perform a significant number of the preventive, primary care, and routine functions that physicians perform now at a significantly lower labor rate, and probably with better patient communication (Dunford, 1993). If there were to be a significant expansion in the supply and use of mid-level practitioners, the physician oversupply would be dramatically increased.

There are significantly more specialists than it is believed are necessary, particularly medical and surgical subspecialists (Harder, Kletke, Silberger, and Willke, 1988). For example, the weekly number of equivalent operations performed by each surgeon in the United States is approximately four or five, less than two days of work. In HMOs, by contrast, surgeons operate the equivalent of five days per week (see Chapter Eleven). Half of the surgeons in the United States are significantly underutilized (Gonzales, 1992; American Hospital Association, 1991; SMG Marketing Group, Inc., 1991). Oddly enough, surgeons report working almost sixty hours a week, but it is not clear what they are doing during this time (Rodgers, 1992). Presumably, they are performing primary care, for which they are not well trained. Despite this oversupply, during the 1980s, the number of surgical specialists increased by 28 percent (Roback, Randolph, and Seidman, 1992).

During the 1980s, the number of general medical practice physicians grew only 17 percent, compared to a 30 percent growth in medical specialists. By contrast, there are shortages of preventive medicine specialists, pediatricians, and psychiatrists.

There is a significant maldistribution of physicians geographically as well (Hicks and Glenn, 1989), with significant shortages in inner cities and rural areas and probable excesses in suburban areas (Roback, Randolph, and Seidman, 1992).

Physicians' offices are the fastest-growing area of employment in the medical care industry. Between 1982 and 1991, employment in physicians' offices grew from 887,000 to 1.46 million. Labor costs have escalated as well. While hours worked stayed constant at an average of thirty-two per week, the average hourly wage almost doubled, from $6.92 per hour in 1982 to $11.35 in 1991 in nominal terms (Sonnefeld, Waldo, Lemieux, and McKusick, 1991).

Utilization. While the volume of physician services, primarily office visits, has grown slowly (in the range of a few percent) over the last fifteen years, intensity, or the number of tests and procedures per visit, has increased dramatically for reasons that do not seem linked to medical need. There was a 20 percent increase between 1975 and 1980, a 23.3 percent increase between 1980 and 1985, and a 37.5 percent increase between 1985 and 1990; this trend is projected to continue at that level for the next decade (Cowan and others, 1992).

Price and Income. Most discussions of the economics of medical practice have focused on physician fees and income, since most doctors have charged for their own time on a per visit or per procedure basis. This has established a convention, even in group practices. "Revenue" is equated here with gross physician income, and profit is interpreted as net personal income to physicians. "Prices" are typically stated as fees.

Physicians' *fees* have increased dramatically since the passage of Medicare and Medicaid and the "follow-me" expansion of benefits by employers. The artificial base for the usual, customary, and reasonable fee profile contributed to this growth (Starr, 1982, 1992). Between 1945 and 1969, physicians' fees rose only 3.8 percent in real dollars (Goldstein, 1972). But then, starting in 1970 and accelerating since at least 1975, price inflation for physician services has been significant. Total price inflation was 14.1 percent from 1975 to 1980 and over 40 percent between 1980 and 1990. It is projected to be in the range of 9 percent between 1990 and 2000 (Sonnefeld, Waldo, Lemieux, and McKusick, 1991).

Physicians' *income* has increased since the enactment of the Medicare and Medicaid laws as well. Annual income rose at 5.9 percent a year in real dollars until the mid 1960s (Goldstein, 1972). At that point, with the rapid growth of hospitals and inpatient technology, a number of the functions of the physicians were assumed by hospital staff and charged for by the hospital. Physicians thus performed fewer services for the same income (Blumberg, 1979). The differential percentage is 50–60 percent more per hour. According to the House Ways and Means Committee, the nominal net income of physicians in practice after expenses but before taxes grew from $32,000 in 1969 to over $164,000 for all physicians (including physicians in training, who have much lower income). The mean is over $200,000 for radiology, anesthesiology, and surgical specialties (Congressional Research Service, House Ways and Means Committee, 1991; Gonzales, 1992; Hammett, 1993).

The increase has been concentrated in the procedural specialties, making them more economically attractive. There are more proceduralists, and in addition they are charging more. For example, the real median surgical net income rose 51 percent over the decade of the 1980s, three times the rate of increase for primary care physicians, and reached $200,000 in 1990 (Gonzales, 1992). Interestingly enough, the total number of operations performed in the United States increased only 26 percent during the same time frame (American Hospital Association, 1991; SMG Marketing Group, Inc., 1991). Incomes rose because surgeons charged much higher fees for new, high-technology procedures that joined but did not replace older procedures (Blumberg, 1979; Eisenberg and others, 1989). For example, between 1979 and 1989, the number of coronary bypass operations tripled; the number of hip replacements nearly tripled. At the same time, the number of appendectomies dropped by 17 percent (U.S. Department of Health and Human Services, 1980b, 1990).

Physicians have historically resisted negotiated prices, keeping prices high. They have also repeatedly threatened to withhold services if their prices were not met. They have lobbied to enact or preserve public financing mechanisms that used inflationary techniques such as usual, customary, and reasonable fee screens (Starr, 1992). There is some change in this resistance now as physicians rely on managed care organizations for an increasing share of their patient base. Large groups of physicians have been more flexible in price negotiations.

This may be something of a moot point in the total scheme of things. Although doctors' fees account for about 20 percent of medical care costs, their decisions dictate about 80 percent of expenditures (Eisenberg, 1986). However, modifying or "containing" their fees under any of the proposed health care reform scenarios, including the recently adopted (and bitterly opposed) Resource Based Relative Value Scale, would only change total medical outlays by a few percent (V. R. Fuchs, 1993). Thus, while this is an important area, particularly because of the power of the physician lobby and the ripple effect on patient satisfaction that fee constraints have, it is not one that will have a great effect on overall costs. A more important issue is the volume of services prescribed or performed.

Responses to Competition and Incentives. Despite the growing supply of physicians, physicians seem to be just as busy as ever. While 36 percent of doctors reported in 1990 that they were seeing more competition for patients than they were in 1982 (Taylor and Leitman, 1990), the percentage whose patient load has actually decreased changed only slightly from 13 percent in 1982 to 16 percent in 1989 (American Hospital Association, 1991). The mean number of patient visits per week has not changed overall since 1984 (Gonzales, 1992). Surgeons saw slightly fewer patients per week over this time period, while internists, family practice physicians, and pediatricians increased slightly.

Physicians state they have responded to the perceived increase in competition by increasing the number of hours worked, by increasing the number of hours their offices are open, and by increasing marketing and amenities. The number of hours worked and total office hours as reported to the American Medical Association rose by two per week (Gonzales, 1992).

Physicians fill a number of roles, ranging from patient advocate to businessperson (Eisenberg, 1986). While the American Medical Association and other professional groups have stressed the former and denied the latter, physicians do in fact appear to respond to economic incentives and conditions. Physicians have maintained what appears to be a target income by increasing prices (Harris, 1992c). This accounts in part for the rise in the income of surgeons.

Two natural experiments have illustrated this. In 1976, there was a change in the Medicaid fee schedule in Colorado. Studies noted that the lower the reimbursement rate for various services, the greater the intensity of service within a given visit or episode, particularly for laboratory services. Likewise, during the wage and price controls in the Nixon administration, prices went up less than 3 percent but visit volume rose 8 to 15 percent. The year after the controls went off, prices rose 23 percent and visits dropped in the range of 10 percent. Similar phenomena have been noted in Medicare (Holahan and Scanlon, 1979). The same phenomenon may well explain rising volume in the workers' compensation arena, where many states have frozen reimbursement according to old fee schedules for some time. In short, an inverse and elastic relationship between price and volume appears to exist. Physicians' preference seems to be to raise prices; when that is not possible and there is no management of medical care, volume is increased.

Despite protestations to the contrary, physicians do respond to economic incentives by increasing volume and adding new services. As noted above, they have also increased prices significantly. They have increased ownership of facilities and participated in joint ventures. There has been some concern that

financial incentives in managed care organizations might lead
in the opposite direction, to underutilization, but that has not
proven to be the case (Hillman, 1991; Hillman, Pauly, and Kerstein, 1989).

Hospitals

Hospitals have been a major cost driver in medical care as well
as a major target for cost management activities. Hospital care
accounted for 39 percent of all medical expenditures in 1991; that
proportion is expected to grow to 41 percent by the year 2000
(Sonnefeld, Waldo, Lemieux, and McKusick, 1991) in spite of
significant growth in the over-sixty-five population (a point only
relevant to employers with employees older than sixty-five and
because of their vulnerability to cost shifting). Hospital care has
comprised between 38 and 44 percent of corporate medical plan
outlays in recent years, down from typical highs of about 48
percent. There seems to be a financial equilibrium of sorts here.
As admission rates and days per 1,000 have dropped steadily
in the last decade, the intensity of services provided has risen
sharply, so that the desired reductions in overall costs have not
taken place. Further, since costs have been shifted from managed
care and government payers to other payers such as individuals, indemnity plans, and workers' compensation, little incentive has existed to increase efficiency. The main cost management tool used has been laying off low-paid support staff.

　　The analysis that follows here should be useful in negotiating with hospitals for unit rates (per day or per hospitalization)
in order to create some financial predictability and foster efficiency and in understanding the pitfalls of discount arrangements. It should also underscore the evidence that hospitals are
capital intensive and apparently inefficient. At the macro level,
massive overcapacity exists. Unfortunately, hospital accounting has not been clear enough to pinpoint areas for improvement. Contracting efforts and supplier improvement projects
could focus on process improvement and reversals of somewhat
unfortunate changes in the labor mix, as well as cost shifting
to ambulatory cost or profit centers. Readers may draw other
conclusions from this summary evidence as well.

Supply. While some beds have been removed from service, there is still significant excess hospital capacity in this country, with the average inpatient occupancy rate at 61.4 percent. The number of beds per 1,000 residents in the United States has not changed substantially since 1965 (Cowan and others, 1992). In other words, even allowing for "surge" capacity, there is a 25–30 percent excess capacity in the hospital segment. Some hospitals have closed, but most were in rural areas. There has been a recent move to mergers in some areas, but whether this will result in removal of excess capacity is unclear. It may lead to some administrative efficiencies (Anders and Winslow, 1993).

As inpatient demand has decreased, hospitals have converted assets to deliver outpatient services, often shifting costs from inpatient cost centers to outpatient ones. There was a 58 percent growth in the number of hospitals providing outpatient services from 1984 to 1989 (American Hospital Association, 1991).

Whether inpatient or outpatient, needed or not, capacity is still being built. Capital (for facilities construction and major equipment purchase) represents 9 percent of the typical community hospital's cost structure. The proportion of these funds going into facilities is much greater than that for equipment. Capital investment in some areas has been increasing rapidly and is out of proportion to the percentage of the population, particularly in New York, Texas, and Florida. However, in California, the percentage of total capital expenditure is about half the typical ratio to the population (Blanchfield, 1992). It may be that new facilities are being added to old ones, rather than closing and replacing unneeded and outmoded plant.

To finance this continued expansion, hospitals have floated bonds at an average of about $11 billion per year. However, this additional debt load is damaging their credit rating and raising interest costs, which are higher for lower-grade debt instruments. There were no hospital bond defaults between 1979 and 1988 but an average of three per year (according to Standard and Poor) from 1989 to 1992. Standard and Poor has consistently downgraded many more hospital bonds than it has upgraded from 1983 to 1991 (Blanchfield, 1992). An average of about fifty bond issues were downgraded each year, as opposed to an average of about fifteen that were upgraded. In 1991, over 40 percent of hospital bonds were triple-B rated.

Employment. Hospital employment continues to grow, even with excess capacity. Despite narrow if not nonexistent operating margins, total employment increased from 3,014,000 in 1982 to 3,674,000 in 1991. This may be due to the increased intensity of patients who are admitted, but keep in mind that the admission rates were declining at the same time. These factors should have evened out. The total number of hospital workers increased, according to another survey, which may have used different definitions, from 4.1 million to 4.3 million from 1983 to 1989; the difference is probably due to the inclusion of governmental hospitals (Anderson and Woottom, 1991). The highest rate of growth has been in the marketing and managerial ranks; the number of marketing, advertising, and public relations managers almost doubled from 1983 to 1989. The number of professional, paraprofessional, and technical workers increased 10.6 percent, and the number of registered nurses increased 13.1 percent. In total, nonsupervisory workers increased from 2.766 million in 1982 to 3.351 million in 1991. However, the number of licensed practical nurses dropped by 21.7 percent, and the number of nurses' aides, orderlies, and attendants dropped by 26.9 percent; building and cleaning services people decreased by 11.9 percent. Downsizing has left higher-paid individuals to perform basic functions that might be done much more cost effectively by other workers, although this is a matter of some debate, with flexible, cross-trained workers as the other alternative (Sonnefeld, Waldo, Lemieux, and McKusick, 1991). As a consequence, the average hourly wage in the hospital industry increased by over 80 percent, from $7.56 to $12.50 per hour.

Price, Costs, and Revenue. The main driver for medical inflation appears to be hospital prices, which have risen faster than those for any other segment of the medical industry, about 44 percent in the 1980s. Prices are projected to rise 19.4 percent from 1990 to 1995 and 16.1 percent from 1995 to the year 2000 (Sonnefeld, Waldo, Lemieux, and McKusick, 1991). However, costs have risen as fast as prices. Operating expenses grew 9.4 percent in 1991 over 1990. Inpatient care was slightly less efficient than outpatient care, accounting for nearly three-quarters of community hospital operating expenses. Payroll accounted for about 54 percent of total costs as of 1991 (Cowan and others, 1992). Hospitals have also been subject to the same pressures as other employers. Benefits have been increasing faster than payroll, now accounting for 4.9 percent of total hospital expenses. Between 1990 and 1991, payroll increased 10.5 percent and benefits increased 14.4 percent (American Hospital Association, 1992). Inflation in labor-related costs partially reflects the need to use temporary nursing help at high cost, again related to the downsizing of lower-paid workers.

While inpatient hospital use was decreasing, outpatient hospital prices and revenues both grew. Prices have inflated slightly more than 10 percent a year, in a rather smooth upward curve since 1975 (American Hospital Association, 1991). Hospitals cope with inpatient pricing pressure by raising their prices at outpatient facilities to up to ten times the Medicare allowables, which are presumably based on cost. Total outpatient revenues accounted for 24 percent of all hospital revenues in 1990. In 1985, they accounted for only 15 percent of revenues.

Combining inpatient and outpatient net income, total hospital revenues increased at a 7.7 percent annual rate, with about 54 percent of the revenues from government sources. Nonservice revenues, which account for hospitals' positive margin, grew at an average rate of 11.3 percent. These revenues include various types of grants, interest on endowments and surplus capital, and concessions (Greene, 1993a).

Efficiency and Profitability. The apparent total margins of hospitals have averaged 4 to 5 percent over the last decade and a half. Operating margins, however, have fluctuated around zero, with a range of about 1 percent positive or negative (Blendon and Edwards, 1991a). (These figures should have been adjusted to label surplus as margin, since many hospitals are not for profit.) These returns are remarkably stable in the face of the fixed price per case offered by Medicare's Prospective Payment System

(PPS) and discounts or unit pricing demanded by managed care organizations. However, at least in the for-profit world, these are unacceptably low rates of return on investment, and one would therefore expect some drive toward greater efficiency. This expectation is reinforced by various published and confidential studies that appear to demonstrate that operationally and clinically, hospitals are very inefficient.

Hospitals as a group may not have had an incentive to become more efficient because they were protected by investment and ancillary income and the ability to charge some payers more than others. Almost the entire margin was generated by donations, grants, and income on investment of a very large pool of capital. The way hospitals have coped with declining unit prices offered by the Medicare PPS and managed care discounting has been to shift costs to other payers than Medicare. In 1986 through 1988, after the PPS went into full effect, hospitals increased the cost to Medicare patients on average less than 3 percent but increased costs to other patients in the range of 7 to 8 percent (Schwartz and Mendelson, 1991). For the most part, hospitals have not taken advantage of the tremendous opportunities that exist to increase both production and clinical efficiency.

It is instructive to analyze the effects the PPS had on hospitals; many hospital administrators feared that it would cause financial distress for hospitals. The PPS was designed at least in part to create financial pressure for greater efficiency and decreased capacity (Wennberg, McPherson, and Caper, 1984). But hospitals have not been very efficient for some time. In 1979, before the PPS, hospitals sustained a 10.6 percent negative profit margin. Operating margins have fluctuated between a fraction of a percent and 1.9 percent over the last eleven years. The greatest margin was 1.9 percent in 1984, the year before the PPS went into effect. The primary reaction hospitals had to the PPS—cutting staff—had its maximum effect at that point. Net revenues then declined slowly to 0.1 percent in 1987 and zero in 1988 and have remained constant at 0.1 percent since then, despite apparent losses on Medicare, Medicaid, CHAMPUS (the insurance program for military dependents and retirees), and uncompensated or unsponsored care (American Hospital Association, 1990). These statistics are dominated by the not-for-profit hospital sector, since they comprise about 85 percent of beds.

On the other hand, Standard & Poor's predicts 12–16 percent annual earnings growth for the for-profit hospital group in the foreseeable future. The investor-owned hospital chains are apparently doing much better than the not-for-profits. This is probably due to more efficient management, although there may be some patient selection and accounting differences involved (Saftlas, 1991). It is not clear whether there is reporting incompatibility caused by not-for-profits' use of surpluses for construction, office subsidies, and equipment acquisition, since they are not allowed to show a profit for an extended period of time, or whether the for-profit hospital sector is in fact more efficient. In 1990, investor-owned chain profits increased 75 percent as a result of cost cutting, the divestiture of unprofitable and underperforming non–acute care operations, and an actual increase in admissions. As of this date, all of the hospital management companies have divested their money-losing HMO and insurance operations. They have also expanded into DRG-exempt psychiatric and specialty hospitals. One could argue that these are financial manipulations rather than increases in operational efficiency, but there are probably elements of both involved in the profitability of for-profit institutions.

The threat of financial difficulties seems greater than the reality at the moment. In a recent survey of U.S. hospitals, 12 percent of hospitals characterized themselves as "distressed." Between 1986 and 1989, as noted, 4 percent of hospitals closed. Interestingly, almost half of hospital CEOs feared failure of their institutions at the end of the 1980s (Deloitte and Touche, 1990; American Hospital Association, 1991). Fear is apparently greater than reality.

Utilization. Excess capacity drives up unit cost and will increase as utilization continues to drop, as it has, sharply, since 1980. The number of admissions dropped 14 percent, from 36.1 million to 31.2 million, and the average daily census declined from

747,000 to 619,000, an even steeper drop of 17 percent. After rising 5.7 percent between 1975 and 1980, the number of days per capita dropped 42.8 percent between 1980 and 1985, perhaps in anticipation of the PPS for Medicare, with a further 23.2 percent between 1985 and 1990, and with another drop of 1.2 percent in 1991 (Cowan and others, 1992). Almost all of this reduction occurred among the Medicare population (Schwartz and Mendelson, 1991). The number of days per person is expected to rise again by about 10 percent by the year 2000, apparently reflecting the aging of the population (Sonnefeld, Waldo, Lemieux, and McKusick, 1991).

The intensity of service, as measured by the number of services per day, at least those billed for, has risen rapidly. There was a 28.6 percent increase between 1975 and 1980, a 60.1 percent increase between 1980 and 1985, and a 41.4 percent increase between 1985 and 1990. A further 15 percent a year increase is expected by the year 2000. This may reflect the fact that more seriously ill patients are now admitted, while those who are less seriously ill are not, changing both the denominator and the relative resource requirements of those patients who are admitted. But it also reflects the increase in the possible (not necessary) technical complexity of medicine, and, in all probability, a certain amount of medically unnecessary services.

From 1975 to 1985, there was an approximately 8 percent increase in the utilization of outpatient hospital services. However, between 1985 and 1991, there was over a 35 percent increase, a trend that is expected to continue at a slightly lower rate until 2000 (Cowan and others, 1992). The intensity of outpatient service also rose at over 30 percent per year from 1975 onward. Thus, there is a marked shift from the relatively managed inpatient setting to the less utilization managed, and certainly less price managed, outpatient setting. It is not clear whether the rapid increase in outpatient services represents shifting of existing services from the inpatient side in its entirety, or whether some of these services are new, adding to the total intensity of service.

Hospitals and Managed Care. Hospitals have been willing in some cases to cut prices to gain share from managed care organizations. However, the managed care industry is still quite fragmented in its use of facilities and market penetration. In one survey, hospital CEOs were divided about the ability of managed care contracts to increase profits. Forty-three percent felt that they decreased profits, 30 percent felt that they had no impact, and 20 percent felt that they increased profits (Louis Harris & Associates, 1988). It is unclear whether these opinions were based on actual data.

Multihospital and Integrated Systems

Multihospital systems have the potential of economies of scale in purchasing and information management and a great but largely untapped potential for increases in efficiencies through benchmarking, procedural standardization, and process improvement, both operational and clinical (Ermann and Gabel, 1985). This in fact is the logical basis for for-profit chains.

Systems have to some extent positioned themselves as vertically integrated providers of care and attempted direct contracting with employers on that basis. This has been more rhetoric than reality to date (Greene, 1993b). There is also a question whether capital- and cost-intensive institutions like hospitals should be the core of a vertically integrated system. The experience of group-model HMOs would argue otherwise.

The hospital landscape has changed, but not to the extent some forecasters have predicted. The wave of hospital mergers and closures predicted when the PPS went into effect in 1985 did not materialize to the extent predicted. However, merger and integration activities have accelerated as administrators and providers anticipate the need for greater efficiency and effectiveness under national health care reform (Kenkel, 1993b). This wave of alliances may not be as sweeping as the last one either, or it could change the face of medical care. It is not clear why administrators feel that hospital revenues and profits are coming under pressure now, since operating margins have been negligible for over a decade, with "profits" resulting in the aggregate from side businesses and investments. Nonetheless, the feeling seems to have increased again, as it had in the mid 1980s. As of 1991, only 31 percent of the hospital beds in the United States were in the approximately 300 systems, although 56 percent of hospitals are affiliated with the systems. Small hospitals were more likely to join a system. For-profit multihospital chains account for about 12 percent of all chains (Standard and Poor, 1992).

Systems have been formed for three reasons. First, administrators, particularly those in for-profit chains, have felt that efficiency could be increased by sharing hotel resources, purchasing, and financial systems. Those efficiencies in fact do reduce operating costs, although the extent is generally proprietary information.

Second, mergers have occurred to reduce excess capacity in local markets. "Excess capacity" has been defined as redundant marketing and administrative functions as well as duplicate or excess facilities. There have been local mergers for almost a decade, peaking in the mid 1980s and accelerating again recently (Blendon and Edwards, 1991a; Ermann and Gabel, 1985). Local mergers are quite different from acquisition by the national chains or their mergers. Local consolidation is felt to be more likely to result in consolidation of services and eventual closure or conversion of duplicate facilities.

Third, hospitals and medical groups have attempted integration of services along the continuum of care. This type of integration makes a good deal of sense from a theoretical standpoint, because health service researchers have recommended continuity of care for decades, even though the specialist- and institution-dominated system in this country has made that difficult. These combinations have taken several forms. The most common appears to be the formation of *physician-hospital organizations,* or PHOs. In these arrangements, hospitals have bought the physical assets of medical groups. Physicians then become either independent contractors or employees. Statistics on the number of these arrangements are not yet available, but there is a significant amount of activity in the legal community setting them up. Another form of PHO is an agreement between a medical group to refer to a specific hospital and to market jointly (De La Fuente, 1993a, 1993b). Some managed care organizations are adding services such as pharmacy management and mental health management to broaden their service package. Some medical groups are forming foundations to hold their assets and combine with other entities (Kenkel, 1993b).

It is not clear that control of primary and secondary care by capital- and procedure-intensive facilities like hospitals makes sense. The style of practice and incentives for parsimonious primary care and institution-based care are quite different. The overhead level for institutions can be much higher than that for ambulatory care, depending on internal efficiency and excess capacity. And there has been tension between administrators and physicians, with covert struggles for control, for decades (Goldsmith, 1993). A key question in any of these arrangements is how to have physicians feel like equal partners (Kenkel, 1993b), although their management expertise may be open to question. Nonetheless, hospitals have been using their large pools of capital for these investments.

Managed care plans have provided the shell for large-scale integration as well. For example, in Detroit, in what is being watched as a national model for an Accountable Health Plan (see Chapter Six), the Henry Ford Health System, the Mercy Health System, and Blue Cross and Blue Shield of Michigan have formed a very large system integrating Henry Ford's clinic-based managed care plan, Mercy's IPA, and the Blue Cross enrollee base to create a plan with over a million HMO and PPO enrollees. The effectiveness of health care delivery integration remains to be seen. Other providers in the area are forming competitive combinations. Some national managed care organizations are accelerating integration as well (Johnsson and Meyer, 1993; Kenkel, 1993b).

For multi-institution systems to have their greatest impact and provide the best care, medical care researchers have long thought that these systems should be vertically integrated. That is, they should provide all services from primary care to tertiary care. In a system such as this, much less incentive would exist for provision of expensive inpatient care. However, to date, while systems have expanded to include nursing homes and home health care and have begun to either provide offices for doctors or actually purchase doctors' practices, they have not become *operationally* integrated vertical systems.

Skilled, Intermediate, and Extended Care Facilities

Skilled and intermediate nursing facilities can provide care needed by recovering patients at a fraction of the cost of acute care hospitals. Hospices perform a similar function for terminal patients. Managed care organizations have used this "progressive step-down" to match needs with resources and better manage costs. These efforts have been constrained, however, by a shortage of available beds. Beds tend to be filled by long-term residents, many of whom could be taken care of at home with custodial care, if that option were available and paid for. Expanded benefits for a range of lower-intensity care would make sense if managed well.

Long-term care facilities include skilled, intermediate, and extended care facilities as well as rehabilitation hospitals. The nursing home industry primarily deals with people over sixty-five, but also with some severely disabled younger individuals. The number of people over seventy-five, who are the primary users of nursing homes, is projected to increase 26 percent from 1990 to 2000 (Francis, 1993). Employers would therefore be concerned with nursing homes for a small number of their beneficiaries who are seriously injured or developmentally delayed, and if they are involved in providing supplemental or long-term care benefits to retirees.

Supply and Employment

There were 16,388 nursing homes with 1.8 million beds and 9,258 residential facilities that provided some skilled nursing care with 1.6 million beds, in 1986, the last year for which accurate data are available, according to the Department of Commerce (Francis, 1993). There were also 734 hospital-based long-term care units at that time, a number that has increased substantially as excess bed capacity is converted, according to industry sources. Whether these units are price competitive with those located outside hospitals is not clear. Skilled and intermediate care facilities were 94 percent occupied, and hospital based units were at 92 percent capacity.

In a more recent but less complete survey, there was 4.9

percent growth from 1991 to 1992 among 4,158 facilities with 489,000 beds. In that report, nine of ten of the largest chains were for profit, with the top five accounting for more than half the reported revenues. There was a shift in revenue to subacute and specialty care from essentially custodial care. The industry is apparently recovering from excess expansion in the mid 1980s, limiting growth. Most nursing homes are owned by for-profit corporations. These groups are diversifying into "life care," which involves supervised residential homes.

The rehabilitation segment is growing at about 20 percent a year in both the number of facilities and the number of beds, almost all in the for-profit sector (De La Fuente, 1993c). This group is fairly concentrated, with the top five chains dominating market share. National Medical Enterprises, a leading for-profit hospital chain, is the market leader. There have been some joint ventures between rehabilitation and long-term care facilities, to optimize bed and other resource use, but these have not been unqualified successes and some have had rocky relationships. Whether there is a genuine medical need for intensive or long-term rehabilitation is an open question. It is true that there is a need for objective management techniques for rehabilitative care, so that it is used only for the steep part of the recovery curve.

The relative efficiency of this industry is not clear. The labor market for long-term care including hospital and nursing homes, home care, occupational, physical, and speech therapy, adult day care, residential care, and nutrition services is expected to grow at twice the rate of the number of persons receiving those services. The employment in the nursing home segment grew from 1.067 million in 1982 to 1.5 million in 1991, an almost 50 percent increase (Sonnefeld, Waldo, Lemieux, and McKusick, 1991). Almost all of the workers are nonsupervisory and are low wage. The average wage in these facilities increased from $4.89 in 1982 to $7.56 in 1991.

Income and Profitability

Nursing homes are presently funded primarily from public funds. According to the Health Care Financing Administration,

Medicaid had accounted for 41.3 percent of total expenditures in 1989, Medicare for 7.6 percent, private insurance for 1.1 percent, and out-of-pocket payments by nursing home residents and families for 48.2 percent (this number includes social security payments channeled to nursing homes, however).

Revenues for all longer-term facilities exceeded $24 billion in 1987 (Darnay, 1992a). According to Standard and Poor's *Industry Surveys* (1991a), the industry had about 16 percent margins in 1992.

Freestanding Ambulatory Facilities

Freestanding facilities can be much more cost effective than hospital-based ones because they do not have the hospital's overhead structure. They therefore could be more price competitive; at the same time, they could also be vulnerable to shadow pricing. There has been a sharp growth in the number of freestanding facilities (M. Fuchs, 1993). These include ambulatory surgical centers, freestanding imaging centers, freestanding laboratories, rehabilitation centers, and others. The vast majority of ambulatory surgical centers were independently owned, usually by physician groups; 590 were owned independently, 190 by corporations and 95 by hospitals in 1987 (Durant, 1989). In recent years, hospitals have been acquiring freestanding facilities to channel patients and capture more relatively unmanaged ambulatory revenue. Nonhospital surgery centers in individual physician's offices account for 23 percent of outpatient surgeries. Office surgery alone increased 20 percent in 1990 to about 1.25 million procedures.

Supply and Employment

Tallies of the number of ambulatory facilities are not as readily available as information on hospitals and long-term care facilities. There were over 900 such facilities in 1988. The growth rate of this sector has been five times that of the inpatient side through 1992 (M. Fuchs, 1993). The greatest growth was in diagnostic imaging, urgent care, and rehabilitation centers. Employment is not usually broken out, being subsumed for the most part under physician office and hospital statistics.

Profitability

Freestanding ambulatory surgical and imaging facilities typically charge somewhat lower prices than hospitals, which still charge private payers several times more than they charge Medicare. The segment has evidently been profitable, since there is still significant entry into it.

Home Care

Home care services range from infusion therapy for infections and cancer treatment to intermittent nursing care to custodial care. It is still covered with some reluctance by most payers, despite its obvious cost efficiencies if operated well. There is a need for medical management methods and quality assurance and improvement. Some five million people "required" home care in 1990, including physician, skilled nursing, physical and speech therapy, supplies, and durable medical equipment. The home care business is growing rapidly, with a 26 percent increase per year since 1980. In 1991, 1.7 million patients were served—twice the number cared for in 1980 (Francis, 1993). Home care agencies are either subsidiaries of hospitals or nursing homes, or freestanding businesses.

Supply

The industry has three large players but is highly fragmented. It included 11,000 companies in 1990 (Francis, 1993). There are a large number of small, independent home care agencies. Several entrepreneurs have bought a number of these "mom-and-pop" operations and consolidated them. There have been several major mergers recently, and the market leader, Caremark, was divested by Baxter. Five companies accounted for the vast majority of the $6.2 billion in service sales, and just two had over 25 percent of sales (J. Burns, 1993; Darnay, 1992a). Caremark has also bought a large multispecialty medical group in

Houston, signaling its attempt to vertically integrate. Meanwhile, Olsten, a temporary employment group, followed Kelly Services into the market.

Revenue and Profitability

The home health care market was estimated at $12 billion in 1990, up 50 percent from $8 billion in 1987 (Standard and Poor, 1991b). In the analysis above, 69 percent of revenues were derived from the personal services of nurses, therapists, and aides; 12 percent was paid for equipment, products, and systems. Respiratory therapy accounted for 10 percent of total services, and 8 percent went for dialysis.

Revenue figures differ depending on the analyst, since different studies apparently include different services. The Department of Commerce reported revenues of about $7.1 billion in 1990 (Francis, 1993), while the Bureau of the Census (1991) stated that revenues were $15.4 billion in 1989, with a projected 17 percent annual increase to $24.3 billion in 1992.

The Commerce Department projects double-digit growth in revenues in the next decade as business shifts from the inpatient setting. However, at least in 1992, there was a 2.4 percent drop in profits on a 25.7 percent increase in sales, perhaps due to restructuring charges or increased competition. Gross margins exceeded 16 percent. Three-quarters of charges were paid by government entities, primarily Medicare, 12 percent out of pocket, and the balance by private insurance (Francis, 1993).

Intermediate Suppliers

There is price competition at the level of supply to managed care plans, physicians' offices, hospitals, nursing homes, and other delivery organizations, since suppliers at this level sell directly to customers rather than being paid on a cost-plus or usual, customary, and reasonable reimbursement scheme. While most employers will not encounter this segment directly, they may become involved with purchasing arrangements in supplier improvement projects with hospitals and managed care organizations. Employers do purchase pharmaceuticals and some durable medical equipment through their medical benefits plans, and their employees purchase many over-the-counter medications, home diagnostic kits, and supplies.

Medical Equipment and Supply Companies

The medical equipment and supply segment includes everything from tongue depressors to sophisticated imaging machines. A number of very large diversified companies that are also involved in the pharmaceutical industry, such as Johnson & Johnson, Abbott Laboratories, and Baxter Travenol, are among the leaders. These companies are beginning to resemble drug companies with large research and development operations, foreign subsidiaries, and target marketing. Research and development cost about 6.2 percent of revenues as opposed to 3 percent for all U.S. manufacturers, according to the Health Industry Manufacturers Association. Almost 22 percent of sales were exports.

The U.S. industry is a leading international supplier, with about 10 percent of the total $71 billion market. The United States commands about 40 percent of markets in the production of medical equipment and supplies in many countries, except in Japan, where the share is 20 percent. There is little foreign competition in most categories, but Japanese and German manufacturers are significant competitors for big-ticket electromedical items. The foreign share of the U.S. market for these items is 27 percent, which is higher than the foreign share of the automobile market.

There are over 130,000 separate items of supplies, equipment, and diagnostic machinery. These are grouped into four broad categories: surgical appliances and supplies (36 percent of shipments), surgical and medical instruments (34 percent of shipments), electromedical equipment and x-ray apparatus, or diagnostic systems (27 percent), and dental equipment and supplies (5 percent). The diagnostic systems market includes x-ray equipment (54 percent), magnetic resonance imaging (15 percent), ultrasound (15 percent), CT scanners and nuclear equipment (8 percent), and radiation therapy equipment (5 percent). These are all high-ticket items that are priced at the top of the experience curve and are available and used at rates several times higher than in other developed countries. Due to tightened Food and Drug Administration requirements and the economic slow-down, new technology introductions have dropped 43 percent from 1991 to 1992, and there has been a 10 percent decrease in device shipments (M. Fuchs, 1993).

Products being offered are changing. Manufacturers are producing customized disposable kits for various procedures, which are more expensive than the same components sold individually. On the other hand, manufacturers should not want to produce thousands and thousands of specific kits for individual surgeons and proceduralists, so that this should lend some degree of standardization and cost efficiency to the industry. New equipment is being developed that can reduce labor costs, improve productivity, reduce patient stays, or facilitate care in less expensive settings. Examples include premixed drug solutions, continuous ambulatory dialysis, parenteral nutritional feeding systems, and cardiac angioplasty.

There are a number of new, very expensive techniques on the horizon, including magnetic source imaging, advanced multiple ionization radiology (AMIR), positron emission tomography (PET), and single photon emission computed tomography (SPECT). These scanners require cyclotrons to produce radioactive tracers. There have been double-digit increases in shipments in most of these areas. If the usual patterns are followed, these techniques — which should replace older techniques — will supplement but not supplant older modalities, driving costs up. Plans will be challenged to determine the medical necessity and cost-effectiveness improvement of these new modalities.

One rapidly increasing market is for laser surgery equipment, which if the surgery is done properly (and this may be questionable, given the minimal amount of training given to many surgeons in this area) should reduce pain, hospital stays, and recuperative time. Recent savings estimates are in the range of $1 billion (Cooper, 1993), despite physicians' propensity to raise charges for an equivalent or less intensive procedure. There is a debate about whether laser surgery has any significant advantage over electrocautery surgery. A number of observers believe that endoscopic surgery may account for 90 percent of the market for certain procedures such as gall bladder and appendix removal and for a substantial number of hysterectomies in the next few years. Laparoscopic cholecystectomies now account for 60 percent of all cholecystectomies, a dramatic change over the last few years (Cooper, 1993). This has created a battle between several leading firms in the surgical product business, as well as among surgeons.

There is a growing market for high-tech cardiovascular products because of the aging of the population and the high prevalence of heart disease among Americans. These products include angioplasty products, implantable defibullators, and ventricular assist devices. The interventional cardiology market is expected to more than double. It is not clear, however, whether these interventions result in survival or improve the quality of life. The angioplasty market is believed to be growing at a rate of 25 to 35 percent a year. These market assessments follow the trajectory of use, not medical necessity or appropriateness.

Of total sales of equipment and supplies, 52 percent goes to hospitals; sales to professionals account for about 20 percent and home care and self-care products for 18 percent. Seven percent of sales were to nursing homes and other long-term care facilities and 2 percent to freestanding ambulatory care facilities. Demand from the outpatient setting is increasing even as the hospital sector contracts. Several hundred thousand people are employed in the equipment and supply sector.

Revenue and Profitability

Medical equipment and supplies are expected to post revenue and earnings growth of at least 15 percent for the remainder of this decade (Standard and Poor, 1992). Margins are reported to be about 8 percent. The dollar volume of all medical and dental equipment and supplies reached $7.9 billion in 1992. There has been an average dollar volume increase of 8 percent from 1990 to 1992, about half due to higher unit volume and half due to price increases.

There is significant competition in this industry (Darnay, 1992b), which has held the inflation rate to a number close to the consumer price index, according to the Bureau of Labor Statistics. For example, prices rose 3.3 percent from 1990 to 1991, while the consumer price index rose 2.9 percent. Over the last five years, medical equipment prices have increased less than the average industrial producer price inflation rate.

Pharmaceuticals

The $60 billion drug industry has come under fire during the national health care reform debate for excessive profit and for production of "me-too" drugs. The return on equity for pharmaceutical manufacturers exceeded that of the Fortune 500 by 50 percent for the last decade, and in 1991, at 26 percent, was twice that of this comparison group because there was no price competition in the industry (O'Reilly, 1991). The Food and Drug Administration has, in fact, classified 80 percent of new drugs introduced from 1985 to 1990 as "copycats" (Carey and others, 1993). Fears of price controls or other consequences under reform proposals and pricing pressures from managed care organizations and organized buyers pummeled stock prices and caused managerial shake-ups in 1993 (Tanouye, Waldholz, and Anders, 1993). It remains to be seen how this will play out. While pharmaceutical prices have risen significantly, the total proportion of a given entity's medical bill they account for is about 7–10 percent, so that gains in this area would not make much difference in the total picture. And constraining development of drugs has negative consequences, as many drugs — for example, cardiac and ulcer drugs — have replaced or reduced the need for surgery (Carey, 1993).

The pharmaceutical industry includes prescription drugs ("ethical" drugs), over-the-counter medications — many of which had been prescription — and generic versions of ethical drugs. Ethical drugs accounted for 72 percent of the total $37.9 billion dollar pharmaceutical market, according to the Commerce Department. Seventy percent of that total is distributed through wholesalers to hospitals, HMOs, and retail pharmacies. The remaining 30 percent is distributed directly. Hospitals accounted for 20 percent of prescription drug purchases; they emphasize the use of generics, as do HMOs, which accounted for more than 15 percent of prescriptions.

Who pays for drugs is significantly different than who pays for other medical goods and services. Medicare paid 5.6 percent of pharmaceutical costs and insurance paid 15.7 percent; 72.4 percent of pharmaceuticals were paid for by individuals. A significant proportion of that was for over-the-counter drugs paid out of pocket. The share of ethical drugs covered by third-party reimbursement is expected to grow to 60 percent by 1995 as employers add drug benefits (Francis, 1993). These programs may provide employers with leverage to negotiate better prices (O'Reilly, 1991). Managed care organizations have recently threatened to boycott major manufacturers if they refuse to discount, leading to a bit more flexibility but lower margins (Weber and Bhargara, 1993).

Three out of four Americans use nonprescription or over-the-counter drugs regularly, with the largest buying group being in the thirty-five to fifty-nine-year-old age group and being primarily women. While six out of every ten medicine purchases are nonprescription, total spending for these drugs accounts for less than $0.02 of every dollar spent on health care in the United States. It is estimated that more consumer access to nonprescription drugs could reduce health care expenditures by more than $35 billion dollars over ten years. Each dollar spent on nonprescription drugs is estimated to save $2 on health care costs, presumably because physician office visits are not involved. The over-sixty-five population accounts for less than 15 percent of all Americans but for nearly one-third of all prescriptions.

Utilization

A recent Health Care Financing Administration analysis indicates that there was no increase in utilization of pharmaceuticals over the 1975–1990 period and that there has been a negative rate of intensity growth since 1980 (Cowan and others, 1992). In other words, any increases in costs have been accounted for entirely by price increases. Other factors that might have contributed to the high earnings of pharmaceutical companies include new-product introduction, cost efficiencies from mergers, strategic alliances, overseas expansion, and so on. Industry shipments are expected to increase in the 4 percent range per year. Almost all of this is physical volume as opposed to dollar volume. Most of that volume is being shipped overseas if the Health Care Financing Administration data are correct.

Supply and Employment

The pharmaceutical industry is fairly concentrated. While there are several hundred drug companies, the four largest players accounted for more than 25 percent of annual sales (Standard and Poor, 1992). A series of recent mergers have occurred. American drug makers account for more than half the total worldwide pharmaceutical shipments, with eleven of the top twenty producers based in the United States (Hurt, 1993).

The pharmaceutical industry is consolidating through joint development, marketing alliances, mergers, and acquisitions. The acquisitions are generally used to obtain desirable products with a constant revenue stream, which is easier than acquiring or building products. There were six very large mergers in 1989 and 1990. Mergers are also done in theory to achieve critical mass for research and development, production, and marketing to lower unit cost. Since a tremendous amount of duplication among drugs exists, this theory makes sense. However, it is not clear that duplicate drugs have been eliminated through the merger process (Standard and Poor, 1992). Merck recently acquired Medco Containment Services, a mail order drug supplier, as well as its data base and customers. This is a new twist on the consolidation theme, representing vertical integration. Name-brand companies have also been acquiring generic manufacturers or entering the field themselves, expanding their reach.

The U.S. generic drug industry is fairly fragmented, with the largest three companies representing only 15 percent of the total market. These companies are all privately held. According to the Commerce Department, 74 percent of all Americans are reasonably confident that generics are as effective as the brand originals. Generics are on average 15 percent less expensive than name-brand competitors.

There are 180,000 people employed in the pharmaceutical industry, of whom about 84,000 are in the production end of the business. The remaining 100,000 are employed in administration, research, and marketing. Productivity is increased in this sector by about 4 percent a year and is projected to increase. However, pharmaceutical companies have not streamlined as other industries have (Carey and others, 1993).

Innovative drug companies are using direct consumer advertising to increase volume. They are also actively seeking to have drugs reclassified when the patent protection has expired, from the "ethical" or prescription category to the over-the-counter category, where a larger market may exist.

The industry spends a tremendous amount of money on marketing. Interestingly, most physicians prefer to be briefed about new drugs by a detail person who is a specially trained salesperson employed by pharmaceutical companies. It is estimated that a detailing visit costs $90 per physician, with a total expenditure on marketing of $6,000 to $10,000 per physician per year. Detailing is being redesigned as an information source, but one wonders what the objectivity level would be (A. Burns, 1993). With the switch to managed care, with restricted formularies, the need for detailing has dropped drastically, leading to significant overcapacity in marketing.

Mail order pharmacies have more than 10 percent of the retail market share, and this is expected to double within five years (Standard and Poor, 1992). These entities have greater price negotiation capabilities than individual or small-group buyers and are likely to put significant pressure on prices. One vendor covering 2.5 million people, for example, claims 15–35 percent discounts (PPO Letter, 1993). Whether they will control utilization depends on the design of the program.

Revenues and Profits

The pharmaceutical industry has experienced 15 percent annual growth in net income in the last decade (Saftlas, 1991). Earnings for drug companies increased 18 percent from 1989 to 1990. Gross margins exceeded 25 percent in 1991 and 1992, with net at about 12 percent. Strong patents protect a good deal of the prescription drug market, creating a near monopoly situation for the drug makers who hold the patents. This leads to monopolistic ability to raise prices and accounted for most of the price increase noted. In 1991, for example, consumer prices for ethical pharmaceuticals increased at 9.6 percent a year—double the consumer price index—while consumer prices increased only 6 percent for nonprescription drugs and less than 3 percent for generics, which are a much more competitive industry. The gain was led by psychotherapeutics (+ 18.2 percent), bronchial therapeutics (+ 11.4 percent), and cold preparations (+ 10.3 percent), reflecting introduction of new drugs at higher prices.

One question is whether prices are fair. Several lines of evidence suggest that some may not be. For example, when levamisole, a livestock worming drug, was discovered to have antitumor properties, the manufacturer raised the price by a factor of more than 100 (Carey and others, 1993). And many drugs are sold in other countries at 20–50 percent of the U.S. cost (Solis, 1993).

The industry was considered to be recession resistant, because illnesses occur regardless of the economic climate. Margins may not continue at these levels. Prices are under pressure from political sources as well as managed care organizations. While there has not been price competition in the ethical segment of the industry, the situation has recently changed (Weber and Bhargara, 1993). In addition, the tax breaks that the industry derives from manufacturing operations in Puerto Rico, estimated at $2.6 for every dollar of wages paid, are under fire (Standard and Poor, 1992).

Drugs declined in price between 1975 and 1980 (Sonnefeld, Waldo, Lemieux, and McCusick, 1991). However, for the next two five-year periods, there were 44 percent and 46 percent increases, for a total increase of over 80 percent in the 1980s. Price inflation is expected to occur at a 41.8 percent rate for the next five years and slow to 23 percent between 1995 and 2000.

Generic prescription drugs make up about 30 percent of total sales. They accounted for $4 billion in 1989 and are expected to reach over $13 billion by 1995. The rate of price increase for generics has been one-third to one-quarter that for branded ethical drugs (O'Reilly, 1991).

Shipments of nonprescription drugs reached an estimated $10.4 billion in 1990 and are expected to increase at close to a 9 percent annual rate over the next five years, rising from $10 billion in 1990 to $17.6 billion by 1996. Much of this growth is based on the premise that prescription drugs will be switched to over-the-counter status, accounting for at least half the new revenues.

Retail pharmacy prices usually include mark-ups of at least 30 percent over average wholesale price (known in the industry as *AWP*). In managed care contracts and dealing with government programs, pharmacists may charge a dispensing fee that can equal the cost of a generic drug. Drugstore chains have negotiated much lower prices with managed care plans.

New-Product Development

There is intensive research and development in the drug industry. The aggregate budget totaled $9.2 billion in 1991 and has been increasing at double-digit rates. However, few of the new drugs represent significant therapeutic advances. Most of these research funds are spent on developing "me-too" drugs. Only 14 out of 225 new drugs offered in the last few years had any significant therapeutic advantage. Fourteen were considered class 1A.

Many drugs under development are intended to care for but not cure chronic illnesses. Half of the industry's research outlay is devoted to discovering treatments or palliation for diseases of the elderly. While this is an admirable social goal, it raises questions about resource allocation and social return on investment and poses a threat to supplemental benefits plans for retirees, particularly if new treatments have marginal benefit, interactions with other drugs, or high complication rates. There are 183 drugs under development for cancer and cardiovascular disease and 76 for chronic geriatric disabilities such as Alzheimer's disease and arthritis.

It is interesting to note that there are no effective drugs to prevent death from AIDS, to ameliorate the symptoms of Alzheimer's disease, or to avert a number of cancers. However, a number of drug industry studies project hundreds of thousands of fewer cases of Alzheimer's disease, AIDS, and arthritis as well as cancers. It is unclear how these projections will be fulfilled since there is no present therapeutic basis for the assumptions. These numbers may be wishful thinking, attempts at supporting stock prices, or based on unrelated preliminary findings.

Administrators/Financers of Care

In describing the administrators/financers of care, we begin with an industry profile and then look at revenue and profitability.

Industry Profile

Several factors are of interest.

Size of the Insurance Market. While the data on the number of Americans covered by private insurance do not completely agree, according to the Health Insurance Association of America (1992), more than 190 million Americans were covered by private health insurance in 1992. Of that number, 71 million were in self-funded employee plans run by major employers, 96 million were insured under for-profit group policies, and 10 million had insurance or individual or family policies. Seventy-three million were insured by Blue Cross and Blue Shield. Presumably these figures overlap (Health Insurance Association of America, 1992).

Of those over sixty-five, 99.7 percent were covered by Medicare. Twenty-five million of those citizens (78.4 percent of the over-sixty-five population) had Medigap insurance to cover uninsured services.

The lowest rate of coverage was for those aged sixteen to twenty-four, with 79 percent covered. Of that group, only 57 percent of the 79 percent are covered by their employers. Presumably the others had purchased individual health insurance, which is much more expensive, or were covered by school policies or their parents' coverage. The highest rate of coverage was for those between thirty-five and sixty-four. Hispanics had the lowest rate of coverage (53.7 percent); African Americans were covered slightly more often (58.4 percent). Over 80 percent of whites had private health insurance.

The proportion of the population that has insurance is directly related to income. In one recent poll, all those with income greater than $75,000 had insurance; the percentage dropped to 78 percent for those with an income of less than $20,000. Almost all married respondents had health insurance, but only 80 percent of single respondents did (Employee Benefits Research Institute and the Gallup Organization, Inc., 1990). Of those without health insurance, 35 percent stated they could not afford it, 14 percent were between jobs, 10 percent did not see a need, 7 percent had employers that did not offer insurance, and the remainder had miscellaneous reasons.

Commercial Insurance. The group health insurance industry has grown rapidly as a result of consumer demand to reduce the high out-of-pocket costs for medical care. Analysts feel that this occurred because corporations increased health benefits to their employees and were attempting to protect them from rising health care costs. This theory is based on the history of the industry. For example, before the 1940s a small number of insurers — mainly casualty and specialty companies — sold primarily individual policies. Between 1942 and 1948, the number of firms offering hospital insurance quadrupled as employers added tax-free benefits and minimum wages. Commercial insurance companies took more than half the market from Blue Cross during this period. Over 1,000 private insurance companies now provide individual and group health insurance in the United States.

Health and life insurers have grown into a diverse financial industry competing not only against other insurers, but also against brokerage houses and banks to provide a complete portfolio of financial products.

There has been a shift in industry leadership from casualty insurance companies to life insurance companies such as Metropolitan and Prudential. Presumably because they had already offered disability and life insurance through employers, these firms now dominate the group market. There is no clear distinction between for-profit and nonprofit entities. Metropolitan and Prudential, for example, are mutual companies owned by policyholders. Surpluses of mutual companies are supposed to be returned to the policyholders but are in fact retained by boards of directors and invested.

HMOs, PPOs, and third-party administrators who administer self-insured plans have eroded insurance companies' market share (Standard and Poor, 1991b).

Blue Cross and Blue Shield. Blue Cross and Blue Shield plans are nonprofit membership plans that serve state and regional areas and offer both individual and group insurance. These plans are coordinated loosely by the Blue Cross/Blue Shield Association. They were developed by providers to reduce risk and ensure payment to hospitals (Blue Cross) and physicians (Blue Shield). Payments were made directly from the plan to the hospital in a service benefit plan form rather than reimbursing the patient. The Blues had been able to secure a significant discount through negotiations and regulations known as "most favored nation status," which ensured that they would have the lowest rates given to any payer in exchange for offering coverage to anyone in the community.

The Blues have been at a disadvantage in competing with commercial insurers because they are restricted by law to offering health insurance only rather than a full portfolio of insurance products. Their local control and loose coordination pose a problem for national employers. They are also at a disadvantage because they are generally required to community rate rather than rate employers on their individual experience. Therefore, their cost of risk is higher. Commercial carriers can offer lower rates because of the "healthy worker effect," in which only healthy people are employed. The Blues have been left as the insurers of last resort to cover individuals who might have chronic illnesses and could therefore not work.

Some Blue Cross plans are now incorporating for-profit entities, and most are experience rating to become more competitive. Many offer administrative service only (ASO) and minimum premium plan (MPP) services. Blues plans had in the past been able to charge less because they were exempt from premium taxes as nonprofits and as a result of provider discounts.

Self-Insurance. Most large employers have become self-insured to avoid premium taxes, administrative overhead, and marketing expenses. Large insurance companies have therefore become transaction processors, providing claims payment services on a cost-plus basis. Continued operating losses and a shrinking fully insured market are predicted to force companies to transform themselves into managed care companies and to improve internal operating and marketing efficiencies. The move toward managed care is raising significant barriers to entry in the health insurance market. It is estimated that only 25 of the nearly 500 group insurance carriers have the capability, finances, management, and patient volume to accomplish these tasks (Abramowitz, 1993).

There are two types of self-insured coverage. ASO contracts provide claims, payment, and cost containment on a fee-for-service basis. Under MPPs, employers self-fund plans and insure a certain number of large unpredictable claims (stop-loss insurance). These two types of coverage accounted for 55 percent of the market in 1990. Thirty-one percent are ASO plans, and 24 percent are minimum premium or reinsured plans. The result of widespread self-insurance was that groups of below-average risk would leave the community pool, providing adverse selection for commercial carriers and Blue Cross and forcing them to raise premiums.

Prepaid Plans. A number of different types of prepaid plans are offered, many through the same companies that offer insured products and claims processing. These are typically newer plans, many of the network or Independent Practice Association model. The older plans, which are parallel entities for financing and delivery of medical care, include the following: the Kaiser Foundation Health Plans and Permanente Medical Groups, which are the largest single financer and provider group in the country, with twelve regional plans offering almost national coverage; the Health Insurance Plan of Greater New York and New Jersey; and the Group Health plans of Puget Sound and Washington, D.C. Prepaid plans generally provide broader coverage than insured plans in that they also cover preventive services and have covered maternity and other such services from the beginning.

Physician groups have developed in parallel with managed care financing organizations to provide services to these plans. Staff and group-model HMOs often have a legally separate physicians' group that provides services to that financing organization. The largest example of this arrangement is the Permanente Medical Group. Very large group practices such as the Mayo and Cleveland clinics now have parallel financing organizations. In Independent Practice Associations, financing organizations contract with a specific group or network of physicians to provide services, either at a discounted fee for service or on a prepaid basis. Some method of superimposed practice organization exists, although there is typically less physician involvement or interaction, monitoring, and improvement of practice patterns as in the staff or group-model delivery system.

Regardless of the arrangement that these plans or their associated medical groups make to hire or contract with physicians, they accept a fixed prepayment to provide all necessary medical care within the scope of their contract with beneficiaries. Recent developments include *point of service options,* in which employees may opt to use providers outside of the designated group or network but at a higher cost to them.

Most prepaid plans contract with providers for scheduled reimbursement, capitated payments, discounts off charges, or per episode payments. Most provider contracts provide for compliance with quality assurance and utilization management activities. This should in theory reduce cost to some extent, as should the emphasis on early care and prevention. In fact, some managed care plans attempt to "shadow price" indemnity plans and neglect operational effectiveness. They still appear less expensive to the extent that indemnity plans did not improve efficiency either and simply passed the cost on to employers.

Revenue and Profitability

The total written premium for accident and health insurance increased about 8 percent a year in the late 1980s. Group health accounted for 73 percent of this total (Standard and Poor, 1992). The group health business was the fastest-growing segment of the life and health insurance industry, with profits growing at a 15 percent annual rate from the early 1970s through the 1980s (Standard and Poor, 1992).

Several segments of the industry, including mutual companies and stock companies, posted operating gains, with actual payouts totaling approximately 75 percent, but experienced net losses because of high administrative and marketing expenses. Nevertheless, the financial structure clearly attracts entrants to the industry, especially as it is an opportunity to make a significant profit through the investment of retained premiums or investing the "float." Statutory earnings increased 21 percent during 1990, according to AM Best. The return on equity for the industry was 14.9 percent in 1990 (Standard and Poor, 1991b).

Cyclicality. While the business is highly cyclical, net losses over time are less than net gains, with profits for commercial carriers and surplus for the nonprofit Blues coming from investment income and sideline businesses (shades of the hospital industry). This financial volatility is usually attributed to the pricing behavior of insurers rather than fluctuating claims expense. The demand for health insurance seems to be much more stable than its supply, because the demand is inelastic. External factors do not seem to explain the price for the pricing cycle. Periods of strong profits are followed by intense price competition and declining profits (known as the *soft market*). After a shakeout of excess capacity, prices rise rapidly and the cycle repeats itself. Profitability follows price increases by about two years (Gabel, DiCarlo, Fink, and DiLissavoy, 1989).

Administrative Expenses. Administrative expenses for insurance policies are directly related to the size of the account, ranging from 40 percent administrative cost for employers of 1 to 4 employees to 18 percent for those with 50 to 99 employees and 5.5 percent for those with more than 10,000 employees (Congressional Research Service, 1988). Some commercial carriers may retain as much as 50 percent on individual policies, presumably to cover higher overhead costs, costs of collection, adverse risk, and so on.

     Overhead structures differ. Apparently, nonprofit status confers some advantage, at least in the administrative and marketing areas. Blue Cross's administrative margin has been 6 percent, Blue Shield's 10 percent, and commercial insurers' about 21 percent. However, it should also be noted that commercial insurers sell many more individual policies, which have much higher overhead (Blendon and Edwards, 1991b).

Conclusion

The American medical industry is now the largest sector of the economy. It has retail or direct delivery elements, such as physicians, pharmacists (for nonprescription drugs), and home health agencies, working through facilities such as hospitals, nursing homes, offices, pharmacies, and ambulatory centers. Physicians control medical care delivery for the most part through the ordering and prescription process, so that while they personally bill for only 20 percent of expenditures, they control over 80 percent. This makes physician behavior crucial to the management of medical care costs, quality, and decision making. Facilities as such may provide the framework for the delivery system, but they are not the delivery system per se. Little price competition has existed in the delivery system because of the mechanics of statistically based or cost-based reimbursement.

Physician income has grown steadily as new procedures have been introduced and as ancillary personnel billed through facilities have taken on some of their duties. Hospitals have had marginal apparent profitability, with positive margins due to investment and ancillary income. The efficiency of both direct delivery and facilities could be greatly improved through process improvement and better information management.

The intermediate suppliers to the delivery system are an industry in their own right, including pharmaceutical, supply, and equipment companies. These are profitable industries; pharmaceutical companies have not competed on price until recently, although price competition has occurred in the equipment and supply areas. Profits have typically been healthy in this group. There appears to be room for negotiation.

The medical care financing industry includes self-insured companies, life and casualty insurers, the nonprofit Blues plans, and managed care organizations. The same entities are now offering both managed and unmanaged products, with various degrees of effectiveness. Over a thousand insurance companies exist, many concentrating on individual and small-group policies, with high administrative costs and stringent underwriting requirements. Managed care plans continue both to proliferate and to consolidate. These plans are basically financing mechanisms, which then contract with providers of care for service delivery. They have varying elements of information and quality management.

Employers can work through financing entities or directly to negotiate prices, standards of care, and delivery packages that are of increased value compared to their present arrangements. To do that requires knowledge of the medical industry, including capacity, supply, profitability, efficiency, and margins, as well as the current efficiency and effectiveness of services used by their employees. This information can then be used as data inputs to the strategic health management process, as we will note in Chapter Five.

CHAPTER FIVE

The Framework
of Strategic Management

Creating a well-managed, high-quality health care *system,* including preventive, acute, and chronic care for employees and dependents, is the most effective way to manage health and health-related costs, but it is not a quick fix. And just as we have seen that managing health has many dimensions, the processes of system development and then proactive health management require data, careful long-range planning, and continuously improving, actively managed execution. Employers probably cannot solve the structural problems with the current medical care industry, but each employer or pool of employers can create a "microenvironment" or subset of the system that functions in better ways.

Many opportunities for change exist if one attacks this large and growing problem in an organized, cooperative way. These opportunities include disease prevention, health promotion, organizational interventions, redesign of financial incentives, more choice to maximize individual utility of benefits, better information, and supplier improvement. Identifying, prioritizing, planning, and executing these improvements are components of the strategic health management process. Designing, monitoring, and improving the process are best carried out by the SHM team. In this chapter, we will describe the SHM team and the attributes of the strategic health management process and then outline the steps in the process. Along the way, we will describe data needed to drive the process as well as several of the steps in more detail.

Attributes of the
Strategic Health Management Process

The strategic health management process in the medical industry is not unlike the strategic management process used throughout well-run businesses, but it has additional organizational overtones and some characteristics of population health management. The strategic health management approach encompasses the following features:

- Wide vision
- Long-term perspective
- Process continuity
- Benefit-cost considerations
- Fit with organizational culture, goals, and objectives
- Internal alliances
- Reliance on data
- Measurement and quality improvement

Wide Vision

The strategic viewpoint is wider than the focus on costs and cost increases. It looks at quality of care so that value or the quality per unit cost is considered. It is wider than illness care, encompassing prevention and even promotion of health. This wider vision includes the effect of organizational climate on health and the effect of healthy employees on the achievement of the goals of the organization. This last implies one of the widest viewpoints, that of actively managing health rather than treating diseases or organizational effects as random events that cannot be managed. Research has shown that life-style, organizational design and style, and the environment account for a majority of health problems (Fielding, 1992). Attention to these issues will have an effect on costs as well as productivity.

Long-Term Perspective

While recognizing that many of today's businesses are driven by quarter to quarter results in rapidly changing marketplaces, we must also recognize that changes in organizational climate, employee perceptions and demands, and health are long-term endeavors. Assuming that the organization plans to exist for a long period of time and maintain a high-quality, stable work force, a time frame of three to five years is not unreasonable to change entrenched behaviors and expectations. There are examples of shorter-term changes that have been sustained, such as smoking cessation driven by smoke-free policies. But a longer time line will prevent rapid changes in direction, which undermine the effectiveness of many programs in sustaining life-style change.

Process Continuity

This point of view recognizes that continuity of care is important to manage medical problems and to prevent them. It also recognizes the continuum from illness to neutral health to positive wellness. It recognizes health itself as a process.

Benefit-Cost Considerations

A strategic approach should explicitly consider the benefits to be accrued for various expenditures. This involves analysis of preventive versus acute care and the cost-effectiveness of various alternative medical treatments, where there are commonly used methods of diagnosis or treatment that are more beneficial than others and other methods that have no proven benefit. It calls into question simply paying for services provided, as compared to assessing and selecting diagnosis and treatment on the basis of results and pricing together. This is particularly germane when considering whether to cover newer drugs and procedures. Benefit-cost factors are especially relevant in considering the volume of services provided. If that analysis can be done by the employer, so much the better, although external assistance may be necessary since this is a fairly technical area.

Fit with Organizational Culture, Goals, and Objectives

The design of the benefits plan is often closely related to the beliefs of management or the culture of larger organizations. If there is an entitlement mentality, benefits will be added continuously and incrementally, and a great deal of resistance to cost sharing will exist. Organizations that value their employees will typically be more open to employee involvement and health promotion. Whether the organization has a short- or long-term focus is important. The financial goals of a benefits program should also dovetail with the financial goals of the organization.

Internal Alliances

Typically, a number of functions and departments in any employer organization have an effect on benefits and medical care programs. These may include in-house medical resources, the benefits department, the finance organization, internal communications, top management, and the purchasing organization, to name just a few. Smoothly functioning alliances between these groups are critical to the effective strategic management of prevention, the purchase of medical care, and the provision of primary care and preventive services. Melding people with different points of view and interests typically requires agreement on common goals and objectives, a facilitated group process, and top management support, like any quality improvement effort. Creating these alliances is based on common interests and diplomatic skills. Employees are key partners in this process as well.

Reliance on Data

This entire exercise should be based on collection and review of pertinent and meaningful data. Given the current, primitive state of data collection, getting carried away with data collection and analysis for its own sake is not a major consideration in most organizations. It is critically important to collect usable data on health risks; medical treatment patterns; costs; and employee preferences, attitudes, and opinions to be able to gauge what one has purchased and what is needed, as well as the success of health management efforts.

Measurement and Quality Improvement

One valid criticism of data collection is that data may not be used in a meaningful way. The purpose of collecting data is to measure progress toward preagreed goals, and to have the means to support continuous improvement of benefits programs, benefits administration, medical care patterns, prevention, and communication efforts. These data will provide the information needed for the strategic health management team and selected vendors to gauge the success of continuous improvement efforts.

Organizing the Strategic Health Care Team

There are at least three reasons to use a multidisciplinary team to plan and conduct a comprehensive strategic health management program. First, the knowledge base for strategic health management is sufficiently broad that several professions are needed to understand and carry out communications efforts, health and financial data analysis, health promotion, provider negotiation, and on-site care. Second, the information about what occurs in these areas is distributed throughout the typical employer organization. Third, there is simply too much to do to have a single function perform it in addition to other duties. In any given organization, it might make sense to create a single department, task group, or matrix organization to deal with health management, but different skill sets are still involved.

The functions that pay for or provide medical care and otherwise affect employee health have typically been scattered throughout employer organizations. Corporate medical departments have traditionally been concerned with screening examinations of various kinds, most commonly to detect the early effects of occupational hazards and less commonly to establish a baseline and screen for unexpected diseases such as cancer. These on-site providers sometimes provide immunization and limited primary care.

Wellness programs have either been placed in the medical department or independent of it. The latter has occurred because administrators have feared, sometimes correctly, that the disease paradigm and other cultural factors would inhibit the growth of these preventive programs. The control of other variables affecting employee health, such as stress levels on the job and organizational design, resides both in the human resource department and in operational groups, with profound effects from the posture and policies of senior management.

Benefits programs are typically administered by separate benefits departments. Payment for medical care may be found in the treasury or finance departments. Management of the workers' compensation program may reside in the risk management or finance functions.

As a consequence, widely differing views and paradigms of the financing, purchase, and conduct of medical care can be present in various parts of the company. No one has a complete picture of both employee health and the cost associated with it. Further, perhaps reflecting the organization of internal health management, most organizations have not had either long-range plans for managing employee health or plans to improve the value of care received. To obtain the necessary perspective and functionality, ad hoc or permanent interdisciplinary teams and cross-functional information must be developed.

The Strategic Health Management Process

Once the strategic health management team has been identified, a specific sequence of steps should be followed. The steps in the strategic health management process are outlined here:

- Assess the current situation

    Data management
    Quantitative analysis
    Qualitative analysis

- "Vision" the future

    Paradigms
    Key quality characteristics
    Goal congruity
    Financial risk

- Analyze the gaps
- Select a strategy to close gaps between present and vision

- Formulate tactics
- Implement the process
- Analyze and monitor the process
- Continuously improve the process

Assess the Current Situation

This analysis should be comprehensive yet concise. It is used as the basis for quantitative future objectives. As such, it is typically presented to the entire team and to senior management for approval and authorization to proceed to the next step. The analysis should cover the qualitative and quantitative areas listed above.

Painting the picture of the current cost, quality, efficiency, effectiveness, and acceptability of the existing benefits program, preventive efforts, and purchased medical care can start with any one of the dimensions. Since many employers are numbers driven, the analysis typically starts with numerical data.

The quantitative data should be collected and analyzed by a task team or subgroup of the strategic health management team made up of experts in population medical care, finance, and statistics. These disciplines are needed to contribute an understanding of the health of the employed population, medical quality and value, and cost accounting. The task team would analyze financial outlays, medical service use patterns, and pooled health risks and would examine correlations between these three areas.

Data Management. The data management task team should also ask a number of questions about data to determine how it is being managed:

- Is the current strategy based on data?
- Conversely, is there an articulated data management strategy?
- What specific data elements are being collected?
- How often are they collected?
- How are they stored?
- How are they being analyzed?

A specific strategy is needed to guide data collection, information systems development, analysis of key management indicators, and continuous improvement efforts. In this preliminary stage, one can note the presence or absence of a coherent information management strategy and the effects and implications of it.

Quantitative Analysis. Once these questions have been answered, the next step is quantitative analysis or "running the numbers": What are the costs and risks of ill health in the past and projected for the future? Basic sources for this exercise include employee demographics, insurance claims tapes, encounter data from managed care organizations, health risk appraisals or surveys of employee and dependent life-style habits, and workers' compensation and related data. This information can be assessed on a rate, or per person, basis for past service use and projected into the future using health risk models.

It is important to adjust the data for the aging of the population, changes in benefits packages, migration to managed care organizations in the case of assessing indemnity plan data, other causes of adverse selection, differences in geography that are typically correlated with differences in medical practice patterns, and any organizational influences. With the exception of the last point, adjustment is fairly straightforward, and observed utilization patterns and costs can be compared to benchmarks and expected levels (Harris, 1992d). Data may need to be "smoothed" or otherwise adjusted if distorted by a few large claims.

It is important to determine the cost drivers for the benefits program. This starts with an analysis of price, volume, and product mix.

Volume. Using claims tapes or parallel information provided by HMOs, employers would want to determine the volume of services used, including:

- Ambulatory visits per employee or dependent
- Inpatient bed days per thousand
- Rates of laboratory use

- Rates of imaging use
- Rates of emergency room use
- Rates of physical therapy use
- Rates of pharmaceutical use
- Rates of other relevant categories of services

These figures can be compared to a variety of benchmarks, from the best-managed care organizations, to means for managed care, to various national means and geographic areas, or even zip code–related means, although those typically reflect highly variable individual practice patterns.

Prices per Unit. The prices paid for major procedures and services such as days of hospital care, the top surgical and diagnostic procedures, various types of office visits, and drugs can be determined in the aggregate and then broken down by business unit or by more specific procedural or drug group. In looking at prices, it is important to compare them to a variety of benchmarks, including managed care contract prices and statistical averages for local and regional geographic areas. There is no intrinsic reason why medical care should be much more expensive in major cities than in surrounding areas (with the exception of specialty referral centers, requiring risk adjustment), since wage differentials are not that great and the cost of equipment and supplies does not change. The cost of physical plant may be more, but that only accounts for about 9 percent of the total cost structure for inpatient facilities.

Price analysis will reveal whether or not the organization has been a victim of cost shifting and whether managed care organizations are actually achieving meaningful reductions in cost per unit. Comparing prices paid to various managed care prices would be a useful exercise. Another useful exercise would be to identify charges that are "unbundled" (for example, procedures broken down into many codes rather than simply billing for a unitary procedure, usually done to maximize revenue) that were identified during use of bill review software programs. If such programs are not in use, one can reprice some claims and determine the total potential financial gain from rebundling or use of global fees.

Costs by Diagnostic Group. In performing these analyses, it is useful to determine which major diagnostic categories, in descending order, accounted for health service use and costs. This can be broken down into more specific diagnostic categories and variance within the major categories examined. For example, it is not uncommon to find that cardiac care in general is close to benchmarks but that certain procedures and diagnoses are either overpriced or overused while others are under much better control. Identifying major costs by disorder or disease would also lay the groundwork for prevention and health promotion programs, since the major risk factors for most life-style and environmentally related problems are well known.

If it is possible to collect information such as copayments and deductibles, contributions and other out-of-pocket costs, and total cost to the employee, it is useful to analyze this by wage or salary level to determine if in fact the lower-paid employees are paying a greater percentage of their salaries or wages for medical care than the higher-paid employees. This is an employee relations equity issue as well as a design issue.

Future Costs. Software programs can be used to project future costs, given risk data from Health Risk Appraisals or employee surveys and employee demographics. This analysis can be compared to another form of projection called *Diagnostic Cost Groups,* which operates on the assumption that expensive categories today will continue to be expensive unless there is a major change in the labor force or life-style.

If possible, it is informative to determine the dollar and physical volume of care provided to end-stage patients compared to others. This is a useful analysis to demonstrate whether the major focus is prevention, acute care, or terminal care (with relatively little contribution to health status).

Quality. Quality analysis is a science in its infancy, but it is beginning to change from retrospective identification of relatively rare adverse events (such as readmissions to hospitals and surgical catastrophes) and more common problems, such as drug reactions or transfers to the intensive care unit to ongoing measurement of improvable parameters. The problem with the "quality assurance" mode of thinking is that it simply identifies relatively infrequent adverse events but does not look at the diagnosis patterns and processes of care that allowed those events to occur.

A relatively "new" way of looking at quality (at least in medical care) is to look for variance from recommended treatment patterns. An example might be some commercial software programs that look at excessive resource use for ambulatory care. (However, as currently used, only the top 5 percent of outliers are typically identified as a problem.) The flow of care and the number of resources used bears examination as well. What might make sense is to look at the resources consumed for specific chronic disease such as asthma, diabetes, hypertension, and coronary artery disease against best professional practice standards. In these cases, inadequate prevention or poor management typically leads to increased resource use or to inpatient care that could largely be avoided.

Another superficial, or screening, way of looking at quality is to match the recorded diagnosis with procedures or surgeries. In many instances, a number of procedures are not correlated with any acceptable diagnosis that should lead to that procedure, and in others, the information is simply missing. This may be nothing more than a record-keeping problem, but that in itself is an element of poor-quality care. If in fact the overview statistical data prove to be correct on audit of the medical records, serious quality problems and a deviation from standard practices exist. Quality improvement programs could then be put into place to create systems to prevent such occurences and to ensure that data collection is improved in the future.

While the best ratios between alternative treatment modes are often not yet known, it is useful to start identifying ratios of alternatives (for example, medical therapy versus angioplasty versus coronary bypass for specific cardiac diagnoses). One or another of these treatments is acceptable only given certain circumstances. However, in a population group, the ratios should remain relatively constant among geographic areas and over time when adjusted for age and gender. A question for further research is what those ratios ought to be and whether any risk adjusting should be done.

Finally, analysis of rates of surgery for some highly variable and sometimes questionable procedures such as Caesarean sections, cataract extraction, knee surgery, back surgery, and some other procedures is useful as a foundation for quality improvement. In this case, one would want to compare adjusted rates of these procedures by practitioners, hospitals, or locations to look for variance. In the case of cataract extractions, hysterectomies, and Caesarean sections, for example, one would want to see the mean reduced (at least from current levels) as well as variance compressed.

Preventive Services. Another important category of analysis is preventive services. One would want to examine the rates of immunizations, mammographies, pap smears, and other preventive services by specific practitioners or locations if covered by the plan. One would look both at the mean and the variance, hoping to increase the mean toward 100 percent and to decrease the variance to a very low level. This is a baseline and periodic tool for quality improvement.

Qualitative Analysis. The preceding analysis concerned itself with internal data only. The external environment must also be carefully assessed, as the state of labor markets and the medical care industry provide important constraints and opportunities (see Chapter Four). A knowledge of the mechanics of the system is important as well.

Paradigms, Goals, and Roles. Assessing the current situation also involves asking some basic questions that expose assumptions about what the organization thinks it is doing with its benefits and health management programs. The questions proposed in the following pages will start to clarify paradigms as well as help with data collection.

Does the organization conceive of itself as involved with the delivery of care or simply the financing of care? If the employer is solely concerned with financing, one might look at contribution rates, plan design, and other financial dimensions. If it is concerned with the delivery of care, involvement might range from quality assessment of delivery organizations to active involvement in quality improvement to the provision of services on site.

Process of Health Management. Is this a medical care or health care program? Is the organization providing or arranging for care, prevention, promotion, or all three? More specific questions to ask in this area include the following:

- Is disease prevention being paid for or carried out on site?
- Is health promotion provided?
- What programs or activities are provided?
- Is the program comprehensive, based on data, or related to programs that employees have requested?

It is important here to distinguish between a comprehensive, strategically designed health promotion or disease prevention program and a series of activities that may have been installed for a variety of well-intentioned but uncoordinated reasons. If the organization is involved in more than financing of disease care, a closer analysis of the health management strategy is in order.

Who is currently involved in developing and executing strategy? This is a question of which departments, functions, or personnel are involved in formulating true health management strategy and managing the program. It would be important to have the proper wide-ranging human resource and management expertise to effectively carry out any sort of comprehensive health management strategy.

How is health risk management accomplished? Here one would want to assess what components of health management are in place: screening, awareness, skill building, self-efficacy training, and incentives and rewards. A common fallacy is to regard screening as an actual intervention program, when in fact it constitutes fact finding, which would then be integrated with data analysis. Skill building is necessary so that employees can make changes once they are aware of the need to do so. Even if skills are added, if the employees and dependents do not have a sense of self-efficacy, they will not move forward. Finally, incentives are frequently helpful to increase motivation to change and to maintain the changed behavior.

Are wellness and illness programs integrated? Integration

with the illness care system is important. Using "teachable moments"—for example, smoking cessation counseling during an acute episode of bronchitis or pneumonia—is frequently more effective than providing abstract information when the person at risk is healthy. Integration of illness care and wellness interventions is important to prevent recurrences of life-style-related illnesses as well.

The next area to examine involves the long-term goals and objectives for health management and the shorter-term objectives for various areas. It is important to revisit any documented goals and measurable objectives that have been laid out for benefits, in-house medical care, health promotion, employee assistance, organizational health and effectiveness, and other areas. One would also want to look at the organization's compensation strategy, since benefits are part of a total compensation package. Such goals and objectives may or may not explicitly exist. Progress toward them may or may not have been documented.

Finally, the organization, staffing, and framework of currently provided services should be evaluated to see if they support and confirm the strategy and are adequate to achieve the stated goals and objectives.

Effects of the Organization on Health. How does the organization itself affect health? Possibly through survey research or focus groups as well as some targeted auditing, it is also important to assess the influences of the particular organization on the health of the employees. These influences can include:

- Management style
- Information flow
- Role definition
- Organization and content of work
- Safety of various processes
- Human resource policy and approach
- Degree of employee involvement
- The sense of threat or security

- Support for healthy life-styles and a healthy environment (for example, a smoke-free environment or provision of healthy food or exercise facilities)

Exploring each of these areas is an exercise in itself and may or may not be part of the initial assessment of the current situation with regard to health management. It is clear that more and more attention is being paid to these influences on health and the use of health services, as well as on productivity and morale of organizations (Harris and Dewey, 1984).

"Vision" the Future

It follows from the preceding discussion that the first step in "visioning" the future is deciding which paradigms the organization will attempt to follow. This would include determining and enunciating a position about relative paternalism and employee empowerment (because this affects human resource policy), a position on advice versus agreement, a position on prescription versus information, and a definition of who makes the decisions about the use of medical care.

Paradigms. Understanding the paradigms in common use in the organization is the key to guiding strategic management. Paradigms are viewpoints or belief systems that are typically below the surface or unrecognized but that guide beliefs and actions about various subjects. A number of these paradigms have to do with medical care, and others have to do with the unspoken culture of the organization.

  Paternalism Versus Empowerment. Enunciating these positions clearly will also provide a basis for contracting with financing and provider organizations. If one position is traditional and paternalistic, probably no further statements are necessary in dealing with suppliers. However, if it is more empowered and shared, it would be advisable to include that as a key quality characteristic in any requests for proposals that are floated.

  Advice Versus Agreement. This paradigm applies to both medical care and human resource management. In medical care, physicians have usually assumed that they should give advice to patients and that that advice should be followed. This is the prescriptive approach. However, it has resulted in a large number of treatment failures, typically known in medical sociology jargon as *compliance problems*. A much more effective strategy is to obtain agreement between the practitioner and the patient as to what a mutually acceptable course of action is. Understanding this paradigm can guide the selection of physicians and other practitioners for medical care networks. Those who use the "agreement" approach tend to be much more effective than groups of practitioners who use the advice paradigm.

Employee involvement in these two paradigms can also be examined. If one uses the advice paradigm, one might accept advice from employees about the structure of the benefits program and how it should be conducted. Then advice can be given to employees in turn about how to use it. However, if there is no general agreement on goals, objectives, needs, and the financial and other capabilities of the organization to meet those needs, employees are likely to act in ways management has not envisioned and may be dissatisfied with what management provides.

Information Versus Prescription. A closely related paradigm is the question of whether one should provide neutral information to a patient or an employee or make a command prescription, providing only the information directly related to the prescribed course of action. Research in both medical care and employee behavior has shown that providing a full range of information — noting the advantages and disadvantages of several possible courses of action — leads to greater participation, and, in medical care, better cure rates. In a society in which the work force is changing and the typical employee or patient is demanding more information and a greater role in decision making, information provision makes more sense than prescriptive or paternalistic behavior.

Balance of Power. In medical care, the balance of power has shifted (if it was ever elsewhere) almost exclusively to the provider side. American consumers have given up their decision-making authority over whether to obtain testing and treatment on various grounds, ranging from lack of knowledge to an unwillingness to make decisions affecting their health and welfare. This can be viewed as transfer or abdication of responsibility.

Providers are not passive participants in this process, since autonomy—a key characteristic of a profession—is based on possession of a unique body of knowledge and set of skills. To the extent that health care providers seek to retain this information, they have retained the decision-making power. However, as noted in discussing the previous paradigms, the general result of this course of action is lack of compliance. A less common but more threatening result is legal action for malpractice based on lack of informed consent. Informed consent still conveys a less equitable decision-making model than agreement.

Quality. A final and critical paradigm has to do with the nature of quality. It has been and is still the case that quality is described as hard to define or only known when one encounters it. In the context of medical care, quality has been assumed and assessed by word of mouth. There is also an underlying assumption that more testing and treatment is better. That paradigm is simply incorrect, based on the science of quality. One must actually evaluate the efficacy of testing or treatment, its appropriateness, the probability of damage caused by the intervention versus its benefit, and its efficiency (or resource use). Quality can and should be measured. It occurs only in a process like medical care as a result of meticulous execution, and it can constantly be improved.

Key Quality Characteristics. Key quality characteristics, derived from reasons for offering the programs, financial constraints, and employee satisfiers, can be used to develop the vision. Key process variables that influence the attainment of the key quality characteristics can be identified, and objective criteria to measure their achievement can be developed.

Employers would be likely to emphasize at least three categories of key quality characteristics for benefits and health management programs. Among employers, employees, and health professionals there is convergence of values and opinion in the areas of wise use of medical care, self-care, health promotion, and value management.

Employment-related key characteristics might include the following:

- The package should be competitive for attracting and retaining needed or valued employees.
- The package should have services that maintain or improve the health of the work force.
- The package should contain benefits that employees value, thus helping to bond employees to the organization.
- The package should protect employees from major financial losses.

Financial key characteristics include these features:

- The package should allow the employer to be competitive in end markets.
- Benefits costs should be manageable.
- Volume should be manageable.
- Purchased medical care should be of optimal value.
- The wage-benefits mix should optimize financial outlays.

Administrative and content key characteristics could include the following:

- The health management program should contain ways of making employers better consumers of medical care.
- The health management program should be preventively focused.
- The program should be as administratively simple as possible.
- Programs should manage the cost and quality of care for workers' compensation.
- The program should have accessible and usable data.
- The program should include a quality improvement framework with identified improvement projects on an ongoing basis.

Goal Congruity. A major issue to deal with in the vision for the future is the continuity and congruity of the health management program with the organizational and human resource goals and objectives of the organization. To be as successful as possible, the program should mirror those goals and objectives and support them. Health personnel sometimes lose sight of the fact that most employment organizations do not exist solely to preserve and promote the health of their employees and dependents, but rather for a specific business or public service purpose. Therefore, while it is important to frame some health goals in terms of desired personal values, or in terms of "loss framing" ("I could have had _____ if I had done _____"), it is also important that the messages are consistent and even overtly stated as aligned with organizational goals.

Financial Risk. An overt decision about who bears risk could also be made. First, the employer should decide whether it is willing to ask that providers of care go at risk for the outcome of their treatment by accepting per diem or capitated payment rather than simply being paid for all services provided on whatever financial basis (be it fee schedules, fee for service, discounted fee for service, or other mechanisms). Second, it should be determined whether employees should bear some of the financial risk for their life-style. This is a hotly debated issue at the present time, but it is clear that smokers and those with uncontrolled high blood pressure, for example, are at significantly higher risk than usual for major catastrophic health events as well as for a series of minor problems.

Analyze the Gaps

The preceding discussion suggested the way an organization would position itself to manage health and related expenditures and how that organization might look. To bridge the gap between that hypothetical approach and the present situation, facilitated strategic planning sessions are often useful to reach consensus or agreement on a number of issues. Subjects to be discussed and resolved would include the following:

- Paradigms
- Goals, objectives, and time lines
- Organizational design
- Skills acquisition plan
- Data management plan
- Monitoring and evaluation plan
- Marketing and communications plan for health management activities and changes in the benefits program

As an organizing point, it is important to frame mutually acceptable goals. Some examples might include:

- Obtaining the "best" care for employees and dependents (it would be important to agree on what "best" means to the participants, just as it is important to overtly agree on what "quality" is)
- Optimizing health satisfaction and productivity
- Optimizing value for both employers and employees

Select a Strategy

The scope and extent of the health management program could be defined at this point. Planners could decide whether the program would include management of health risks, education and training and self-care, education and training and wise use of the medical system, and/or care during and after illnesses, whether provided through a benefits program or on site. Each of these sounds like a decision to add a specific activity. But in reality, whether or not to do each of them devolves directly from paradigms such as the degree of empowerment and activism desired for employees and dependents in dealing with the medical system, or the organization's intent to be proactive rather than reactive and to make an investment that is long term but that should pay off significantly.

To execute the strategy and achieve the vision for the future, it would be important to create an organization that can support the strategy. This might be a matrix organization that is cross-departmental, or one might name a single person in charge of the various functions that relate to health and medical care. That person would need to have appropriate responsibility and a small staff to carry out the administration of the program. Organization and lines of authority should be relatively clear, since completely matrixed organizations tend to spend a fair amount of time deciding who is in charge of what.

It is likely that the skill set of the people in the organization would have to be upgraded to encompass benefits management, data analysis, population medicine, prevention, communications, and other key aspects of executing this program. Staffing could be outlined with the understanding that while multiple disciplines are needed, the use of multiskilled individuals is probably more efficient. It also is consistent with a philosophy of job expansion and enhancement.

Information Management and Communication. A specific strategy for data collection, analysis, and management should be built into the program from square one. As the old management saying goes, "You can't manage what you don't measure." An information strategy could be enunciated at this point.

The communication strategy follows to a large degree from a paradigm of empowerment or top-down communication. One key would be the amount of employee contact that is desired. At this point, it would be advisable to broadly outline which types of media might be used for communication. This should probably be consistent with the usual communication channels in the organization.

All of these strategies and tactics should be based on a clear understanding of what plan design, service delivery techniques, and communications techniques are both efficient and effective. Offering health promotion activities or cost containment activities because they are the "latest thing," without either theoretical or empirical proof of their effectiveness, is an invitation to waste more money and create unrealistic expectations.

We will discuss specific strategies in Part Two. The groundwork has been laid here, by discussing the flaws in the current acute medical care approach and the misalignment of industry structure, resource allocation, and function with typical employer and employee needs and wants.

Conclusion

The strategic health management process is a structured, logical, business approach to the analysis, planning, and consistent execution of a longer-range, data-based strategy that will manage health as well as illness in a cost-effective and cost-beneficial manner. The first phase involves characterization of the present and recent past expenditures on medical care as well as the quality of care and its value. Projections of the future costs of life-style-related illness and injury are also helpful.

In the second phase, employers, and hopefully employees, identify desirable characteristics for their health management system. This is a form of intellectual "zero-based budgeting" to identify the real reasons for the benefits program and its optimal shape and performance, tempered by the realistic ability of medical care to deliver those characteristics. A comparison is then made between the current and the desired state, and plans are made to bridge the gaps over a period of time.

A variety of specific strategies can be selected to move from the current state to the future one. These will be explored in some detail in Part Two.

PART TWO

Strategies
for Proactive
Health Management

Managing the costs of medical benefits, let alone the services purchased, has been a daunting task. To be fully effective in the longer term, it requires a broader perspective than a purely financial one. Managing the factors that cause health problems and use of medical services (the two are not synonymous, since services may or may not be used for symptoms, feelings, and overt illness or injury) is needed to move upstream from the point of service and become more effective. That in turn implies participatory management of the health of the work force and their dependents.

Part One of *Strategic Health Management: A Guide for Employers, Employees, and Policy Makers* described the current dilemma employers find themselves in and presented a strategic management framework to analyze cost drivers, factors that affect the use of health services, and the effect of these factors on benefits plans and on employee and dependent health. Determining what the health management program and the benefits plan should look like, and the gap between the present situation and the desired future, provided a concrete framework to actively manage health, costs, and care.

As each critical gap between the desired health management program and the current situation is identified, it can be listed and prioritized. Strategies can then be developed to close each gap. The remainder of this book will discuss a number of strategies that have proven successful and that are based directly on the known mechanics and environment of the medical care system as it exists in the United States. Which strategies

141

are most appropriate for each employer is a decision to be made as part of the strategic management process. This book offers some general guidelines.

We will first deal with potential political solutions, since they are now at the forefront and will continue to appear on the public agenda as long as costs continue to rise, removing funds from other endeavors, and as long as access is a problem (Chapter Six). If activity fades at the federal level, it will most likely continue and even increase at the state and local levels. But political change in itself will likely address only part of the picture, and when and if it will occur, and in what form, are uncertain.

To provide a wider and more effective approach to health management, I would recommend increasing employee involvement in decision making (Chapter Eight) and health promotion (Chapter Nine) to any employer or group of cooperating employers with a reasonably stable work force. In a community, work-force stability is less of an issue, since health maintenance and promotion will benefit the community regardless of job change. Employee involvement is a cornerstone of preventive and promotive programs and is part of the foundation for the total compensation approach to the wage and benefits package (Chapter Ten) as well as for productivity improvement and better human resource management. It also improves the flow of information needed for supplier improvement.

Health promotion is economically better than care or cure after illness has developed and will become more cost advantageous as prices rise and more technology is introduced. The extent of a health promotion program is a tactical rather than a strategic decision.

The remainder of the strategies are part of a continuum from pure financing of care (conventional indemnity insurance) to close supplier-purchaser partnerships. Managed care falls somewhere in the middle of the spectrum. I would recommend moving toward supplier improvement in the long run, because it has the potential to decrease the expenditure on management structure and return control of the health process to providers and patients. How rapidly to get there is again an individual or collective employer and employee decision based on employee acceptance, financial constraints, the typical organizational time horizon, the existence of suitable providers, and internal or collective resources.

Most employers still have conventional indemnity plans for at least some of their employees. They may have overlaid utilization management, but the basic structure and incentives or disincentives still bear revisiting to ensure that they match the goals of the program, address specific objectives such as distribution of payment between employer and employee, and are as effective as they could be (Chapter Seven).

Many employers are moving toward managed care, but they have done so without great enthusiasm, judging by the small number that actively advocate these programs and by the relative price tags assigned to options offered to employees. They also offer many managed care options, diluting focus and leverage. In addition, how well managed care works depends on the contracts, information feedback, and operational execution of each managed care organization. Some plans work well and others do not (Chapter Eleven). Operational improvement therefore plays a key role in managing costs and health through such plans. This is a step in the direction of a true supplier improvement program.

Direct contracting allows for more intensive supplier improvement (Chapter Twelve). If that is not possible or could be more efficiently accomplished by "insourcing," then employers can vertically integrate and provide the services themselves, as some have done (Chapter Thirteen). This progression of strategies is summarized in Chapter Fourteen.

The more crucial issue here, if one accepts the need for management of care, management of health, and more active involvement, is the chain of tactics used over time to accomplish the strategies. These must be tailored to the organization's culture, financial goals, human resource objectives, and top management direction to ensure some measure of success and to avoid nasty surprises. Figuring this out and articulating it is a central part of strategic health management.

CHAPTER SIX

A Political Solution:
Changing Public Policies

Providing efficient and effective medical care for employees and their families is clearly a critical challenge for employers if they are to retain the advantages of offering medical benefits and avoid the disadvantages. Various strategies to reach this goal are available, some active and some passive. Leading the list of passive strategies is waiting for government to change the rules of the game, from the shape of the benefits package to the form of the delivery system to the "rules of engagement" such as community rating, taxability, and portability. Being able to shift the blame for dissatisfiers in medical care to the government is attractive, but is it viable? Will the executive and legislative process result in a new "system" that is more efficient, effective, and affordable than the old? Will it do it in a reasonable time frame? Might the government solution be worse than the current scenario?

President Clinton has elevated the issue of "national health care reform" to the forefront of the political agenda. Since employers provide the majority of financing for medical care for those under sixty-five, and that connection will be maintained under the Clinton proposal and most other "reform" scenarios, employers should want a major voice in the outcome. The questions they should raise may well be different than the ones raised by government policy makers. Should a political solution be applied to a private industry that contracts with private buyers? One might argue that leverage is necessary to improve value or that some political action is necessary to prevent cost shifting from Medicare, Medicaid, and county medical funds, but it is a real political question whether that is appropriate, or whether the private sector should solve its own problems. From a policy standpoint, the most obvious employment related issue is the consumption of a greater and greater share of the total compensation package and public resources for other programs by the undamped escalation of medical care costs.

On the other hand, a number of facets of a well-functioning, true *health* care system are not addressed in reform proposals (for example, consumer information and empowerment, wise use and self-care programs, health promotion (as opposed to preventive services), and integration of medical benefits into the total compensation package). Employers would do well to provide these to avoid further cost escalation and erosion of value.

It remains to be seen whether President Clinton (or anyone else, for that matter) can orchestrate and execute a quantum change in the system. The history of American politics is that of "creeping incrementalism" (Starr, 1982). The history of attempts at national health care reform since the Truman administration has been that vigorous objection by the medical establishment has prevented any quantum change. Since that time, the health care industry has grown from less than 1 percent to over 15 percent of the national economy. Thus, the amount of resistance to change has increased tremendously.

State sovereignty and action are a tradition as well. States have provided some medical care for some time. A number of states, among them Hawaii, Florida, Minnesota, Maryland, New Jersey, Tennesseee, Washington, Oregon, and Vermont, have enacted or are actively debating proposals ranging from insurance rate caps to managed competition (Rogal and Helms, 1993). They have felt the need to move ahead in any area they can, despite barriers such as Federal Medicaid requirements, which interfere with managed care, and the ERISA preemption of mandated benefits for self-insured employers. Some analysts feel that the current administration may be using the states to clear the way for its agenda, or as a laboratory to see the actual effects of various reform models. These will be discussed below. It should also be noted that state reforms may make life more complicated for employers with facilities or personnel in more than one state. Administration will be more complicated, and it may be difficult explaining to employees why benefits are different in different states, leading to pressure to raise benefits to the highest common denominator for labor relations reasons.

Advantages of Health Care Reform for Employers

A number of employers have become involved in the debate on "national health care reform" — for example, in the area of access. One might well ask whether this is an offensive or defensive maneuver on their part, since the present primary concern of most employers is cost management. While it is true that adding thirty-five million uncovered Americans and thirty-five million undercovered Americans to the medical care system would probably decrease cost shifting to private payers, it is possible that it might exacerbate the problem by adding them in a way that does not pay full costs or full charges, or adds them to an essentially unmanaged system, exacerbating the overall cost spiral and shifting more resources to the medical care industry.

Employers should have an interest in moderating medical care costs for several other less obvious reasons. A primary one is that medical care costs for government employees, Medicaid beneficiaries, and the balance of Medicare costs in excess of premiums are eroding the ability of the public sector to provide the infrastructure on which industry depends (Starr, 1992). Federal spending on medical care is now double that for education, defense, or public works and is growing at a much faster rate. State budgets are constrained and dominated by rapidly increasing Medicaid costs. The results have been deteriorating highways, airports, rivers, and seaports, and declining quality of public services and public education. That in turn makes transportation and communication more difficult and government research and support and promotional services less available, and it reduces the quality of the work force. Taxes may have to be raised if any improvement is to be made, unless medical care cost increases are restrained.

If medical coverage remains employment based, some of the current proposals could increase employer bargaining power with providers by forming groups for purchasing purposes. Employers and employees benefit to the extent that price and volume are better managed and/or quality is increased.

Multistate employers would have an interest both in state reforms and in provisions in a federal program for state variations and control. Costs might vary by state, affecting siting or expansion decisions, especially if ERISA provisions are preempted or repealed. Employees are also concerned about perceived companywide equality of benefits. If states have different requirements, administrative costs could increase. So state action is of concern for a variety of reasons.

Another reason, but one that applies only to certain businesses, has to do with retiree medical care costs. Some employers, particularly those in the auto industry, are involved in calls for national health insurance, or a single-payer, tax-financed system. They are suffering a major financial burden from medical benefits for early retirees and supplementary benefits for retirees over age sixty-five. Because the use of medical services increases with age after age thirty-five in the absence of health promotion programs, costs rapidly escalate in the retiree population; those costs are very unevenly distributed, with 10 percent of enrollees accruing 70 percent of the cost (Harris, 1989; Riley and others, 1986; Garfinkel, Riley, and Iannacchione, 1988). Further, the adoption of Financial Accounting Standards Board Rule 106 requires reporting of liability for retirees. Moving this liability into a national health system would make sense from their standpoint, but probably not from the standpoint of the rest of the economy.

Evaluating and Supporting
Reform Proposals: A Scorecard

In evaluating the options for political solutions, employers would do well to focus on their public policy and employee benefits goals. They should analyze what their costs might be and what the effects on the quality of care might be. These costs would be net of any tax advantages or disadvantages.

The vision of political reform for any given employer depends on its goals; which proposal to support or advance would clearly be linked to this intent. As discussed, health management goals, if they address the external environment or if adequate benefits are not available to an employer at a reasonable price, might include access, universal coverage, cost management, targeted decreases in cost shifting, and so on. Internal goals and objectives for reform might be appropriate if one were attempting to measure and manage a firm's political activities.

Some of the questions to be answered are listed in Table 6.1. These tests should be appplied to any proposal before it is supported or before changes are suggested.

One of the major pieces of data needed to assess various proposals would be a comparison of the provisions of the proposal (particularly those including a minimum or basic benefits package) with the benefits currently offered by the employer. It is likely that any benefits offered above that level would be outside the basic package and probably not tax advantaged. A careful assessment of the labor market and the probable moves of competitors if these benefits were not tax free would determine the company's position on use of benefits to attract and retain desired workers. The relative supply of skilled or unskilled workers, depending on the industry, would dictate the needs for additional incentives to attract and retain labor.

Generic Proposals

The central organizing point of most "health care reform" legislation proposed at both the state and federal levels is a change in the economic incentives in the financing of medical care. One key presumption underlying these financing reform concepts is that extending coverage to all Americans will solve access problems.

Cost Shifting from the Uninsured and Underinsured

The large and growing number of un- and underinsured pose several problems. In addition to issues of social equity, providers shift the 30–75 percent of costs not paid by these patients to private patients, leveraging price increases in a much steeper curve

Table 6.1. Framework for Political Proposal Analysis.

Issue	Question
Total cost	What would the effect be on the total cost of medical care?
	Are tax incentives changed for both employers and employees — that is, are both contributions no longer tax sheltered?
Financial mechanics	How will coverage be financed and will that introduce further distortion into the system?
	Is there a global budget?
	Is there a provision to manage risk selection among plans?
	Are there provisions to manage capital investment?
	What is the effect on pricing to private payers?
	Has the proposal adequately addressed cost shifting, both interemployer and from government programs?
	Does the proposal contain a way to introduce realistic pricing into the medical sector?
	Does the proposal give buyers any more leverage?
	Does the proposal provide financial incentives for prevention and primary care rather than specialist care, procedures, and intensive terminal care?
	Is there a provision for better consumer information?
Capacity	Is excess capacity effectively addressed?
	Is there a provision for retraining or outplacing medical workers likely to be displaced?
	Is there a mechanism to reduce excess physician specialist supply?
	Is there an effective mechanism to reduce excess facilities and technology?
Utilization	Is there a mechanism to discourage excess utilization?
	Is there a framework to determine and provide for appropriateness of testing and treatment?
Technology	Does the proposal effectively deal with assessment of new technology?
	Are there provisions to prevent duplication of technology?
	Are there provisions to manage the diffusion of technology?
Efficiency and effectiveness	Are there provisions to assess efficiency and effectiveness of testing and treatments?
	Are there incentives to improve clinical effectiveness and process efficiency?

Table 6.1. Framework for Political Proposal Analysis, Cont'd.

Issue	Question
Quality	How would quality be managed?
	Is data collection mandated?
	Is there an appropriate way of feeding back data on quality to providers?
	Are providers involved in quality assessment?
	Is there a quality improvement mandate?
	Is there a plausible mechanism for quality improvement in the plan?
	Is information on the quality of plans or providers readily available to employees as they choose competing plans?
Staffing issues	Will this proposal affect the company's ability to attract and retain needed workers?
Compensation and benefits	What is the wage benefit trade-off net of taxes?
	Will there be a universal or standardized benefits package? Is it better or worse than the present coverage?
	Will employers be free to offer additional coverage?

than would otherwise occur. One of the main benefits of any of these programs would be to cover the uninsured.

The Employee Benefits Research Institute has reported that there were 36.3 million uninsured Americans in 1991, an increase of 12.4 percent over three years (Employee Benefits Research Institute, 1992). The overall percent of uninsured has remained relatively stable for some time. Apparent changes in statistics may occur because of the sensitivity of estimates to survey frames, methods, and questions, as well as the business cycle (H. S. Luft, personal communication, Aug. 1993). Workers or their dependents make up 79.3 percent of the uninsured. According to the Employee Benefits Research Institute report, the proportion of Americans covered by group health care plans has declined over the last several years to 57.2 percent of the population, down from 59.7 percent in 1988. Workers at small firms account for more than half of the increase in uninsured workers; these workers and the self-employed were 13.1 million of the uninsured in 1991.

Almost all of the uninsured are under sixty-five, since virtually everyone (about 97 percent of those) over sixty-five is covered by Medicare. If the over-sixty-five population is factored out, the percentage of the population that is uninsured is considerably higher. The rate of lack of insurance is much higher among Hispanics and African Americans than among whites. Almost a majority live in the South, as opposed to other regions of the country.

It is estimated that the uninsured use about one-third less hospital services than the insured; services are used but are paid for by public agencies. Thus, if they become covered and no changes are made in the medical care delivery system, total costs should rise. It is also estimated that the uninsured have only about one-third of the access to inpatient hospital services that insured people have. Whether this has an effect on health is a subject of debate. Much of the uncompensated care that hospitals do provide is outpatient and ambulatory care (Fuchs, 1991; Long and Rogers, 1989).

Another 20 percent of the population are "underinsured." These Americans have possibilities of catastrophic loss that exceed 10 percent of their income. These people are not completely uncovered.

Aside from the structural and access issues raised above or perhaps because of them, questions also arise of medical necessity versus risk. There is also the central issue of exactly how much of the national economy should be devoted to a palliative (and occasionally curative) system rather than building "real wealth" (V. R. Fuchs, 1993). It could certainly be argued that maintaining a healthy population is a national priority, but whether to do that through intensive medical care after disease has been developed, as opposed to disease prevention and health promotion, and how much these vast expenditures actually do improve health and function, are clearly open to question (Leaf, 1993).

Incentives to Change Provider Behavior

The other key presumption, based on economic theory, is that changes in financial incentives of one sort or another will change provider and supplier behavior. While this last is true in organized delivery systems with a restricted number of providers (Hillman, Pauly, and Kerstein, 1989; Hillman, 1991), it remains to be seen what the effects would be in an open system with a great oversupply. A number of proposals have been advanced to change the financing mechanics and eligibility provisions of the de facto medical care system. I will summarize each of the generic financing mechanisms but not specific proposals, since they can change rapidly and are typically altered in debate. In the following section, I will discuss structural changes beyond payment and eligibility that will be needed to change the process of care and some of the responses to financial incentives.

Managed Competition

Alain Enthoven, a Business School professor at Stanford University, and his associate Richard Kronick, now at the University of California, San Diego, have advanced a proposal known as *managed competition*. The concept has been adopted by the Jackson Hole Group, a group of academics and policy analysts.

The basic theory of managed competition is that large groups of purchasers could negotiate with large groups of providers to determine price and some other terms of services in advance (Enthoven and Kronick, 1989; Iglehart, 1993). These have intrinsic appeal, but the market has failed in medical care because of the mechanics of the reimbursement system. In most of these proposals, *affordable health plans* or AHPs are offered to purchasing cooperatives, which would then choose a few of the best plans to offer their combined enrollees. Presumably, there would be competition on price and quality. According to one estimate, at most three plans could be supported in approximately 71 markets with greater than 180,000, which would cover approximately 71 percent of U.S. population (Kronick, Goodman, Wennberg, and Wagner, 1993). Therefore, some other supplementary mechanism would be needed to manage care in the remaining areas of the country. An unresolved issue is whether, and at what employee population, employers would be allowed to opt out of an AHP, diffusing its effectiveness. Managed competition as proposed by the Clinton administration, with a single-sponsor health alliance, is more restrictive and in fact perhaps even more noncompetitive, as opposed to the more open and pluralistic model proposed by the Jackson Hole Group.

While total managed competition has not been tried on an area-wide basis, there are examples of large purchasing groups exerting leverage in dealing with providers. The California Public Employees Retirement System, or CalPERS, with over 800,000 retirees and public employees eligible, has bargained aggressively for rates for a basic benefits package with managed care plans, holding increases to low single digits. The plan still allows many suppliers, as long as they meet the terms of the lowest bidder. The Federal Employees Health Benefit Plan pays only for the lowest-cost plan, as does the State of Minnesota and Stanford University (Enthoven, 1989). The State of Florida has capitalized on the experience of several employer purchasing cooperatives in the state by creating regional purchasing authorities much like AHPs. The effects remain to be seen (Brown, 1993).

Employer Mandate

Employer mandate or "pay-or-play" proposals continue the present employment basis for medical care financing, requiring employers greater than a certain size to provide coverage for all employees who work more than a certain number of hours per week. Most of these proposals have a threshold of hours worked (typically somewhere between 17.5 and 32), so that part-time workers would not be covered. Employer-based financing has been folded into the Clinton Task Force recommendations, although it is not intrinsic to managed competition. An employer mandate per se does not address the tax-advantaged status of medical benefits and therefore the incentive to overinsure. A pure employer mandate program does not have cost management provisions. It is aimed primarily at stopping interemployer cost shifting from small to large employers, which is substantial (Moran and Sheils, 1991). In many scenarios, employer mandates are combined with expansion of the public "system" (Medicare and Medicaid) to provide near-universal coverage.

There are several potential problems with employer mandate programs. First, they do not cover all Americans. Second, a number of people might lose their jobs, or wages might be reduced in low-income jobs to the minimum wage floor in order to pay for health insurance. There would be some declines in the Medicaid roles because previously uncovered individuals would be covered (but total tax-supported coverage might rise if the object is universal coverage). The number of individual medical insurance policies would also be reduced. While these policies are very inefficient, they are a substantial business.

Small employers have been strongly opposed to these proposals because they presently do not offer insurance and see employer mandates as increasing their cost of doing business. While they have had to pay higher money wages to attract employees in some cases, they may have attracted those with a preference for money rather than benefits, such as young healthy workers and those who are not risk averse. These employees do not *want* medical insurance but prefer cash wages.

Expansion of Public Programs

Expansion of public programs to cover the uninsured and underinsured would address both the access issue and possibly cost shifting. Medicaid expansion, for example, would decrease the number of uninsured Americans depending on the threshold of eligibility, but might not cover everyone because the programs would probably still be categorical. Some expansion of public programs would be needed to provide universal coverage in the absence of a single program or single-payer system. A number of plans combine Medicaid expansion and an employer mandate. This approach would most likely increase the burden on middle- and upper-income taxpayers. It might create a two-tier system of medical care as well.

Universal Insurance

Universal Insurance (UI), also known as *National Health Insurance,* has been proposed and repeatedly failed to win approval since the 1920s. A number of advocacy groups favor this mode of reform rather than managed competition, for reasons that will become clear shortly; some analysts believe that managed competition may be a stalking horse for UI. In that scenario, managed competition, without specifically addressing structural reform, will result in a further cost spiral, or at least not adequately suppress cost escalation, creating a demand for a single budgeted system.

UI has been proposed for a number of related reasons — to ensure uniform coverage for all Americans, to impose a global budget for all medical care expenditures, and to reduce administrative costs. UI is essentially a single-payer system with the government providing payment to all providers, at least for a basic benefits package. It does not necessarily dictate who provides the services. This system should decrease administrative overhead, marketing expenses, and some duplication of services, depending on the exact details. Depending on the model, the insurance industry would either become a much smaller government-contracted claims payer or be abolished except for supplemental coverages, as in Canada and the United Kingdom.

UI might have little effect on large employers. They would not have to provide benefits but might have to raise money wages to compensate for the loss of previously provided benefits in order to have a competitive total compensation package. Small employers would have an easier time attracting workers, since they would not have to raise wages to compensate for the inability to offer insurance at reasonable rates compared to larger employers, or the cost increases might be hidden in the tax structure or at least uniformly applied. Cost shifting, at least for the basic benefits package, would probably stop, since there would be only one payer (Morrisey, 1991). It should reduce or eliminate interemployer cost shifting, or the "free-rider" phenomenon.

A single, central source of funding and administration might significantly reduce processing cost and administrative overhead. There is some controversy about the magnitude of these savings, but one estimate is that it might be as great as 8 to 10 percent of the nation's total medical bill or as much as

$85 to $100 billion, which would clearly fund a basic medical package for every underinsured and uninsured person in this country. These estimates are derived from comparisons of the American system, with its multiplicity of payers and financial intermediaries, each with its own set of rules, paperwork, review appeals, and so on, to systems such as the Canadian and British systems, which have a single payer and one relatively small payment mechanism (Woolhandler and Himmelstein, 1991; Woolhandler, Himmelstein, and Lewontin, 1993). This type of change would mean the virtual elimination of the insurance industry for the basic benefits package and may not be politically viable because of opposition from that quarter.

If UI follows existing models elsewhere in the world, preventive services would be covered. Taxes for employees would rise to support the system. Currently uninsured and underinsured people should benefit from easier financial access to medical care. It is unclear whether industrial competitiveness would be improved, since medical care costs are a significant element of the total cost of production in only a few instances. The country's infrastructure would in theory be improved if funds were again available for roads, schools, and so on.

Employee Mandate

A different type of proposal is the employee mandate, which removes many of the economic anomalies from the current financing system. It would cover almost all the uninsured. This option has been proposed by a group of economists from the Wharton School and the University of California at Irvine, as well as by the California Business Group on Health (Pauly, Danzon, and Feldstein, 1991; Kerr, 1992). In this scheme, all Americans would be required to have insurance through their employer or a government-run pool. Employees rather than employers would receive the tax deduction for the purchase of a basic insurance package; those who pay no taxes would receive a refund. Vouchers would be issued by the local social welfare agency for those who could not afford insurance. Coverage would be recorded and enforced through the W4 form. The authors believe that this plan would provide coverage for almost all Americans, eliminate tax-based distortions in the reimbursement system, eliminate wage benefit trade-off distortions, and eliminate cost shifting between employers and employers and government funding agencies. Portability of coverage would be most easily accomplished by an employee mandate. It is not clear whether the overhead now devoted to marketing and attempts at risk selection among carriers would be addressed or solved by this proposal.

Provider Proposals

The proposals put forward by some provider groups are centered around coverage or access. Universal access without any other changes would increase their revenue base and might not manage costs, quality, or value. These proposals are outlined here as a baseline and to introduce the provider perspectives that have been put forward, since providers have had powerful positions in past debates. They may change as the debate on reform progresses.

The American Society of Internal Medicine and the American College of Physicians have only two basic demands: that there be a basic benefits package and that preventive services as outlined by the U.S. Preventive Services Task Force be reimbursable.

The American Medical Association's Health Access America program is considerably more complicated, but it includes the same basic provision of universal access through a public and private partnership and an affordable minimum benefits package (Yang and Anderson, 1993). It, too, advocates portability, community rating, and no preexisting clause. The American Medical Association proposes that a tax deductibility cap be set at 150 percent of the minimum benefits package, with an optional unlimited benefits package that would not trigger the cap, and deductibility for all out-of-pocket expenses. In addition, it proposes health-related IRAs for long-term care that could be tax free.

The American Medical Association has a number of other provisions that might be seen as self-serving, such as federal regulation of utilization review to reduce the "hassle factor" for physicians, the medical profession being empowered to enforce ethical and clinical standards, no third-party payer challenges to professional judgments, and resistance to single-payer systems. It does advocate a universal claim form, which should reduce administrative costs to some extent.

In the financial arena, physicians should be free to charge patients their usual fee, and the American Medical Association should be free to negotiate fees with carriers and the government. It also maintains that patients should have freedom of choice of physicians and/or delivery system. This last is somewhat nebulous. Some observers have characterized universal access with free choice of provider as effective restraint of trade, stemming from the guildlike properties of professions in Western countries, particularly the United States (Weller, 1986). If it were free choice of physician at any time, managed care would be impossible. Free choice of plan would subvert attempts at supplier improvement.

Organizations concerned with public health, preventive medicine, and primary care have forwarded more balanced and wider-ranging proposals. The Association of State and Territorial Health Officers proposes communitywide preventive health services, universal access to basic health services (with a guaranteed minimum benefits package, including preventive and educational services, as well as financial reform and strong cost containment measures), and quality assurance — type unspecified. The American College of Preventive Medicine advocates, among other things, assessment of the health of communities to prioritize needs, health education, prevention of infectious and chronic diseases, outreach screening and linkage to identify those in need of health care, and reform of financing of graduate medical education to increase the number of primary and preventive practitioners.

The American Academy of Family Practice proposal addresses financing, structure, and process. Key points include universal coverage through employer-based and state-sponsored plans, a cost-effective, comprehensive benefits package, insurance reforms to guarantee the issuance and renewal of portable policies with community rating, coordinated work-force changes to achieve at least 50 percent generalist physicians, and protection and enhancement of quality.

International Comparisons

Much has been made of comparisons with medical care financing and delivery systems in other major developed countries. The usual suspects are Canada, Germany, Great Britain, Japan, and sometimes France and the Scandinavian countries (Harvard Community Health Plan, 1990). However, there are limits to the lessons to be learned because of cultural differences and because of entrenched differences in each country's medical industry or delivery system. In almost all cases, the national government exerts considerable control over the supply and type of physicians; in many cases, it controls the supply of other resources as well (see the Appendix).

Most other countries that have significantly lower per person health care expenditures, health care expenditures as a percentage of the gross domestic product, and growth rates of health expenditures have public systems or global budgets or both (Schieber, Poullier, and Greenwald, 1993). While there is some fee-for-service payment, it is contained in a global budget in most cases (Harvard Community Health Plan, 1990).

Perhaps the main point to be gained from this discussion is that health status does not seem to vary in direct correlation with expenditures, nor does satisfaction (Table 6.2). There are some interesting anomalies to be noted, included the long hospital stays in Japan, which may constitute medically unnecessary service. Almost all of these countries have much higher ratios of primary care doctors to specialists than the United States does. Most of them also have a much lower concentration of high-technology equipment and many fewer unoccupied hospital beds. There would appear to be a lesson here in the relationship between the availability of resources, the training of the physicians, and the use of these resources. Employers can emulate these systems by specifically designing or buying private networks that share these characteristics.

Table 6.2. International Comparison of
Medical Care Expenditures and Health Status.

	Per capita health expenditure	Health expenditures as percent of gross domestic product	Infant mortality rate (per thousand)	Life expectancy (years)
United States	$2,051	11.2	10.4	75.6
Sweden	$1,328	9.0	5.9	77.7
Switzerland	$1,301	7.9	4.9	78.9
Germany	$1,212	8.6	5.6	77.2
France	$1,178	8.7	6.3	77.6
Netherlands	$1,071	8.4	7.0	77.6
Canada	$1,054	8.5	7.3	79.2
Italy	$995	7.3	6.1	78.0
Australia	$990	7.0	8.2	76.6
Japan	$978	6.5	4.5	79.3
Great Britain	$795	5.9	7.3	76.3

Source: Adapted from Harvard Community Health Plan, 1990.

Structural Issues

Structural issues in the population and the medical "system" will shape the effects of reform. Some of these are recapped below to bring perspective to the evaluation of present and likely future proposals.

The United States has not had a clear, overt, comprehensive, articulated health policy, just as we have a medical care industry rather than a health care system. However, service, research, taxation, and funding programs have been added incrementally, creating de facto public and private policies. To the extent that the United States has a health care policy, it is manifested by:

• Categorical programs, including Medicare for the elderly; Medicaid for disadvantaged women and children; the Veterans Administration programs; U.S. Public Health Service programs for Native Americans, the Coast Guard, the Merchant Marine, and prisoners; military medicine; and the CHAMPUS programs

- Categorical funding for research, primarily on illness rather than prevention or health promotion, through the National Institutes of Health and the National Science Foundation
- Relatively small public health programs funded through state and local health departments and the U.S. Centers for Disease Control
- Capitation grants to medical schools, which have encouraged an oversupply of specialists
- Government loans for health professional students, lowering the cost of entry, particularly for physicians
- Support of hospital construction through the Hill-Burton Act and tax-exempt bonding capacity

There are several other apparently disconnected public policy decisions that have arguably exacerbated and perhaps even caused the current cost spiral. It is not clear what the political background was. However, when Medicare was passed in 1966 against the initial violent opposition of both the American Medical Association and initially the American Hospital Association, a "floor" for physician payments based on a statistical average that included a large number of newly graduated specialists was established. This limit was considerably above market prices at the time (Starr, 1982).

The existence of that large and growing supply of new specialists was in itself the result of a public policy decision made in isolation from a broad overview of what would happen to medical expenditures. As employers and insurers have often done, they followed the federal government's lead in expanding benefits package and coverage, using the usual, customary, and reasonable statistical payment method. Another public policy decision—that of making benefits pretax—encouraged overinsurance, untrammeled consumption, and a price spiral. In short, the private sector followed the government's lead in establishing an indemnity-based pricing and reimbursement policy and offered ever-expanding benefits packages because of the public policy of making these expenses tax exempt. Rational targets for policy reform therefore might include taxation policy and pricing policy.

The Mechanics of the Medical Industry: A Brief Review

Recall that the payment mechanism for medical care is

- Disassociated from the purchase decision
- Based on statistical parameters rather than market prices
- Set up in such a way that cost can be shifted from one payer to another without consent
- Based on a retroactive casualty insurance model rather than proactive contractual terms
- Not adapted to assessing new technology before it is used
- Set up in such a way that large pools of capital are available to build new facilities and fund the development of new technologies and pharmaceuticals that may or may not have incremental benefit

There is no global budget for medical care in the United States, no central planning, a significant oversupply of medical staff and facilities, and minimal emphasis on prevention and health promotion. This means that the system is essentially unmanaged. The oversupply consists of specialists, with the ratio of specialists and generalists reversed, a 30 percent oversupply of hospital beds, a significant excess of imaging, other radiological equipment, and probably laboratory facilities, and a significant oversupply of therapeutically similar drugs. There are a plethora of technologies that partially duplicate each other and tend to be additive rather than replacing each other.

This excess capacity would not exist in a competitive industry, because excess capacity and services with low marginal utility would not be paid for. However, because the financing system is disassociated from the development of supply, virtually any new therapy is paid for. While it is becoming more expensive because of the cost of medical education and offices, market entry is not that difficult, particularly given subsidies available from hospitals and organized practices.

What Is Not There

Note that none of the financing proposals just summarized deal with issues such as tax-supported professional training and facilities expansion, or technology assessment, that are driving costs. The issue of oversupply should be addressed for several reasons.

According to most projections, the supply of physicians, particularly specialists, will continue to grow under current training scenarios. Although there has been a recent change, primary care training programs have been underfilled, with the proportion of physicians in training selecting true primary care declining for the past fifteen years (Page, 1993). In addition, primary care physicians receive grossly inadequate training in prevention. Further, there is some debate whether internists and pediatricians are in fact primary care physicians, since they are trained more to seek and exclude esoteric diseases than they are to understand the dynamics of health, illness, growth and development, social support systems, and family dynamics. The oversupply of specialists drives the use of new and marginally useful technology (Ginzberg, 1990). As noted in Chapter Four, there may well be a significant oversupply of other health care workers, facilities, technology, and pharmaceuticals as well.

Consumer information, the balance of power between practitioners and consumers, and quality improvement are not central components of any of these proposals, but they are critical areas to address to make the system function effectively.

A Model Proposal

As a model proposal, the following might fit most employers' objectives (Harris and others, 1993):

- An employee/uninsured American mandate with a basic benefits package is the core of the proposal. This would cover essentially all Americans. It should remove financial barriers to medical care. It should stop cost shifting. At the same time, because there is no hour threshold, all Americans would be covered. The wage-benefit trade-off would become a nonissue because everyone would be covered. The effect on small businesses is unclear. Some analysts maintain that they should not have to lower wages to pay for coverage.

However, this assumes that they compete only against each other. They would be at a larger disadvantage relative to larger companies who already provide benefits if they had to add the cost of benefits to their other costs; low cost is presumably one of their current competitive advantages.

- Preventive services should be emphasized and made reimbursable through the basic benefits package. There should be reimbursement for work-site-based primary care and preventive services (see Chapter Thirteen).

- The benefits package should be tax deductible to employees. Supplementary insurance should not be tax deductible.

- Pricing should somehow be restored to a reasonable relationship to other goods and services and should be set by the market rather than usual, customary, and reasonable (statistical average) fee screens.

- Some form of budget, whether it be global or per person, is needed to create some force in the direction of efficiency and effectiveness. This may have to be enforced through statewide purchasing alliances or other quasi-governmental means.

- Cost sharing should be high enough that employees are aware of and guided by financial elements of their decisions to seek care.

- Health education and wise-use education should be mandated along with the basic benefits package. Further, health education should be a meaningful element of the curriculum at all educational levels from kindergarten through twelfth grade.

- Workers' compensation, disability benefits, and group health coverage should be merged to create a single standard of care and income replacement regardless of the source of injury or illness.

- Excess capacity and maldistribution should be addressed by changing the graduate medical education formulas and providing financial incentives to locate in underserved urban and rural areas. Excess capacity should not be a deductible business expense. (How to determine this remains to be seen.)

- There should be a standard claims form and standard data set, including enough clinical information to perform outcomes research and quality improvement efforts.
- Technology assessment, consisting of proof of effectiveness and improved cost benefit, should be required of all drugs, devices, and procedures. This would have to be a fairly standardized set of criteria and procedures to avoid "gaming" the system.
- There should be substantial support for outcomes research, which includes patient satisfaction, perceived utility, functionality, resource use, and morbidity and mortality.
- There should be a requirement that service delivery organizations engage in continuance quality improvement in a meaningful sense.
- The malpractice situation should be reformed in such a way that it does not induce excessive testing and treatment to avoid legal liability. Tactics may include arbitration, caps on awards, or other methods that preserve the rights of patients but keep awards reasonable. (Note also that malpractice awards have not apparently been successful in reducing malpractice or in improving quality.)

If these guidelines are followed, many of the inequities of the systems would be corrected. Employers presumably have an interest in creating such a system in the longer term, although in the short term, such changes could produce financial dislocation and some changes in business practices to adapt to new tax and wage structures.

Conclusion

A coherent, overtly articulated *health* policy for the United States would go a long way toward clarifying the patchwork and competing interests of the present nonsystem. At best, the new system would be just that — a true system with goals, objectives, management, and continuous improvement. This will be difficult, as many interests would prefer things as they are, and states have already taken things into their own hands. But a national system would offer advantages to multistate employers and might reduce administrative costs, depending on its structure. At a minimum, a national system would provide financial access to care for all Americans, removing us from the company of South Africa as the only industrialized country without such access.

Ideally, the new system would be prevention based and involve consumers in well-informed, joint decisions about their life-styles and medical care. Such a vision requires information and education to implement. But it may well be the most efficient way to manage health.

CHAPTER SEVEN

Revisiting Conventional Benefits Plans: Where They Succeed and Fail

Most employers offer both conventional indemnity medical benefits plans and fully managed plans. The latter, typified by HMOs, offer a fixed price for a package of services. Employers have exercised limited flexibility in designing benefits or financial provisions, although more options are becoming available. They can and do spend a good deal of time deciding on the relative contributions, price tags, and coverage of self-insured indemnity-based plans (including managed indemnity and PPOs), or comparing and selecting the provisions of fully insured plans. These design features should be used in the service of long-range objectives. Further, the mix of employee cost-sharing provisions, coverages, and the contribution "price tag" assigned to each plan will determine the likelihood that employees will select one option or another when several choices are offered. Such engineered incentives will support strategic moves toward managed care or specific providers engaged in cooperative improvement (see Chapters Eleven and Twelve).

The design of benefits plans has a number of objectives. Defining what is available to employees is perhaps the basic purpose. Defining what is *not* to be paid for and what costs are to be shared has become at least as important. In the current environment of cost pressure and uncertain medical quality, plan design is used as a financial management tool and a way to influence employee purchasing behavior.

These last goals may exceed the capabilities of many plan terms for at least two reasons. First, typical employee contributions may be too small relative to other purchases or may

168

occur at the wrong time to influence purchase behavior. Second, economic incentives without information are a relatively blunt instrument to change behavior and may not achieve the desired effect.

Many employers are less sanguine about what conventional plan design can accomplish. They generally expect plan design provisions to, among other things:

- Encourage responsible use of medical services.
- Manage the distribution of costs between employers and employees.
- Limit employers' exposure to cost increases.
- Prohibit payment for medically unnecessary or unproven diagnostic tests or treatments.
- Channel employees and dependents to specific plans.

Because of their historic importance and central role in the thinking of plan administrators, we will start our description of tactical options to support a benefits design strategy with a review of plan types and financial mechanics. Prepaid plans are now emerging as an effective way of managing costs and creating provider accountability. The service benefit type of plan, which was eclipsed after the Second World War by indemnity coverage, also deserves a second look as a contractually based cost management tool. The divergence of expectations and actual functionality for indemnity plans in particular makes it important that health managers understand what benefits plan type, copayments, deductibles, contributions, and other financial mechanisms can and cannot do.

Types of Insurance

Three basic types of medical benefits coverage, with different philosophical bases, have been popular at different times since the development of "health" insurance in the late nineteenth century. Indemnity plans grew out of life and casualty insurance, which compensates for unexpected events. Service benefit and prepaid plans were developed to provide payment for a specific service and a specific scope of service, respectively.

Indemnity plans will typically pay for coverage services using some sort of fee screen such as the usual, customary, and reasonable screen. Some will effectively pay all charges for covered services. There is no contract between provider and payer and therefore virtually no control over what is charged (Feldstein, 1988; Starr, 1982).

Service benefit plans were designed to pay for specific services, such as listed surgical procedures. They are similar in theory to defined benefit pension plans. These plans negotiate directly with hospitals and physicians for fixed rates as a way to define financial liability. Blue Cross and Blue Shield pioneered such arrangements in the 1930s. However, commercial indemnity plans, which pay bills as submitted, gained market share rapidly. By the mid 1950s, the proportion of Blue Cross enrollees with service benefits plans dropped from 96 to 76 percent (Somers and Somers, 1972). Indemnity plan design eclipsed service benefit design shortly thereafter.

Service benefit plan lists did not keep up with the discovery or addition of new services and procedures that were at least perceived to offer some benefit to patients. The rapid decline of service benefit plans occurred at the time that commercial insurance companies began offering major medical insurance with a stop loss. This type of coverage, which paid for all care, was much more attractive to organized labor and to individual consumers (and not coincidentally, to providers, who were freed of contractual constraints and procedure lists).

However, precisely because they are contractual, have fixed fee schedules, and can be used to pay only for proven effective treatments, arrangements of the service benefit type have a number of cost management advantages. Managed care plans sometimes use defined benefit and fixed contract arrangements to arrange care with providers. Many PPOs have a type of service benefit feature in that their providers have agreed not to balance bill patients, and bill the plan directly, eliminating the need to file claims and wait for reimbursement. Some employers are now installing their own fee schedules and have arranged direct contracts, resurrecting some aspects of these plans.

Under a *prepaid plan,* providers agree to care for any illness or injury at a fixed price per person. These plans were designed initially during the Depression to solve providers' cash flow problems and in most cases provide incentives for efficient care. Some of the earliest were the Baylor University Hospital Plan (the precursor to Blue Cross) and the Kaiser Foundation Health Plans. There are typically contracts between providers and the financing organization running the plan that specify the reimbursement level, agreement to cooperate with utilization management, and some structural parameters of quality such as credentialing.

Prepaid plans should not be confused with the delivery organizations with which they typically contract. Because of some state laws against the corporate practice of medicine, which were installed largely at the behest of medical societies, financing organizations in most areas cannot be the same organizations as those delivering care. For example, the Permanente Medical Group is a separate but parallel organization that delivers services through the Kaiser Foundation health plans.

It should also be noted that prepayment per se does not specify how or even whether care is managed. There may be a contract for prepayment with absolutely no hands-on management from the plan or from the participating providers. It would clearly be in the providers' best interest to manage care if they are paid on a capitated (or fixed-budget) basis. And it would be in the plan's best interest to do so if it were paying the providers on a fee-for-service or discount basis. However, a number of prepaid plans have not actively managed care, with negative to catastrophic financial consequences.

Types of Coverage

In theory, financial risk and the type of services covered could be limited by offering certain defined types of insurance coverages. It therefore makes sense to review them. As a practical matter, however, most employers now offer a package of coverages that mirror comprehensive, integrated policies (which are best exemplified in practice by managed care contracts). There are few limits or controls. However, coverage definition could be used as the basis for specifications for fees and the type and quality of services that would be paid for.

Most specific coverages are now folded into "basic" and "major medical" plans. Within these packages, *hospital expense* coverage provides defined benefits for daily room-and-board charges and ancillary services and supplies. *Room-and-board benefits* (an embedded service benefit) either reimburse for the actual charge up to a specified maximum or the full cost. *Basic policies* typically cover room and board and physician or surgeon's expenses. *Major medical* policies provide broader coverage. The two are typically linked in most employer plans, and integrated plans are now becoming more common. These plans cover a wide range of charges with a few internal limits at a high overall maximum (Health Insurance Association of America, 1992).

Preventive services have not typically been covered in most plans despite the fact that there is ample evidence that they reduce costs in the midterm and long-run. This may be because the insurance industry is founded on the theory of statistical prediction of random events. Preventive services are not random events. However, recent research, notably the INSURE project (Logsdon and Rosen, 1984), has documented significant cost savings when preventive services such as immunizations, mammograms, pap smears, and in some cases type-specific cancer screening were performed at appropriate intervals. The project further calculated the additional premium cost necessary to cover these services. This evidence would suggest that employers would do well to fund the full scope of preventive services as a cost management tool (Fielding, 1992). The U.S. Preventive Services Task Force has recently reviewed the literature and clearly defined those preventive measures that are cost effective for various age, gender, and risk groups (Lawrence, 1989). Final evidence on the ultimate cost savings of these steps in the aggregate awaits further study, but the task force did analyze the benefits accruing for the cost of each individual service, applying the WHO guidelines, as it framed its recommendations.

Long-term care insurance is an expanding market, particularly with the growth of the elderly population. Policies may cover chronic diseases and/or custodial care. In 1990, about 140 companies offered long-term care insurance, which covered about two million people. This represents a 40 percent increase in companies and a 43 percent increase in covered lives just since 1988. However, the premiums are quite expensive and costs increase exponentially as the person ages (Standard and Poor, 1991b; Piacentini and Foley, 1992).

Cost Management Tools

Most plans require employee cost sharing, both as a budget-balancing tool and as an attempt to create some price sensitivity. A brief review of conventional risk sharing and cost management techniques is instructive to describe the current dimensions of employee financial involvement in most group health coverage. The evidence on their effectiveness at current levels will then be described.

Out-of-Pocket Expenses

Cost sharing by employees is thought to create cost sensitivity and certainly is used to manage employer outlays. For their employees, employers pay on average 70 percent of the total premium following contributions, copayments, and deductibles. The average total out-of-pocket expense for medical benefits, a combination of the effects of the cost management tools described below, was $524 in 1990 (Piacentini and Foley, 1992). In one recent survey, for 30 percent there was no out-of-pocket cost, since all insurance was paid by their employer. Thirteen percent of respondents had no idea what they paid per month (Piacentini and Anzick, 1991).

Contribution Rates

Employees typically contribute some amount toward their health insurance, but traditionally this has been very small. In recent years, however, the amount, while still a fraction of the total cost, has risen rapidly, becoming a dissatisfier for employees. The average contribution has risen from about $9 for individual coverage in 1982 to about $19 in 1988 and $25 in 1990, and from $27 for family coverage in 1982 to $60 in 1988 and $72 in 1990 — the last year for which comprehensive data are available (Piacentini and Foley, 1992). These figures are for medium and large employers (those with more than 100 employees). The rates were significantly higher for family coverage for government employers ($118) and smaller establishments ($109) in 1990. Even with these increases, contribution rates have not kept pace with inflation.

Until recently, there had been little differentiation based on family size, so that people with large families paid proportionately less per person for care. Family contribution rates have typically been about 10 percent of the actual cost of family coverage (Harris and Custer, 1992). Although only about 60 percent of a typical work force has dependent coverage, dependents account for half or more of the total expenditures of most plans. The contribution rate affects only the demand for health insurance, not the demand for care itself. It does not affect the demand for services at the point of care. In addition, it is such a small amount that its effect on demand is likely to be small. Nonetheless, contributions tend to be regressive in that they are not pegged to income. A number of employers have recently created sliding-scale contributions based on salary.

Determining an appropriate employee contribution rate is a difficult decision. Contribution rates should be set to encourage responsible selection of benefits features, direct employees toward more cost-effective delivery systems, and reduce the number of vendors, if those are in fact strategic objectives.

There is a further problem if contribution rates are not set carefully. If equal contributions are set for all levels of efficiency of plans, sick employees with an established source of care and specialists who are not members of managed care networks would tend to select the indemnity plan; those without an established physician relationship, who are usually healthy, would select a plan with easier access and more comprehensive benefits, such as a managed care organization. This selection may lead to a "death spiral" for the indemnity plan, in which more and more costly employees are left in a least-cost-effective plan, the cost per employee spirals, and the plan becomes unaffordable (Gold, 1992).

There are two corollaries to this problem. First, the chronically ill, who are arguably most in need of the managed quality and comprehensive services that managed care can afford, do not get them. Second, if plans are split in this way and the cost of the indemnity plan cannot be managed effectively, employers cannot manage to a "global budget" for their benefits program.

Deductibles are amounts to be paid by the employee prior to reimbursement of expenses by the health insurance plan. They were traditionally used to decrease the administrative cost caused by processing many small claims. Since many employees may not have expenses that exceed the deductible, the total number of claimants is decreased as well. Plans with high deductibles still provide catastrophic coverage. Deductibles may pose a significant barrier to care for low-income families (Feldstein, 1988).

In 1989, conventional insurance plans averaged deductibles of $150 for individual coverage, with a median of $100, and $300 per family (Gold, 1992; Piacentini and Foley, 1992). Deductibles have a limited effect on price sensitivity unless they are fairly large and exceed the amount many families would use in benefits per year. What services are included in the deductible is also an important issue. Once the deductible is met, the price of the service to the employer or dependent is zero, except for the copayment.

Coinsurance

Copayments are the portion of medical expenses paid by the employee. They have historically been set at 10 to 20 percent for outpatient services and zero for inpatient service, providing a perverse incentive to increase the use of hospital services. This structure is more common in the Eastern United States than in the West; this pattern was set by unions and Blues plans through major medical policy design. Physicians have been known to admit patients to the hospital if the out-of-pocket expense is less when they perceive themselves to be acting as an economic agent of the patient (Harris, 1992e). In 1990, 79 percent of large-employer indemnity plans, 71 percent of government plans, and 80 percent of small-employer plans included coinsurance levels of 20 percent (Piacentini and Foley, 1992).

The effectiveness of copayments as a method of increasing employee price sensitivity is related to income and other insurance coverage. Through *coordination of benefits,* families with more than one insurance policy can effectively negate the effect of both deductibles and coinsurance. This makes the cost to the patient zero (Feldstein, 1988). Employees with higher incomes, who also use more discretionary medical services, would tend not to regard this level of copayment as a major issue. Therefore, consideration should be given to eliminating coordination of benefits provisions to restore price sensitivity.

Out-of-Pocket Maximums

Price sensitivity is blunted by provisions that limit the total amount employees could pay in a given year. Most private employer insurance plans have limits in the $1,000 to $5,000 range, while government employers typically have maximum employee payment limits between $500 and $750.

A few companies have now started indexing the stop loss to income. These provisions are designed to protect patients from catastrophic losses. However, with the rapidly rising cost of health care, out-of-pocket maximums can be reached quickly and negate the effect of copayments or deductibles. The cost of almost any procedure or one day of hospitalization may exceed the limits, at which point price sensitivity is lost. These maximums are typically less than one-third the average price of medical care per employee (Dwyer and Garland, 1991; Garland, 1991).

Exclusions

Exclusions are generally established in insurance contracts to bar coverage for preexisting conditions for a period of six months to a year. Some plans also schedule exclusions of specific procedures that are deemed discretionary, experimental, or "not medically necessary for function." Examples include cosmetic surgery, self-inflicted injuries, therapeutic abortions, and a number of popular tests and procedures that have no proven efficacy. Exclusions could be used to a much greater extent based on the emerging results of outcomes research. Medical input into exclusion lists seems to have been limited. Exclusions are often not well communicated during plan enrollment, creating a significant amount of ill will and pressure for benefits exceptions.

Limits or Caps

Limits or caps have been placed on some services to control the use of treatments that have no clear time-related benefit or that may have outpatient alternatives. This has mainly been done in the mental health and substance abuse arena, where there is only tenuous evidence that long inpatient stays have a positive impact on the ultimate outcome of a problem, especially when compared to outpatient treatment. This is most true of substance abuse disorders and adolescent conduct disorders (which are arguably disciplinary rather than medical problems). The professional consensus for the optimal length of inpatient treatment for these disorders have changed from "unknown" to fifteen days to thirty days and back to fifteen days for no obvious reason.

Lifetime Maximum

Most indemnity plans define benefits or limit total payments through a total lifetime payout limit. The lifetime maximums of most plans has ranged from $500,000 to $1,000,000 (Employee Benefits Research Institute, 1991). Lower lifetime benefits levels have been used in service industries. It is unusual to reach this maximum, so its impact is limited to acting as a stop loss for financial protection for the employer.

Evidence of Effectiveness

Many measures of effectiveness exist.

Copayments

Most of the evidence about the effects of copayments comes from a few nonexperimental studies and the RAND Health Insurance Experiment. There are a number of beliefs about copayments that are not consistent with research findings. For example, it is widely believed among managed care and some indemnity plan managers that adding a $10 copayment for office visits results in a marked decrease in visits that could have been taken care of by self-care. This may be true temporarily because of the shock value in a previously fully paid plan, but does not hold in the long term.

The major and perhaps only controlled study of the economic and health consequences of different payment structures is the Health Insurance Experiment conducted by the RAND Corporation and funded by the U.S. Department of Health and Human Services from 1974 to 1982. Almost 7,000 people were enrolled in fourteen experimental health plans or health maintenance organizations in six cities and rural sites. This was a fairly stringent experiment, with 0, 25, 50 or 95 percent copayments, an income-related stop loss, and an out-of-pocket maximum of $1,000 (Newhouse, 1985).

As out-of-pocket expense was increased, the use of service was decreased without apparent regard to what type of service was sought or the appropriateness of the services. That is, appropriate as well as inappropriate services were discouraged according to retrospective explicit reviews of medical records by the researchers. The Health Insurance Experiment validated earlier research that the "elasticity" of medical care is about -1; in other words, if the price goes up 1 percent, the dollar volume goes down 2 percent (Feldstein, 1988).

Hospital Admissions. For the 25 percent copayment plan, there was a 21 percent drop in hospital admissions and a 10 percent drop in costs. With a 50 percent copayment, there was a 29 percent drop in hospital admissions and a 31 percent drop in admissions for the 95 percent copayment plan. In other words, the relationship is curvilinear rather than linear for hospital care.

Physician Visits. For the 25 percent plan, physician visits dropped 7 percent. A comparison of the 50 percent plan to the 95 percent plan shows that physician visits dropped by 40 percent. Ambulatory care displays a linear decrease, with elasticities of -0.33 (a decrease of $0.33) and cost for every dollar in cost sharing. Somewhat ominously, for well care this elasticity was 0.43, while for chronic illness it was 0.23. For the care of children, it appeared to be about 0.25. For ambulatory care in total it was 0.41 (Newhouse and others, 1981; Manning and others, 1987; Leibowitz and others, 1985).

Mental health service is more price elastic. Use declined 50 percent comparing the 95 percent copay plan to the free plan. This cost-sharing effect was seen in the outpatient setting only and was income related (Manning, Wells, and Benjamin, 1986).

As copayment increases, the demand for medical care becomes much more responsive to time costs such as queuing and waiting times (Phelps and Newhouse, 1972).

Other Services. Prescription drug use is affected by cost sharing. In the 95 percent plan, there was a 43 percent decrease in the use of pharmaceuticals (Leibowitz, Manning, and Newhouse, 1985). Dental services were similarly elastic (although dental care is not the subject of discussion here).

Emergency Services. Emergency room services are basically patient initiated in contrast to office visits and hospital admissions, about half of which are initiated by physicians. A curvilinear relationship was noted, with a 40 percent decrease in emergency room use with a 95 percent copayment compared to the free plan. Medical record review revealed that these visits were for minor complaints, so that they probably did not have much of an effect on the patient's health. It was also noted as an incidental finding that low-income people were using the emergency room for ambulatory care (O'Grady, Manning, Newhouse, and Brook, 1985).

Another study that looked at the effects of copayments and deductibles using insurance claims data was performed by the Employee Benefits Research Institute for eight Houston employers (Custer, 1989). Coinsurance rates did not vary across employers and were not a factor in this study.

Deductibles

Using deductibles that range from 0 to $500 per year, the researchers estimated that a plan's deductible *increases* the average inpatient charge by about 5 percent per $100 per year. This is believed to result from the reduction for low-cost inpatient care, raising the average charge per episode. Postponement of needed care was thought to be unlikely because increasing deductibles were associated with decreasing lengths of stay.

High deductibles were associated with lower mean charges for drugs, surgery, and laboratory and x-ray services in the Houston study (Custer, 1989). They were associated with higher mean per person charges for medical visits, again believed to be due to reductions in the use of low-cost or discretionary visits.

Contribution Rates

Increasing employee contribution rates was associated with a decrease in total hospital charges of 4 percent, with a decrease in inpatient physician charges of 8 percent. This was believed to be due to increased consumer awareness of costs. However, contributions were unrelated to charges for outpatient services and negatively related to charges for prescription drugs, in that there was no effect on total cost.

Caps

There is a wide variation in service use and effectiveness of mental health services (Rodrigues, 1984). In the Employee Benefits Research Institute study, caps on benefits reduced inpatient charges and hospital charges by more than 32 percent but were not significantly related to inpatient physician charges. Total charges dropped by 7 percent (Custer, 1989). In another study in the Houston area, at Tennaco, implementation of a cap on mental inpatient days resulted in a halving of bed days per thousand (Tsai, Reedy, Bernacki, and Lee, 1988).

However, there is some evidence that mental health services can reduce the use of medical services by effectively treating somatic complaints (Schlesinger and others, 1986). This may explain the Houston coalition's finding that the restrictions on mental health benefits were also associated with an increase in the mean charge for medical visits of more than 35 percent.

Total Out-of-Pocket Costs

When employee out-of-pocket costs or net price differential between prepaid and indemnity plans become large (including contribution level), copayments, deductibles, and other costs, including uncovered services), the vast majority of individuals (particularly those without an established physician relationship) join the lower-cost option (Long, Settle, and Wrightson, 1988). The easiest way to solve this problem is to offer only one efficient plan, but this may not be acceptable since employees are demanding a choice.

A Further Exposure

In 1988, 43 percent of all Americans forty and over had retiree health coverage through their own or their spouse's current or former employer. Under the Financial Accounting Standards Board statement 106 (commonly known as FASB 106) adopted in December 1990, companies are required to record liability for these retiree benefits on their balance sheet beginning in 1993. This in fact accounted for the world's largest loss by an industrial company of $23 billion posted by GM in 1993. Similarly large losses were posted by Ford, IBM, and other major employers. As a result of this recent action, employers have become acutely aware of the fact that they have very large future liabilities for benefits to retirees, particularly early retirees. Many of them have reacted by dropping supplementary coverage for retirees. Those who retain retiree coverage would do well to

manage these liabilities very carefully (Employee Benefits Research Institute, 1991).

It is important to note that while 12.5 percent of Americans were over age sixty-five in 1989, the percentage is expected
to rise to 22 percent by the year 2030. Many of them have
"Medigap" insurance frequently sponsored by employers. The
proportion of those with chronic illnesses increases dramatically
after age sixty-five for those who have poor life-style habits. This
would suggest that employers should manage not only cost but
also health for their retirees as a prudent business decision.

Is Benefits Design Satisfying the Customer?

Satisfaction with medical benefits has dropped substantially in
the last decade. In 1982, 87 percent of employees rated their
hospital and medical insurance as very good or good. By 1990,
this percentage had dropped to 45 percent (International Survey Research Corporation, 1991). This drop in benefits satisfaction has paralleled a drop in morale. In addition, the percentage of those satisfied with the medical care that they had
received in the last few years, purchased through those plans,
dropped from 84 to 71 percent from 1987 to 1992 (Henry J.
Kaiser Family Foundation and Louis Harris and Associates,
1992a). More tellingly, the percentage of employees who are
dissatisfied has doubled — from 13 to 26 percent — in the same time
period.

Not only is satisfaction with plans dropping, but the cost
management provisions most favored by benefits managers have
the distinct potential to be dissatisfiers. In a Louis Harris and
Associates poll of Americans in 1991, the most acceptable solution to the medical care cost problem was thought to be accepting limits on the right to sue for malpractice (61 percent).
Obtaining prior approval for emergency care garnered only
57 percent support, and being a member of an exclusive provider
organization that excludes non-cost-effective providers garnered
42 percent. Queuing and being a member of a plan that does
not cover some expensive procedures and treatments got only

36 percent support, and having to pay substantially higher out-of-pocket costs (the most popular option among benefits managers) was acceptable to only 22 percent (Taylor and Leitman, 1991a).

As recently as 1991, about 90 percent of consumers oppose restriction of choice of physicians. Yet people do not actually seem to shop for medical care. Only 30 percent report ever having compared the price of a specific medical procedure between two or more physicians. In addition, there is a serious lack of information about plans where there may be some limitation of access, presumably in exchange for lower cost or better quality. For example, many consumers do not know about the relative cost of managed care plans such as HMOs, whether they get a choice of doctor, and whether they get more preventive care. Even fewer understand PPOs (Employee Benefits Research Institute, 1990).

What Employers Have Done and Intend to Do Next

A curious disconnection exists between employers' desires to use benefits as a way of satisfying employee demands and needs and their actions and intentions to manage costs, which are in general known dissatisfiers. Careful consideration of employee research data, or perhaps an expanded set of options, might lead to more acceptable solutions.

Contribution rates have increased. The percentage of large and medium-sized employers offering completely paid health insurance dropped during the 1980s. In 1980, 72 percent of employers wholly financed employee coverage; by 1988, this had fallen to 51 percent. Similarly, fully financed family coverage dropped from 51 to 34 percent in that decade (Bureau of Labor Statistics, U.S. Department of Labor, 1980, 1982, 1984, 1986, 1988).

Employers surveyed by *Business and Health* magazine indicated that increasing premiums, deductibles, and copayments were the options they would most likely use to cut their health care costs in the future (*Business and Health,* 1990). Eighty-one percent of employers said they would increase contributions

or premiums. Eighty percent said they would increase deductibles, and 71 percent said they would increase copayments.

Fifty-seven percent of employers have in fact raised the
level of employee cost sharing. Forty-four percent have limited
coverage for expensive technologies, but only an additional 6
percent say they will expand the option or do so in the future
(Taylor and Leitman, 1989).

Fifty-four percent of employers stated that they are self-
insured, with an additional 25 percent considering that in the
future. Over half, or 54 percent, said that they will change insurance companies (or third-party administrators), presumably
because they are dissatisfied.

Conclusion

Conventional benefits design tools are primarily financial and
contractual mechanisms defining who pays for what medical
care. When used in service benefit and prepaid plans, these tools
can be used to limit payment for unproven or medically unnecessary treatment. This is more difficult in a classic indemnity plan. But simply using financial and definitional tools without tying them to employee involvement, prevention, total
compensation, and defined long-range total cost and cost distribution goals runs a significant risk of increasing employee
dissatisfaction and missing financial targets.

Benefits design tools have been used to define coverage
and to allocate costs between employers and employees. Stop
losses, exclusions, and maximums are used to limit plan liability. Contribution rates can be used to steer employees to more
efficient plans if there are multiple choices. Significant contribution differentials have not been used widely to induce employees to select the most efficient plans.

It is widely believed that copayments and deductibles at
the present level will create enough price sensitivity to moti-
vate wise use of medical care, but this belief is not supported
by well-structured studies. Much higher levels of cost sharing,
at the point of purchase, appear to be needed. If employers wish
to use cost sharing and coverage limitations to increase employee

cost sensitivity in order to encourage responsible purchasing of medical care, they should first increase employees' fund of information about the costs of the plans, the effects on total compensation, and value in medical care. It is also important to increase meaningful employee involvement in discussions of design options. Employees may need additional analytical and decision-making skills as well.

Benefits design is a key element of strategies intended to encourage wise use of medical care, move employees to managed care, and support greater individual choice and utility through a flexible total compensation approach. As such, design features should flow from the overall strategy, rather than being temporizing measures to meet short-term budget targets.

CHAPTER EIGHT

Increasing
Employee Involvement
in Decision Making

Employer-based financing of medical care has traditionally been a top-down activity. The employer or its consultant would frame the benefits design, package, and options and provide them to employees with only financial or structural information about the choices. This approach has two intrinsic flaws, however. First, it is not consistent with employee expectations and needs at the current time. Second, it contributes to the medical care cost spiral because it leaves the end consumer without the information and skills needed to make the most cost-effective decisions.

Customer Satisfaction

The prescriptive approach to benefits selection worked well from a "customer relations" standpoint until the mid 1980s, when satisfaction with benefits began to decrease. In 1982, 87 percent of employees rated their hospital and medical insurance as very good or good. By 1990, this percentage had dropped to 45 percent (International Survey Research Corporation, 1991). The drop in benefits satisfaction has paralleled a drop in morale. Further, the percentage of those satisfied with the medical care that they have received in the last few years has dropped from 84 to 71 percent from 1987 to 1992 (Henry J. Kaiser Family Foundation and Louis Harris and Associates, 1992a). More tellingly, the percentage who were dissatisfied doubled from 13 to 26 percent in the same period.

Benefits are clearly important to employees in choosing jobs. According to a recent survey by the Employee Benefits

186

Research Institute, nearly three out of five employees said they consider benefits very important when deciding whether to accept or reject a job. An additional quarter said they were important (Employee Benefits Research Institute and the Gallup Organization, Inc., 1990). Employees seem to realize that benefits have significant value, since a majority of those interviewed said they would not accept a job if it did not provide them with health insurance, and health benefits were by far most often mentioned as the most important employee benefit.

However, as noted in the previous chapter, employees do not favor the methods most employers use to manage the costs and quality of care provided by these programs. Employees are also quite interested in preventive activities and services. However, these are not often provided by employers in a comprehensive or cost-effective manner.

Employees are in an interesting position. They have come to depend on medical benefits for financial protection and income supplementation. However, they have essentially no responsibility for a medical benefits plan and little say in how it is designed or executed. Their collective demand has certainly speeded its development and expansion. Employees certainly have not been loath to accept benefits. They have become willing participants in a system they did not create. Employee (and dependent) involvement may be a key element of benefits design in the future to increase the perceived value of benefits to each employee, and their greater involvement in the medical decision-making process may be needed to make demand more rational — based on logic and financial values, not impulse buying of apparently zero-cost services.

Medically Related Decision Making

Employees and dependents must make a series of decisions about medical care. Most remote from the process of care, they may decide which of a series of alternative benefits packages or programs to select. This decision has consequences in terms of financial and temporal access to care that certainly affect satisfaction and may affect health. Then, many authorities and most managed care plans recommend choosing a personal physician before there is an immediate need for one, to communicate one's medical history and preferences and to obtain preventive services. Again, a mismatch with expectations or a wrong choice can at the least provoke anxiety and at worst result in a medical mishap.

At the point at which acute care services are needed, each person or family will have to decide (or default to a physician) what diagnostic and treatment options to select. To be made most effectively, each of these decisions requires knowledge of the mechanics of organized medical systems, what works and what does not in prevention and medical care, what the risks and benefits are, and what the costs in inconvenience, potential embarrassment, lost time, pain and suffering, and money are.

Objective knowledge alone is not enough. To maximize the personal benefits to be obtained for the tangible and intangible costs of prevention, diagnosis, and treatment, each person should decide how the benefits and risks fit his or her value system. Understanding this match and making plans and decisions, especially in such a personal and anxiety-provoking area as health, is difficult without some skills to evaluate and quantify information and values (or "gut feel") (Reiser, 1992; Harris, Goldstein, and Tager, 1986).

Thus, information and skills are needed for a series of critical decisions. However, few Americans have such a fund of accurate information or those learned skills. The situation is compounded by erroneous beliefs about what medical care can do, by popular misconceptions that everyone should always be young, healthy, beautiful, and pain free, and sometimes by misleading advertising and press coverage. Providing objective, understandable information and skills training would go a long way toward rationalizing the selection and use of health behaviors and medical treatments.

Objectives for Involvement and Skill Building

Employers might therefore wish to involve employees in decisions about benefits design, election, and use. In our strategic continuum and scheme of things, we might be concerned about employee involvement to increase individual utility of benefits, thereby increasing satisfaction and moderating cost increases. So reasons for employee partnership in benefits design and use might include the following:

- To increase the perceived utility of benefits to each employee
- To encourage a "total compensation" view by employees
- To increase satisfaction with benefits
- To foster innovation in benefits design
- To improve the appropriateness of use of medical care
- To increase self-care skill

Why Involve Employees in Benefits and Health Management?

As with any other service, when consumer satisfaction drops as rapidly as it has with health benefits, it would behoove the organization offering that service to find out why consumers are dissatisfied and what options they would find more acceptable. Unless the organization does that, most of the reasons why benefits are offered become moot. The program may even become counterproductive and a dissatisfier. In addition, consumer involvement generally leads to improved products or services. In this case, if customer utility can be increased, overinsurance and use of marginally necessary services might be constrained.

At the same time that satisfaction is dropping, the costs of benefits programs are going up at a rapid rate. So employers are faced with hard choices about trade-offs between compensation and benefits. If cutbacks or changes are needed, employee involvement in their design and communication may allow better acceptance of the changes and the need for them.

In the core business activities of organizations, when the competitiveness, cost structure, or survival of an employer was threatened, employee involvement has made it easier to arrive at solutions. The results have been good to innovative to excellent. Examples of success stories built on a foundation of employee involvement include the Emerson Electric Company, the turnaround of Weirton Steel, and a whole panoply of quality improvement–based successes such as General Motors' Saturn, Toyota, and Nissan cars, and Motorola's 6-Sigma program. There are a few medical care examples, such as West Pace's Ferry Hospital in Atlanta.

Determinants of Satisfaction

The reasons for the decline in satisfaction have not been well researched. However, they probably include dissatisfaction with increased cost sharing (however minimal) and limited choice of providers and may also reflect changing needs and demands. As the work force has diversified, single-focus benefits packages no longer meet the needs of young singles, single parents, various ethnic groups, double-income families, part-time workers, and older workers. Workers have also become accustomed to a greater voice in defining their work environment and are demanding a greater voice in their terms of employment. This would include benefits design as well.

Better Decision Making

It has also become apparent that employees must become more involved in their choices of benefits, physicians, treatment, and life-style. Without this involvement, there is little chance that they will take control and make cost-effective decisions about when to seek care and what treatment options to select or agree to. They will not, in short, become wise consumers.

Cost-effective choices, wise use, and self-care require specific knowledge and skills (Vickery, 1993; Harris, Goldstein, and Tager, 1986; Bandura, 1991). Most Americans do not have this information and the appropriate decision-making skills. Comprehensive health education is not generally available in the schools or the lay literature. While one could argue that these areas are not an employer's responsibility, employers are paying for the consequences of those decisions and therefore have an interest in making them the most cost-effective ones.

One of the original reasons for offering benefits was to improve the health of the work force. If that were still the case and the American worker were in need of medical care much of the time, one might argue that wise use training is not needed. However, there is little evidence at this point that the working population in this country is less productive because of a lack of medical care. In fact, given the long lengths of absence many physicians grant as compared to consensus standards (often as a result of patient demand), the working population is probably less productive than it could be as a result of medical care (Starr, 1982).

Knowledge of Health and Medical Care. A number of people have noted that employees — and the general public, for that matter — do not have adequate knowledge to understand many medical conditions or to be active, let alone equal, participants in medical decision making with practitioners. In fact, in the RAND study, expert medical reviewers — who reviewed the records of patients to determine whether the care they received was medically necessary or not — determined that when copayments were increased, medically necessary and medically unnecessary care were affected to the same degree (Newhouse, 1991; Siu and others, 1986). This means that when demand became patient initiated, patients refrained from seeking both medically necessary and medically unnecessary care. One might conclude from this that patients are not knowledgeable enough to distinguish between the two.

A number of studies bear out the conclusion that wise-use training and information would result in decision making that more closely reflected the patient's personal values about function, risk, and benefit. In studies using interactive videodiscs to educate patients about the risks and benefits of surgical procedures compared to nonsurgical alternatives, and emphasizing function and well-being, researchers noted a dramatic decrease in the number of patients choosing surgery (Mulley, 1992; Darby, 1993b).

Knowledge of Costs. Employees generally do not have enough information about the actual costs of medical care. They have been known to overestimate the amount of money being spent on benefits. They also state that the amount of the company contribution is reasonable and that their contribution should not increase, even if it is minimal.

Some interesting results are obtained when one asks employees what they think the value of benefits is. According to a Gallup poll, employees believed that employers would have to pay them $4,219 to give up their current medical benefits (Employee Benefits Research Institute and the Gallup Organization, 1990). Slightly more than half of employees would choose health insurance rather than an equivalent amount of after-tax cash. Employees seem to recognize that employers obtain better deals because of their market power. Sixty-six percent of employees in that survey answered that they would have to pay more if they had to pay the insurance themselves.

In one large telecommunications company, the employees thought that the company was contributing about $7,500 to their medical benefits. In fact, at that point of time the contribution was just over $3,000. These employees also felt that their monthly contribution rate of about $80, their deductible of $200, and their co-payment of $100 were about right. What is missing from this picture is the fact that the value of benefits paid by the employer was a quarter of the average wage at this particular company, a not-insignificant number, particularly since it constrains cash wage increases. This type of uninformed judgment is not uncommon.

It appears that employees are not completely aware of the wage-benefit trade-off they are making or even of the effects of benefits expenditures on the continued profitability and survival of their employer. While benefits are generally determined by competitive levels of coverage in a given labor market, wages are generally a reflection of the skills and output of the individual employees in that particular industry. It is therefore not inconceivable that in lower-paying occupations or lower-margin industries, benefits could be equal to one-half to three-quarters of the wage rate, although in those industries benefits tend to be scaled back. Employees must understand the cost-benefit trade-offs among the medical resources they use and the trade-offs they are unwittingly making between wages, benefits, and even continued employment.

Health Promotion

Involvement offers the chance to achieve greater health for employees and dependents, through health promotion as well as wise use. Employees must understand the effect that their lifestyles are having on their employer's benefits costs and therefore their wage levels, and they should take action to reduce both medically unnecessary use of medical care and life-style risks that are raising costs. (In this context, we are defining *life-style* to include behaviors of demanding and using unneeded services and not engaging in self-care first.)

Support for Public Policy Initiatives

Another reason for employee involvement is to increase awareness of the possible political solutions to the "health care crisis." Unless employees become more fully aware of their personal situation as it relates to the medical care industry's pricing, practices, and the use of "gray-zone" technology and therapies, they will not be able to be fully informed participants in the current debate about health care reform. The outcome of that debate may, of course, have a significant effect on individual benefits plans.

Improving Communication

Involving employees to design and test communications makes sense as well. Since benefits are a fairly technical area, communications materials may make sense to the specialist designing them but not to the average employee. Repeated testing with employees significantly enhances the understandability of the issues discussed above as well as the specific benefits and assets of the benefits program. This is true whether the communication is print, interactive voice, computer-based video, or face to face. Communications should also be tested with the spouse, since that person may make health-related decisions for the family.

Increasing Utility

In a more global sense than just choosing a benefits package, employees should become more involved in "point-of-need" choices about which diagnostic and health treatment alternative to take. This is also an argument to increase utility, but a noneconomic one. It is based more on personal preferences, which in many instances have turned out to be more rational in overview than narrow medical recommendations (Gardner and Sneiderman, 1992; McNeil, Weichselbaum, and Pauker, 1978).

Data Analysis to Focus Involvement and Skill-Building Activities

Employers should have a knowledge base about what employees know and believe about health and medical care to quantify the additional information and training that are needed, and they should be aware of preferences for services and benefits options, including price points. Surveys (customized for literacy level and language) are useful to gather baseline and generic information about the following topics:

- Perceived costs of the benefits program
- Satisfaction with the program, providers, and specific services
- Choices for coverage, access to care, plan choice, and options for various benefits
- Current life-style habits
- Preferences for other options and services

This information is a form of market research and can be used to shape benefits design, communications programs, and skills training. It is particularly useful to formulate options for a "megaflex" or total compensation program (see Chapter Ten). Surveys are also useful as a source of baseline data to help shape programs to convey information about health and disease, self-care, the effects and effectiveness of medical treatments, and wise use of the medical care system. A good way to determine where to start these programs would be to survey employees and dependents to determine their current beliefs and levels of knowledge.

It is also important to ask about feelings, process, and results in interactions with physicians and other health care providers, about whether respondents were getting the information they needed to make a decision, who they thought was making the decision, whether they felt uncomfortable about that, and what information or skills they would like to better take care of themselves and better use the medical care system. Survey topics that might be included are listed below; surveys can be done in annual cycles to track progress or changes for program quality improvement.

- Knowledge about general symptoms such as fever, cough, sore throat, abdominal pain, urinary tract problems, superficial infections, and so on
- Knowledge about how to care for minor symptoms, illnesses, and injuries
- Knowledge about when it is important to seek medical care (specific "red-flag" symptoms)
- What questions to ask health care providers about the tentative diagnosis and proposed treatment alternatives, including benefits and costs (monetary, discomfort, and potential side effects)
- Employees' and dependents' general grasp of the use of probabilities to evaluate risks of developing disease and of alternatives for treatment
- Knowledge of how to evaluate the price of medical care services (cost to employees and the benefits plan)
- Where employees and dependents seek information when they think they need care
- Preferences for sources and types of information
- Comfort with making their own decisions about medical care
- Beliefs about whether they could make effective decisions
- Who else they rely on to help make medical decisions
- What additional skills they would like or need in order to make decisions

- Perceptions and definitions of the quality of care
- How they would judge medical quality
- What additional information or skills they would need to judge the quality of care

Health Risk Appraisals can be used to determine pooled life-style risks, but if they have not been obtained or a health promotion program is not in effect, it may be easier to combine life-style questions with other questions in surveys.

Focus groups are often an effective way of obtaining employee opinions, beliefs, and attitudes and exploring a number of options about program redesign and other issues such as repricing and potential options. By stratifying these groups by compensation or education level, one can obtain information about income- or education-related preferences for benefits and health-related activities.

Ongoing task forces of appropriate employee representatives are another effective way of obtaining employee input and buy-in. If the task forces consist of elected representatives rather than those appointed by management, they can also effectively carry information back to their constituents in addition to providing information to those managing the benefits program. It should be made clear, however, that this is an advisory capacity rather than a decision-making one, unless management feels otherwise.

Medical insurance claims and utilization management tapes are a source of data to approximate the costs of failure to use self-care and wise decision making. Areas to examine are listed below:

- Inappropriate use of emergency facilities
- Costs and frequency of "nonspecific complaints"
- Costs and frequency of targeted minor illnesses and injuries treated through the medical care system
- Assessment of medically unnecessary treatment either paid for or detoured through utilization management

Another good source of data, but one that is often unavailable, is logs of the frequency, type, and content of health plan member or patient complaints. These might have been registered either with the benefits program office at the employer or with organized systems of medical care such as group practices and managed care programs.

Intent and Direction

In the strategic health management process, the vision for employee involvement in health management is directly related to management's emphasis on employee involvement with other human resource issues and perhaps in the work process as a whole. The organization's posture in this regard must be consistent with management style to be credible. Two-way communication and marketing of some elements of medical benefits as they appeal to employee preferences strengthens the program. This is clearly true for other goods and services.

Whether or not employees are (heavily) involved in the design and execution of the medical benefits program is integrally related to the way the program is framed. In turn, their involvement or lack of it will be reflected in the way they use the program and interact with the medical system. The mission statement of the health management program should therefore include statements about supporting employees in making decisions that maximize their personal utility (although phrasing it using that term might not make sense to some people). The concept, as noted earlier, is that people's preferences for various courses of action are different. To the extent that the "right treatment" advocated by providers turns out to be much more invasive than the individual wishes, this constitutes inappropriate care and unnecessary expense (Fowler and others, 1988; Darby, 1993b). Utility can probably be modified by education, so that a high utility for immediate access to medical advice for minor complaints, which many providers feel is inappropriate, might be changed through self-care and wise-use education.

The mission statement might also include comments about the appropriate use of medical care and could even address ways of providing employees with the knowledge to make appropriate decisions. In addition, if it fits with the corporate culture and the intent of the program, the mission statement might note the goal of working with community resources to improve health education for dependents and others in the community. The mission statement for the health management benefits and health management program should therefore reflect:

- Interest in meeting employee needs and wishes
- An intent to understand and satisfy the reasonable needs and desires of employees or candidates regarding benefits and medical care
- An intent to involve employees in the design process and in testing options and materials
- An intent to involve dependents, especially decision makers and high utilizers of care, in preventive services
- An intent to fund or provide only efficient and effective medical care

Program Design

The process used in continuous or periodic design and redesign of options, pricing, and mechanics of the health management program is directly related to the emphasis placed on employee involvement. Employee sensing (survey research and focus groups), information testing, and means of interactions such as focus groups are tasks that should be built into the health management process (if it is compatible with the corporate culture). The shape of the program, within the financial constraints established by the chief financial officer, would be heavily influenced by the nature of employee feedback and tempered by labor market and competitive information (which presumably would be given to any employee group working on or reacting to the program).

   The program would also be shaped by the commitment — or lack of it — to fully involve employees and dependents in managing their own health. Involvement could range from assistance with improving life-styles, to purchasing with maximum personal utility, to purchasing appropriate and most cost-effective care, to building self-control, self-efficacy, and a shared balance of power into preventive health management and disease diagnosis and treatment. If those goals underlie the program, the specific design should include mechanisms to convey information, reinforce that information, make usable information accessible at the "point of need," and build the skills and self-efficacy necessary to effectively use the information.

Gap Analysis

If the vision of the program is that it become interactive and cooperative, goals should be set to realize that vision by structuring and administering surveys, administering health risk appraisals, conducting focus groups, providing for employee representation, obtaining information feedback, and whatever other mechanisms have been decided on.

Goals should be set to operationalize all of the various facets of support for employee decision making implied by the mission statement. There might be goals for:

- Increases in knowledge
- Increases in perceived self-efficacy
- Decreases in complaints about medical care (or possibly increases as the consumers become more sophisticated)
- Decreases in changes of primary care providers within managed care networks
- Increases in skills for dealing with providers
- Satisfaction with interactions with providers

Other "softer" projections may be made that have to do with changes with employee satisfaction with their benefits and satisfaction with the medical care system. Objectives would be related directly to the creation and use of various involvement mechanisms and communications packages.

Forward projections for costs under a variety of different scenarios proposed either by management or employees could be used to guide the program. Projections can be made of cost and utilization increases or decreases from nonspecific complaints, symptoms, and inappropriate treatment. This would likely be a fairly steep upward curve, given the growing number of diagnostic techniques to "rule out" esoteric problems that may be masquerading behind common symptoms (but with a very low probability). Concrete objectives could also be set to reach these goals:

- Decreases in costs for specific diagnoses or lack of them (that is, lack of specific symptoms)
- Decreases in the incidence of nonspecific complaints and life-style-related illness
- Decreases in medically unnecessary care
- Decreases in inappropriate use of emergency and urgent care facilities

As a precursor to these process and outcome objectives, program managers might want to establish structural objectives such as the following:

- Formation and use of employee task groups
- Implementation of a self-care program
- Implementation of a wise-use program
- Integration of these programs with the benefits package
- Specific activities with managed care or other networks of providers to make the interaction with patients more balanced events, and to mutually change paradigms by both consumers and providers

Management Support

Clear management support for employee involvement drives its success. Management introduction of the involvement initiative should be participatory. The degree of employee involvement in benefits design, communication, and selection should reflect the degree of employee involvement elsewhere in the company. If the employer is very hierarchical and has no other employee involvement in its processes, it is not likely to be taken seriously in this context, and employees may not be as forthcoming as they otherwise could be.

Communication and Involvement Program Elements

A number of targeted activities have proven important to actualize employee involvement and change the balance of power in health and medical transactions. These initiatives are generally supported by employees and managed care organizations. Some or all of them would benefit most employers.

Informed Consent

Some observers maintain that the most important health-related decisions an employee can make is the selection of a benefits package. Because the underlying delivery systems vary significantly in form and structure, the employee should realize that benefit selection may well influence the extent of coverage, the ability to select one's own physician, and the site of care. Therefore, some have advocated informed consent for these choices (Grodin, 1992). Informed consent includes completely divulging:

- Available benefits
- Relative costs, both to the employee and in total
- Quality of care as far as is known
- Degree of choice of providers permitted
- Eligibility requirements
- Options within plans
- Possibility of switching during any given year

Employers may also have information about employee understanding and experience and about implications of choices. This is part of the utility model in which employees, if given adequate information, may be able to make choices that maximize their own utility and therefore minimize medically unnecessary care.

It would be useful if nondirective advice could be given while the employee retains the right to make the final choice about testing and treatment options. A consistent strategy should be developed to determine what information should be provided and when it would be most effective.

The employer must protect employees' rights to autonomous choice and should also be concerned for employee welfare. The benefits group should be aware of what is driving the system: Are employees' choices driven by costs, perceived quality, satisfaction, the opinions of others, or a desire to improve work or health? Observers feel that the selection of benefits should focus on the best interest of employees through open communication.

General Health Knowledge

Few published surveys of adult health knowledge exist, but informal surveys done by corporate medical departments show a significant lack of information about basic anatomy and physiology, ignorance of the relative effectiveness of treatment, and inability to judge quality and the effectiveness of new or "fringe" treatments. It is not clear that the general public (or more specifically, employees) understands the concept of watchful waiting, or the use of proven effective therapies rather than faddish but marginally effective therapy. Specific services that seem to be significantly overused are listed below.

- Antibiotics for viral infections
- Long-term physical therapy for either tension symptoms or mechanical problems that were misdiagnosed
- Treatment programs for substance abuse and conduct disorders that seem to depend on the availability of reimbursement for their "medical necessity"
- Psychotherapy for post-traumatic disorders (when structured peer groups might be more effective)
- Continued or misapplied use of tranquilizers, sedatives, and sleeping pills
- Esophagogastroduodenoscopy
- Coronary artery bypass grafts
- Caesarean sections
- Prostatectomy
- Hysterectomy

(See the discussion in Chapter Three on misuse or overuse of tests and treatments.)

One key need, then, is to increase the basic level of knowledge about health problems, their origin, their prevention, their self-treatment, and their treatment in the medical system. Employers should devise ways of conveying this information to employees and dependents. In many organizations, it is unlikely that classes of any intensity could be offered during work hours, although time sharing might be possible. Various kinds of media can be used, including print, audiotape, videotape, interactive voice response for specific queries, CD-ROM retrieval for the more technically oriented, or other means. Some market research would no doubt be useful to determine what format employees would prefer and then to test market the messages.

This information must get into the hands of the spouse, because in many instances the spouse is the actual decision maker about medical care. If there are dependents such as teenagers who become high users of medical care, getting this information to them as well would be important.

One alternative is to make specific information available at the point of need. Several programs now exist in which, through print or voice communication or sometimes even face to face with a "health counselor," employees (and less often dependents) can get information about specific proposed treatment alternatives or discuss how to make a decision about the different alternatives. Point-of-use information tends to be much more useful than general information that people may not grant the highest priority. Some anecdotal research suggests that this results in significant decreases in benefits costs (Gardner and Sneiderman, 1992).

Self-Efficacy Training

Frequently the gap between knowledge and action is a lack of a sense of self-efficacy — the belief that one can change or carry out some action. Bandura and others have developed specific self-efficacy training that might be very useful in this regard.

The combination of knowledge, a structured approach to information gathering and decision making, and a sense of self-efficacy should change the balance of power between providers and patients to a more nearly equal one (or perhaps one even skewed in favor of the patient). This contrasts with the present situation, where over 90 percent of the power resides with the provider. The provider is really unable to assess the proposed alternatives for each individual without exploring them in detail, and even then cannot act within the patient's value system (Vickery, 1993).

Controlled trials of the use of self-efficacy training to better manage chronic diseases such as diabetes, asthma, and arthritis are ongoing at Stanford University. Preliminary data indicate that this training is accompanied by a dramatic drop in the use of medical resources, a decrease in the use of the medical system, a decrease in disability, and an increase in functionality and satisfaction with life (Bandura, 1991; Pelletier, Joss, and Locke, 1992; Lorig, Mazonson, and Holman, 1993).

Wise-Use Education and Training

Employees and dependents could clearly use structured information on how to interact with health care providers. This should probably consist of a generic list of facts to acquire and generic ways of solving problems so that specific information or decision trees are not necessary at an initial level. This mental approach would be analogous to a "review of systems" undertaken in a medical history. Patients might want to know what the provider thinks the problem is, how the provider reached that conclusion, what the proposed course of treatment is, what the natural history of the untreated disease is, what the alternatives are, and what the probabilities of success of various treatments are. They might also like to know the expected length of disability or impairment and the effects on function. The line between wise-use education and general health education is unclear, because some knowledge about symptoms, medications, and common diagnostic and surgical procedures is necessary to intelligently ask questions about specific problems.

Some hard data exist that can be used to project the effectiveness of wise-use programs for interactions with the medical care system (Vickery and others, 1983). Anecdotally, a number of corporate medical departments have observed that with wise-use training (which is not terribly popular), increases in the appropriate use of care — and, in particular, in appropriate management of chronic disorders — have occurred. A few analyses of medical claims data focusing on nonspecific complaints have demonstrated this effect as well (Dalton and Harris, 1992).

Self-Care Education

One important facet of wise use, based on a fund of knowledge about health and illness, is how to care for minor illnesses and injuries without using the medical system. A fair amount of misinformation exists about simple remedies that can be used to take care of minor symptoms and injuries. At least judging from those who use emergency rooms, particularly at off hours, there is a lack of knowledge about when to use the medical system and when not to. This can probably be tied to a lack of effective health education. Yet many minor complaints do not require medical attention. They do just as well with self-care. In fact, most providers would prefer not to see minor complaints because they do not really require their services and are not all that intellectually challenging. (This, of course, does not address the issue of provider income enhancement through seeking a long progression of minor complaints that may not be susceptible to medical treatment, any more than they are to over-the-counter medication or watchful waiting.)

A specific skill set is required in order to be able to assess the need for medical care and then care for one's self or one's family in an effective way (Vickery and Fries, 1993).

A number of commercial packages are available to teach self-care, or they can be customized or developed for individual work sites. In addition, a small but growing number of managed care organizations are now developing these materials or courses. Some face-to-face instruction is frequently helpful to revalidate what someone has learned. Providing books, videotapes, and other materials is certainly part of this effort. Employers sometimes resist offering a $5 to $10 book because this appears to be a large initial expense, but compared to the cost of one office visit, or certainly one emergency room visit, it is a relatively minor investment.

Three types of information are available on the effectiveness of self-care. There are a few controlled trials of advice lines that provide information at the point of need. In one classic example at a health maintenance organization in Rhode Island, utilization was cut by about 30 percent with this technique (Vickery and others, 1983). There are also a number of proprietary self-care programs that have been in existence for over ten years. It appears that when they are used, a significant decrease in inappropriate use of the medical care system occurs (Vickery, Golaszewski, Wright, and Kalmer, 1988). A number of worksite based programs have been shown to be cost effective (Lorig, Kraines, Brown, and Richardson, 1985; Dalton and Harris, 1992).

Media and Messages

It is not yet clear whether electronic media are more effective in conveying self-care and wise-use information. Some experiments with interactive voice response and video have indicated that electronically engaging employees or dependents can increase their involvement with the material. Flowcharts and graphics are particularly useful for self-care and wise-use materials, which can be integrated into health promotion materials.

Conclusion

Creating a partnership with employees to design benefits, prevention, and medical care programs can increase satisfaction and manage costs by matching needs and demands with program offerings. An effective partnership in this area does require more basic knowledge and more benefit-cost information than most people currently have. Effective transmission of that information presupposes a desire to know, effective media and technologies, and a perception that the information makes a difference. Transmitting the information will most likely also require additional skills.

Given the growing dissatisfaction with benefits and medical care, rising costs, and concerns about the appropriateness and quality of medical care, employee involvement is a critical factor in managing health, care, and costs.

CHAPTER NINE

Encouraging
Health Promotion
and Disease Prevention

Life-style and the environment (including the work environment) affect health to a significant extent, being associated with over half of postponable deaths and at least that percentage of medical care costs. Given the complexities of managing medical care, it would be preferable and less expensive to avoid using the system entirely by staying healthy, or at least to reduce use as much as possible. Further, medical care may be a less effective alternative for improving health than better nutrition, less smoking and drinking, greater use of seatbelts and child safety restraints, more social support, and better income and education (Harris, 1992b; Lundberg, 1992; Fielding, 1992; Harris, 1993b).

It can be argued that given the turnover in some industries, promoting health is really a social endeavor that public agencies should undertake. However, even in health care reform scenarios, the employer (and ultimately employees) pay the bill for the consequences of unhealthy life-styles. Alternatively, employers could look at health promotion as one aspect of their community service program, since health behavior change among community residents who work for them will remain in the community even if workers change employers.

Promoting health is a logical next step after wise use and self-care. Health promotion activities are much in demand by employees and dependents in many surveys and are being offered at more and more work sites.

Employers therefore have a number of good reasons to offer health promotion programs:

- To reduce life-style and environmental risk
- To reduce associated costs
- To improve well-being, morale, and productivity
- To improve employee satisfaction
- To meet employee demands for preventive information
- To meet demands for assistance in changing unhealthy life-styles
- To increase involvement with work
- To increase productivity (at least availability for work) and morale and reduce turnover

Why Health Promotion Makes Sense

Although public knowledge about the connection between *health risk behavior* — as dangerous life-styles are called — and disease is increasing, it is useful to review it. There are still many misconceptions, especially about some popular methods of reducing these risks. The scientific evidence is often useful as a basis for employee surveys, to focus program budgeting and design, to frame communications, and to make the business case for health promotion to top and mid-level management.

Links Between Life-Style, Environment, and Health

The major causes of disability and death in industrialized nations have changed dramatically from common infectious diseases around the turn of the century to life-style-related illness today (Fielding, 1992). The knowledge of how to prevent or postpone these types of health problems and the technology to do so were undeveloped until recently. Prevention was confined to the avoidance of infectious disease until the last several decades. The turning point probably came in 1964, with the use of epidemiology (the study of the rates and distribution of disease) to demonstrate conclusively — although not to the satisfaction of the tobacco industry — that smoking was causally linked with cancer and a number of other diseases (U.S. Surgeon General, 1964). The U.S. Centers For Disease Control have

continued to update this information. Recent composite estimates of the overall impact of life-style–related illness and injury using these and other data are shown in Tables 9.1 and
9.2. The former shows the number of "years of potential life
lost" (YPLL), or population mortality impact of life-style. The
latter demonstrates some impacts of these health problems in
terms of morbidity, mortality, and cost.

Table 9.1. Estimated Years of Potential Life
Lost Before Age Sixty-Five (YPLL = 65), United States, 1988.

Cause of death	YPLL = 65 for persons dying in 1988
All causes (total)	12,281,741
Unintentional injuries	2,319,400
Malignant neoplasms	1,309,289
Diseases of the heart	1,466,629
Suicide/homicide	1,361,473
Congenital anomalies	671,709
HIV infection	472,800
Prematurity	432,342
Cerebrovascular disease	245,722
Chronic liver disease and cirrhosis	236,944
Pneumonia/influenza	172,712
Diabetes mellitus	130,666
Chronic obstructive pulmonary disease	128,126
Sudden infant death syndrome	296,304

Source: In J. S. Harris, H. D. Belk, and L. W. Wood (eds.), Managing Employee
Health Care Costs. Beverly, Mass.: OEM Press, 1992. Reprinted with permission.

In the late 1970s, the U.S. Surgeon General summarized
the available knowledge about the connections between life-style
and health in *Healthy People: The Surgeon General's Report on Health
Promotion and Disease Prevention* (U.S. Surgeon General, 1979).
A parallel document to *Healthy People* set quantified targets for
health promotion for the 1980s, including work-site objectives.
A number of general population objectives, such as reducing
in levels of high blood pressure and cholesterol and increasing
levels of exercise, were also targets for work-site health promotion programs. A similar report in Canada quantified the burden of disease associated with life-style, environmental factors,
genetics, and lapses in the medical care system (Lalonde, 1978).

Table 9.2. Costs of Treatment for Selected Preventable Conditions.

Condition	Overall magnitude	Avoidable intervention[a]	Cost per patient[b]
Heart disease	7 million with coronary artery disease; 500,000 deaths/yr; 284,000 bypass procedures/yr	Coronary bypass surgery	$30,000
Cancer	1 million new cases/yr; 510,000 deaths/yr	Lung cancer treatment Cervical cancer treatment	$29,000 $28,000
Stroke	600,000 stroke/yr; 150,000 deaths/yr	Hemiplegia treatment and rehabilitation	$22,000
Injuries	2.3 million hospitalization/yr; 142,500 deaths/yr; 177,000 persons with spinal cord injuries in the United States	Quadriplegia treatment and rehabilitation Hip fracture treatment and rehabilitation Severe head injury treatment and rehabilitation	$570,000 (lifetime) $40,000 $310,000
HIV infection	1–1.5 million infected; 118,000 AIDS cases (as of Jan. 1990)	AIDS treatment	$75,000 (lifetime)
Low-birthweight baby	260,000 LBWB born/yr; 23,000 deaths/yr	Neonatal intensive care for LBWB	$10,000
Inadequate immunization	Lacking basic immunization series: 20–30%, aged 2 and younger; 3%, aged 6 and older	Congenital rubella syndrome treatment	$354,000 (lifetime)

[a]Examples (other interventions may apply).
[b]Representative first-year costs, except as noted. Not indicated are nonmedical costs, such as lost productivity to society.
Source: In J. S. Harris, H. D. Belk, and L. W. Wood (eds.), *Managing Employee Health Care Costs.* Beverly, Mass.: OEM Press, 1992. Reprinted with permission.

A comprehensive study for the Carter Center at Emory University — *Closing the Gap: The Burden of Unnecessary Illness* (Amler and Dull, 1987) — demonstrated that alcohol use, tobacco consumption, injury, and unintended pregnancy are the top precursors of illness, disability, and death in the general population. These data are useful to the extent that an employed group is typical of the general public. The authors suggested that approximately two-thirds of deaths in the United States are attributable to a "preventable precursor," by which they meant that these deaths could be postponed to the end of the natural life span if the precursors did not exist. The study concluded that 24 percent of deaths, 21 percent of years of life lost before age sixty-five, 21 percent of hospital days, and 16 percent of direct medical costs were attributable to certain lifestyle behaviors.

Tobacco use, high blood pressure, "overnutrition" (including high fat consumption and excess caloric intake), and alcohol use alone accounted for approximately a million postponable deaths per year. Tobacco was responsible for 27 percent of premature deaths, high blood pressure for 24 percent, and overnutrition for 23 percent. Subdividing the deaths caused by tobacco in those under sixty-five, circulatory disease (including heart attack, stroke, and diabetic complications) accounted for 36 percent of the deaths, cancer for 34 percent, infant death for 18 percent, lung disease for 6 percent, fires and burns for 5 percent, and ulcers for 1 percent. Subdividing the years of life lost due to alcohol, 47 percent were due to motor vehicle injuries, 36 percent to other injuries, 14 percent to cirrhosis, and 3 percent to cancer. Similar estimates for individual worksites or employers can be derived using population-based health risk appraisals (HRAs) or survey estimates of risk factor prevalence applied through HRAs. An example of premature mortality for a large technology company using this method, prior to implementation of a comprehensive health promotion program, is shown in Figures 9.1a–d (Harris, 1989).

The first three risk factors also accounted for four million potential years of life lost and for 45.5 million days of hospital care. At an average cost of approximately $2,000 a day, this

Figure 9.1a. Causes of Premature Mortality (Males < 35).

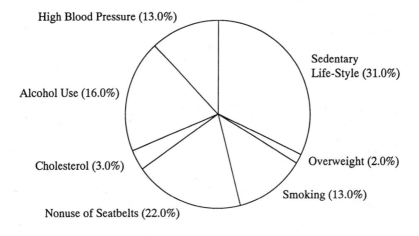

Figure 9.1b. Causes of Premature Mortality (Females < 35).

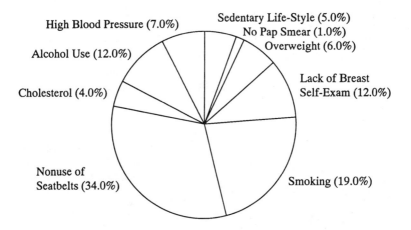

Figure 9.1c. Causes of Premature Mortality (Males > 35).

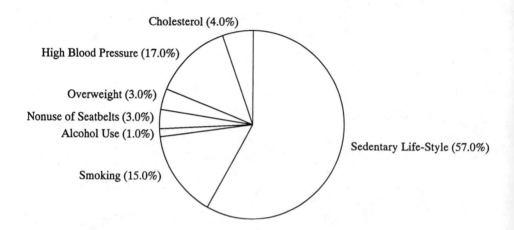

Figure 9.1d. Causes of Premature Mortality (Females > 35).

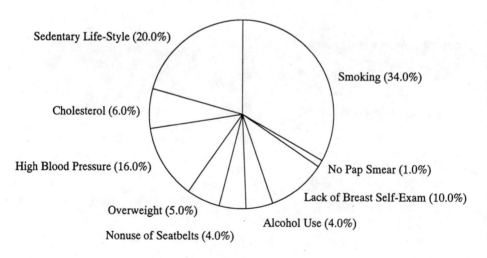

Source: Harris, 1989, pp. 181–182.

avoidable inpatient care would account for at least $90 billion of the nation's medical care bill.

Gaps in screening, injury precursors other than alcohol, and alcohol itself accounted for most of the remainder. In looking at gaps in primary prevention, 67 percent of years of life lost were due to infant deaths, 17 percent to infection, 15 percent to suicide, and 1 percent to cancer.

In terms of premature years of life lost before the age of sixty-five, injury precursors excluding alcohol such as violent behavior, depression, and unsafe machinery contributed 21 percent, alcohol 18 percent via injury and 4 percent by other means, tobacco 18 percent, and gaps in primary prevention 15 percent. Unintended pregnancy contributed 6 percent, handguns 4 percent, high blood pressure 4 percent, and other causes 10 percent. The burden of illness by life-style factor is shown in Table 9.3, and the detailed effects of these precursors are shown in Table 9.4. In all, life-style factors were associated with 11,897,000 potential years of life lost before age sixty-five.

All life-style-related causes were estimated to account for 1,195,000 deaths and 274,500,000 days of hospitalizations in 1980. Extrapolating these figures, at today's hospital charge rates, approximately one-quarter of our national health care bill can be identified as connected solely to hospitalization due to life-style-related diseases.

Since 1980, there has been an upswing in research linking specific behaviors, environmental influences, disease prevention maneuvers, and other factors to today's major causes of disability and death, which include (in rank order) heart disease, cancer, injuries, stroke, and pneumonia. The spectrum of disease has changed somewhat over the last ten years. Only one of the ten leading causes of mortality (pneumonia) is now directly attributable to an infectious agent, although HIV-related disease has now assumed the number eleven position and will probably move up on the list. Both these infectious diseases are related to life-style. A detailed review of the evidence linking life-style with morbidity, disability, and premature death can be found in *Health Promotion in the Workplace* (O'Donnell and Harris, 1993) and *Healthy People 2000* (U.S. Surgeon General,

Table 9.3. Major Precursors of Premature Death,
United States, 1980: Attributable Deaths, Years Lost
Before Age Sixty-Five, and Days of Hospital Care.

Precursor	Deaths	Potential years lost before age sixty-five	Days of hospital care
Tobacco	338,022	1,497,161	16,098,587
High blood pressure	297,162	340,752	9,781,647
Overnutrition	289,502	292,960	16,306,194
Alcohol			
Total	99,247	1,795,458	3,348,354
(Injury)	(53,683)	(1,497,206)	(2,229,824)
(Other)	(45,564)	(298,252)	(1,118,530)
Injury risks (excluding alcohol)	64,169	1,755,720	25,470,176
Gaps in screening	56,592	172,793	3,647,729
Gaps in primary prevention	54,027	1,273,631	4,651,730
Inadequate access to care	21,974	324,709	2,141,569
Occupation	16,807	102,065	581,740
Handguns	13,365	350,683	28,514
Unintended pregnancy	8,000	520,000	n/a
Total preventable	1,258,867	8,425,932	82,056,240
(percentage)	(63.1)	(70.8)	(29.9)
Total all causes	1,995,000	11,897,174	274,508,000

Source: Amler and Dull, 1987, p. 184. Reprinted with permission.

1991; National High Blood Pressure Education Program, 1985; National Cholesterol Education Program, 1990).

Links Between Life-Style Changes and Better Health

Changes in population disease rates have been correlated with changes in life-style risks. For example, the age-adjusted death rate for coronary disease has dropped in the United States by over 50 percent from 1950 to 1985. These declines have been correlated with population reductions in hypertension, dietary fat consumption, and tobacco consumption (Blackburn and Luepker, 1992). Stroke mortality has been dropping in the United States since the early twentieth century, but the rate of decrease accelerated after the introduction of drug treatment of hypertension.

Injury rates have dropped as well in association with

Table 9.4. Studied Health Problems and Major Precursors, United States, 1980.

Studied health problems	Quantified precursors	Other identified precursors
Alcohol dependency and abuse	Alcohol	Gaps in screening, gaps in primary prevention
Arthritis and musculoskeletal diseases	Gaps in primary prevention	Socioeconomic level
Cancer	Tobacco, alcohol, occupation, gaps in screening, dietary fat, inadequate dietary fiber, gaps in primary prevention	Socioeconomic level
Cardiovascular diseases	Tobacco, high blood pressure, overnutrition, diabetes	Inadequate physical activity, socioeconomic level
Dental diseases	Gaps in primary prevention, tobacco, inadequate access to care	Socioeconomic level
Depression	None	Gaps in primary prevention, alcohol, inadequate access to care
Diabetes mellitus	Overnutrition, tobacco, inadequate access to care	Socioeconomic level
Digestive diseases	Alcohol, tobacco, gaps in screening, gaps in primary prevention	None
Drug dependence and abuse	None	Gaps in primary prevention, inadequate access to care, socioeconomic level
Infectious and parasitic diseases	Gaps in primary prevention, gaps in screening, inadequate access to care	Tobacco, alcohol, occupation
Respiratory diseases	Tobacco	Occupation, inadequate access to care
Unintended pregnancy and infant mortality and morbidity	Tobacco, gaps in primary prevention, inadequate access to care	Alcohol, socioeconomic level
Unintentional injury	Alcohol, injury risks exclusive of alcohol, tobacco, handguns	Socioeconomic level
Violence: homicide, domestic violence, and suicide	Alcohol, handguns, gaps in primary prevention, gaps in screening, inadequate access to care	Socioeconomic level

Source: Amler and Dull, 1987. Reprinted with permission.

reductions in risk factors. The injury death rate for motor vehicle crashes declined by almost 30 percent between 1970 and 1990 and was attributed to lower rates of alcohol use, increased use of occupant restraints, motorcycle and bicycle helmet laws, and lower speed limits (Chorba, 1991). Restrictive licensing of handguns in some locations has been followed promptly by a decline in both homicides and suicides (Loftin, MacDowell, Wiersema, and Cottey, 1991). Violent incidents declined with decreases in alcohol and drug use as well.

Maternal and perinatal death rates declined significantly during the 1970s as the prevalence of early prenatal care and prenatal nutrition counseling increased. These decreases also were associated with a decline in smoking rates among women of childbearing age (U.S. Surgeon General, 1991).

The rates of syphilis, gonorrhea, HIV, and hepatitis B infection have dropped in areas and during periods when there has been extensive health education, public health case finding, and increases in condom use. In some test programs, use of disposable needles has cut the HIV and hepatitis B infection rate as well (Cates and Holmes, 1992).

Clinical trials in cholesterol reduction, in high blood pressure control, and in multifactorial risk reduction for men at high risk have demonstrated that intensive intervention by health care professionals can result in impressive reductions in mortality and morbidity and gains in healthy years of life and function (Lipid Research Clinic Program, 1984; National High Blood Pressure Education Program, 1985; National Cholesterol Education Program, 1990; Multiple Risk Factor Intervention Trial Research Group, 1990).

Public health interventions, using entire communities as experimental groups, have demonstrated changes in disease rates and mortality with communitywide health promotion activities in Belgium, Switzerland, Norway, Finland, the United States, and other countries (Puska and others, 1985; Vartiainen, Heath, and Ford, 1991; Shea and Basch, 1990).

Two studies conducted by Stanford University—the *Three Communities Study* and the *Five Community Study*—targeted smoking, high blood pressure, and high cholesterol as key risks for heart disease. The studies used intervention techniques similar to those used in North Karelia, Finland, with matched groups receiving intervention or no intervention consisting of media-based information and, in some cases, face-to-face counseling. In the *Three Community Study,* after two years there was a 23 percent reduction in cardiovascular risk. In the short run, counseling and the media were more effective than the media alone, but in the long run there was no difference (Shea and Basch, 1990).

In the *Five Community Study,* use of low-intensity media involving social learning theory, a behavior change model, community organizing principles, and social marketing methods resulted in a significant drop in mean population cholesterol level, blood pressure, smoking prevalence, body mass index, total mortality risk, and cardiovascular risk (Farquhar and others, 1990). The Minnesota Heart Project has demonstrated similar results.

Community-based attempts to reduce smoking provide instructive evidence of effective techniques that might be used in the workplace. These include emphasis on warning labels, bans on promotion, statements from opinion leaders, educational efforts, smoking restrictions or smoke-free workplaces, and restricting distribution — that is, removing cigarette machines from anywhere near the workplace (MacKay and Davis, 1991).

While not a work-site intervention per se, it should be noted that tax increases have had a linear effect on reduction and cigarette smoking. Tax increases in the United States have shown a 4 percent drop in use for every 10 percent increase in taxes (an elasticity of -0.4), and a 14 percent drop in use among teenagers (an elasticity of -1.4). Overseas, increases in import taxes have caused significant drops in imports.

Effects of Work-Site Health Promotion Efforts

There is increasing evidence that work-site health promotion programs result in increased job satisfaction, increased morale, decreased life-style risks, and changes in medical care expenses. The Johnson & Johnson "Life for Life" program demonstrated that the program site had half the mean annual increase in inpatient medical care costs, due to both lower admission rates and total hospital days. There was no effect on outpatient care or costs. This was a three-year study, with effects seen in the last year; follow-up data have not been published but are expected to confirm the original findings (Bly, Jones, and Richardson, 1986). In other studies of this program, individual participants showed significantly greater fitness, smoking cessation, seatbelt use, self-esteem, opinion of working conditions, organization commitment, morale, job satisfaction, and fewer adjusted absentee hours and reported sick days than nonparticipants (Breslow, Fielding, Hermann, and Wilbur, 1990).

Participants in a comprehensive health promotion program at Blue Cross and Blue Shield of Indiana showed 24 percent lower medical care costs than nonparticipants, accompanied by decreases in smoking and blood pressure and increases in exercise level (Gibbs, Mulvaney, Henes, and Reed, 1985).

Northern Telecom, Inc., published results of an integrated comprehensive health management program. Dimensions of the program included coverage for preventive services, utilization management, a renewed emphasis on safety, primary care at the work site, and a comprehensive health promotion program that included screening, mass communication, counseling, skill building, social and environmental support, wise use of self-care education, an employee assistance program, and incentives for healthy life-styles. Surveys revealed significant decreases in heavy drinking, smoking, hypertension, and work stress, and an increase in seatbelt use. Analysis of insurance claims data after five years of the program showed significant reductions in cost per case for those specific diagnostic categories expected to be affected by changes in life-style. Hospitalization rates were reduced for these target diagnoses as well (Dalton and Harris, 1992).

An evaluation of the relationship between participation in the work-site fitness program at the Travelers Taking Care Center and absence from work demonstrated a significant decrease in absence, after controlling for age, gender, and baseline absence level (Lynch and others, 1990).

Work-Site Health Promotion Is Evolving Rapidly

Because those with higher levels of certain risk behaviors ("risk factors") will develop diseases at a higher rate than those without these risks, people have been both encouraged and trained to reduce their level of risk and therefore reduce the burden of ill health. By some estimates, these life-styles and choices are responsible for over half of present medical care expenditures. It is clearly in the best interests of both employers and employees to reduce health risks so that employees and dependents lead healthier, more productive lives. Presumably, they would be happier and feel better as well. Costs to both employers and employees would drop.

Prevalence and Content of Work-Site Health Promotion Programs

Work-site health promotion activities have become common, but comprehensive programs are still the exception rather than the rule. Sixty-six percent of work sites in a 1985 survey reported some health promotion activities, with the percentage increasing to more than 80 percent with work sites of over 250 employees. The most common activity was smoking cessation, followed by back injury prevention, health risk assessments, stress management, and exercise. Twenty-seven percent offered stress management programs in 1985. Sixteen percent of work sites offered high blood pressure activities and 16.8 percent offered nutrition education activities in 1985. Ten percent of work sites of fifty or more employees offered nutrition education activities for employees that included healthy food selections (Fielding and Piserchia, 1989).

Twenty-two percent of work sites with fifty or more employees offered physical fitness "activities." However, the majority of activities consisted of provision of information; 65 percent were group classes or workshops, 22 percent provided facilities, and 27 percent provided subsidized memberships (Fielding and Piserchia, 1989).

In 1985, the national survey found that 27 percent of work sites of fifty or more employees had formal smoking policies. In 1986, that number had increased to 36 percent; by 1987, it was 54 percent (Harris, 1993b). However, it was not clear how many of these work sites restricted smoking and how many banned it. Small companies are less likely than large ones to have work-site smoking policies.

Broad-brush work-site health promotion programs initially focused on smoking cessation, weight control, exercise, high blood pressure control, and stress management. With increased knowledge about life-style-related disease, programs have expanded their scope to include nutrition activities aimed at reducing cholesterol levels and fat intake as well as sodium consumption. They also focus on smoking prevention, establishment of smoke-free environments, organizational as well as individual stress management, risks for prematurity and low birthweight, injury prevention, violence prevention, healthy relationships, prevention of AIDS and other sexually transmitted diseases, and the entire range of preventable injury and illnesses that cost employers and employees tremendous amounts in anguish and dollars (Harris, 1993b).

Examples of quantified goals are now available to guide these activities. In 1991, following an extensive consensus development process, the Office of the Surgeon General issued a second assessment and set of targets, *Healthy People 2000*, which should guide work-site, medical care sector, and public health programs toward the attainment of a new set of goals by the year 2000 (U.S. Surgeon General, 1991). Concise summaries are available in O'Donnell and Harris (1993), Harris (1993c), and elsewhere.

Health Promotion Process

The initial phase of health promotion is aimed at modifying unhealthy life-styles by building awareness, knowledge, skills, and interpersonal support. Health promotion includes environmental and social support for health behaviors and conditions. Environmental changes might include removing passive smoke from the workplace, providing healthy food, making exercise facilities or showers available, and providing social support for healthier life-styles. Health promotion programs at the work site are placing increased emphasis on the organizational environment, including corporate culture, health-related policies and benefits design, and the physical environment, in support of health behaviors (Roman and Blum, 1988).

Characterizing the Present Situation

The basic information to determine the need for health promotion programs comes from two sources: employee health risks, and current and projected claims and other costs for life-style related diseases. Health risk data can be obtained either from individually administered Health Risk Appraisals or from employee surveys. If a health promotion program is not in place, surveys may be a faster and less expensive way to obtain the data, although obtaining individual identifiers or conducting follow-up evaluations may be problematic.

Medical insurance claims data can be analyzed to determine the prevalence and cost of specific disease categories known to be associated with life-style or environmental factors. By applying the population-attributable risk (Amler and Dull, 1987), the attributable fraction of cost can be calculated. If individual identifiers are available, the cost of life-style-related diseases can be linked to health risks, creating a more complete profile for that population (Harris and Theriault, 1993).

Health risk appraisal data can be used to project costs forward based on the age and gender distribution of the employee population. This is a hypothetical model to some extent, because it typically uses mortality data rather than morbidity data, but the mortality curve that increases sharply with age is a useful model to start to explain the observed hyperbolically increasing cost levels in the absence of preventive and promotive intervention (Harris, 1985a).

In constructing a benefit-cost scenario to evaluate health promotion programs, one can project the probable impacts of the activities shown in Table 9.5 using sensitivity analysis predicated on various participation and success rates.

Table 9.5. Probable Short-Term Benefits of Health Promotion Activities.

Activity	Reduction in
Smoking cessation	Upper respiratory infections Pneumonia Asthma Bronchitis Sinusitis Low-birthweight premature births Otitis and upper respiratory infections in dependent children Sudden cardiac deaths
Cessation of heavy drinking	Trauma and domestic violence Seizures Nutritionally related disease Dependent use of health service
Self-care counseling or classes	Medical services for minor complaints
Wise-use classes, counseling, or hotlines	Ambulatory care and emergency room use Elective surgery Diagnostic testing Medication costs
Immunizations	Influenza Pneumonia Tetanus
Cardiac and neurological rehabilitation	Absence Total cost Retraining Replacement
Diabetes education and control	Ketoacidosis Hypoglycemia
Seatbelt safety	Motor vehicle trauma
Work and/or home safety	Trauma

Source: In J. S. Harris, H. D. Belk, L. W. Wood (eds.), *Managing Employee Health Care Costs*. Beverly, Mass.: OEM Press, 1992. Reprinted with permission.

Program Framework

The mission of the health management program should clearly include prevention and health promotion. It might be framed as an intent to maintain and improve the health of employees and dependents, or it may be more specific. The shape of the program will depend to some extent on the corporate or employer's culture. In participatory cultures, there would be more of an emphasis on employee involvement in program design and perhaps employee representatives to guide publicity and implementation of the program and to assist with support groups. Corporate attitudes about preventive services and the extent of support for health promotion may guide the provision of screening programs, on-site health promotion activities, and facilities.

Gap Analysis

Using the data collected to determine the life-style and the environmentally related effect on disease and risk rates, goals might be framed as follows:

- Becoming smoke free
- Having a fit work force
- Improving employee morale
- Having the healthiest possible place to work
- Providing a health-promoting work-site culture

Concrete objectives to achieve those goals are shown below:

- Offering certain activities
- Reducing specific health risks
- Increasing health status
- Reducing disease levels
- Reducing health care costs for specific diseases
- Increasing positive employee attitudes
- Reducing turnover
- Increasing productivity (although this is somewhat difficult to measure)

Program Structure

Health promotion programs have tended to be a collection of activities that address specific risks or behavior changes rather than an integrated, synergistic whole that builds on common values through behavioral and communication techniques. An integrated program focuses on core values and effective behavioral technologies. It also provides an opportunity to develop cross-disciplinary skills and to increase the efficiency of the "delivery system" for health promotion. Such a system includes not only health professionals, facilities, supplies, and equipment, but also employees, dependents, and the environment in which they live and work. Employees and dependents must be active rather than passive participants for health risks to change and for change to be sustained (Harris, 1993b).

Health promotion programs have been developed in-house as part of medical departments or as independent entities or have been provided by outside vendors. Which approach to take depends on the cost-effectiveness of each system and the degree of management commitment to the program. It is also essential to coordinate health promotion activities with any on-site medical care that is provided and with managed care and referral networks. In addition, it is important to form alliances with departments that have common purposes or techniques, such as Organizational Development or Effectiveness, Human Resources, Benefits, the medical department, and so on.

Stages in the Health Promotion Cycle

The key steps in coordinated, well-sequenced health promotion programs are the following:

- Determining high-impact and desired target areas
- Raising awareness
- Changing individual health risk habits
- Sustaining behavior change
- Building healthy environments
- Evaluating and improving the program

This cycle bears a remarkable resemblance to the *plan-do-check-act* cycle inherent in the continuous quality improvement approach. We have already discussed data analysis and determination of the areas of greatest effect on costs and health. We will now describe the remaining parts of the cycle (Figure 9.2 provides an example).

Figure 9.2. Health Enhancement Program Design Cycle.

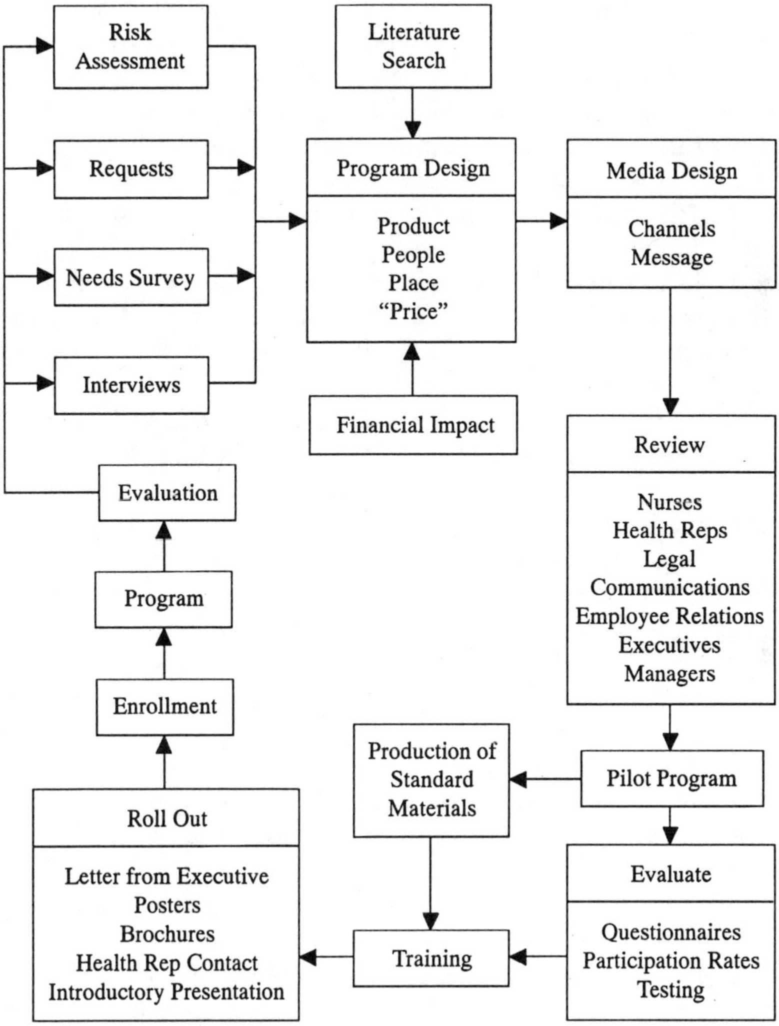

Source: In J. S. Harris, H. D. Belk, L. W. Wood (eds.), *Managing Employee Health Care Costs.* Beverly, Mass.: OEM Press, 1992. Reprinted with permission.

Raising Awareness. Awareness can be raised through provision of information. Information can come from various kinds of media, including print, video, and multimedia. Seminars and classes are a time-honored method of attempting to convey information that may work for some people. However, many employees and dependents are not particularly interested in sitting still to listen to health information. Seminars can be enhanced by using interactive multimedia, turning the seminars into discussion groups, or sharing experiences.

It is important to get the information to those who make many family life-style decisions, particularly spouses. It is often cost effective to send materials home. One interesting variation on information provision is a series of newsletters chained together to provide a coherent set of information about reducing health risks.

In framing messages, it is important to use available psychological techniques to change values as well as knowledge. One of the more effective ways of framing messages is what is known as *loss framing* (Wallston, 1993). In loss framing, the message is that you "could have had something if you had not become ill." Loss framing is more effective than talking about positive goals for a significant proportion of the population, particularly the "late adopters" or those resistant to changing their behavior. Attractive graphics and step-by-step flowcharts are also quite useful to some segments of the population.

Point-of-use health promotion information, while not as specific as point-of-use information to make decisions about acute care (for example, what you need to know about fevers if you have one) is quite helpful. A hybrid of these techniques is to provide informative self-care and preventive information during an episode of acute life-style-related illness. For instance, if someone has acute bronchitis, information about smoking cessation is probably going to be more effective when provided at this time than when the smoker is not experiencing acute health problems.

Media provision can be orchestrated into campaigns. It is usually quite helpful to sequence a series of media campaigns centered around either general health promotion or specific life-style change issues. Forward planning over a long period of time will maximize the effect of these campaigns and avoid confusion or cross messages (Dalton and Harris, 1992). Multiple channels of communication such as the following should be used for reinforcement and to maintain interest:

- Messages from opinion leaders
- Print material
- Audiovisual material
- Brief reminders mailed home
- In-plant or in-workplace information sequenced synergistically

(Also see Figure 9.3.)

This organized, practical approach to information provision and motivation for change has often been referred to as *marketing health behavior.* It closely resembles both social marketing, which has been used to "sell" values and concepts and effectively change behaviors in social change campaigns (Kottler, 1988), and product marketing. Social marketing uses the well-known and effective techniques normally used to market products and services (Fredrickson, Soloman, and Brehony, 1984). A good deal of supporting evidence from the social psychology and decision-making literature suggests that culture change can be orchestrated and sustained while building social support for new life-styles.

Unfortunately, little available research documents the differential effectiveness of various types of media and messages in this area. Research is clearly needed to be able to focus efforts and increase cost-effectiveness. There is also little research to document the relative effectiveness of specific activities or combination of activities, messages, and other tactics such as health promotion classes, sequences of classes, and so on.

It is clear that this type of research to improve "behavioral technology" is needed (Harris, 1993a). However, using the classic public health approach of taking action when a threat is reasonably clear (in this case, the threat that life-style poses to health and to the financial stability of the medical care system), wait-

Figure 9.3. Promotion Channels for a Health Enhancement Program.

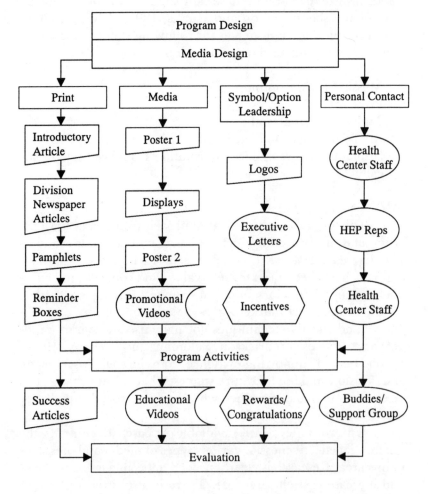

Source: In J. S. Harris, H. D. Belk, and L. W. Wood (eds.), *Managing Employee Health Care Costs.* Beverly, Mass.: OEM Press, 1992. Reprinted with permission.

ing for further research is not a reason to slow down implementation of behavior change techniques.

Changing Individual Health Risk Habits. After awareness has been raised, the next stage of health promotion is to make more information available and to offer activities and build individual skills to change behavior. A variety of activities targeted at specific health risks are listed below.

- Screening (preferably cost-effective, parsimonious screening)
- Smoking cessation
- Fitness activities
- Weight management
- Stress management
- Nutrition
- Cholesterol management
- Hypertension management
- Employee Assistance Programs
- Substance abuse prevention
- Healthy baby education
- AIDS prevention
- Healthy relationships
- Women's health
- Men's health
- Violence prevention
- Suicide prevention
- Vehicle restraint use
- Safety and injury prevention

An extension of information provision that makes decision-making easier is preventive counseling. Counseling can either follow identification of health risks through health risk appraisals and screening or be at the point of need. One very useful counseling technique is *behavioral contracting*. In this approach, an individual agrees with a health professional on specific risk behaviors and achievements over a period of time, signing a contract in writing to reinforce the commitment toward change (Kottke, Batista, and DeFriese, 1988; Harris, Casperson, DeFriese, and Estes, 1991; Mullen, Green, and Persing, 1985; Tolsma and Coplin, 1992).

A core skill of many health promotion programs, and particularly substance abuse prevention activities, should be the skills to resist peer media pressure to use or abuse alcohol, prescription drugs, cigarettes, and other drugs that alter perception (Schuster and Kilbey, 1992).

Sustaining Behavior Change. One key to enhancing the long-term effectiveness of health promotion activities is to make them part of a structured sequence over a long period of time rather than isolated events. The latter will probably not sustain change. In addition, creating a social support network geared either to a specific or generic change is often important to promote and sustain those changes.

Covering preventive services in the benefits package is a good strategy to support the message as well as the execution of health promotion programs. Various surveys have found that between 39 and 80 percent of companies provide some kind of preventive coverage, including cholesterol screening, hypertension screening, and early cancer detection. Another survey reported that 39 percent of large employers provide periodic physicals and 44 percent provide well-baby care (Fielding, 1992).

The INSURE project, sponsored by the commercial insurance industry with additional foundation support, demonstrated the effectiveness of having primary physicians include a package of preventive services as part of their periodic examinations. The project also showed that the cost can be predicted and that the results were cost beneficial. Patients who received these services were more likely to report positive changes for exercise, seatbelt use, weight loss, decreased alcohol consumption, and monthly breast self-examinations (Logsdon and Rosen, 1984; Logsdon, Lazaro, and Meier, 1989).

Incentives can be important as well to inspire a sense of competition. They may be short, long term, or "point-of-practice" incentives that reinforce behaviors immediately. Coupons for observed seatbelt use or safe work practices have been at least partially responsible for up to a fourfold increase in seatbelt use and marked decreases in the frequencies of on-the-job accidents (Dalton and Harris, 1992). Fitness programs often give away T-shirts or bags for reaching exercise participation or aerobic capacity goals. These incentives are symbolic but sometimes effective. In the medium term, one successful incentive is a partial or full tuition refund for health promotion activities if an employee sustains a behavior change such as smoking cessation, seatbelt use, or weight loss after a given period of time.

"Risk rating" benefits is an emerging concept that sets contribution levels for benefits commensurate with a controllable risk. The basic idea is that people who experience excess medical and absence-related costs because of voluntarily modifiable health behavior should pay for the consequences of their behaviors. Control Data Corporation has documented that high-risk groups have claims costs sometimes 100 percent higher than low-risk groups in areas such as smoking, overweight, exercise, seatbelt use, and high blood pressure (Brink, 1987). One particularly well-documented area is smoking; smokers are conservatively estimated to cost between $450 and $1,200 a year more than nonsmokers (in 1990 dollars) (Kristein, 1983). This is a negative long-term incentive.

Building Healthy Environments. A variety of environmental features are known to be effective in facilitating healthy life-styles. They include space for various health promotion activities, healthy food in cafeterias and vending machines, removal of tobacco vending machines or facilities, and a workplace free of cigarette smoke and other indoor air pollution. In addition, healthy environments include attention to ergonomics and workstations designed to facilitate a reasonable amount of social contact.

It is important to be sure that the workplace is safe before embarking on health promoting environmental change. A safe workplace ranks high on Maslow's scale of needs, being characterized as a basic survival need. Organized labor has emphasized this point. Attention to it will gain labor's support for health promotion; neglecting it will often engender opposition to health promotion activities.

While facilities can be capital intensive and may not be necessary for successful program execution, they do have advantages. Providing facilities encourages desirable behavior by increasing convenience and social support. Facilities are evidence of management commitment to health life-styles. Useful facilities include fitness centers, health centers, and educational rooms or complexes.

Exercise facilities can include fitness equipment, shower and locker facilities, endurance equipment such as stationary bicycles, rowing machines, cross-country ski trainers, and areas for aerobics. Lower-cost hydraulic equipment seems to be just as effective as other more expensive types. Jogging tracks and swimming pools are welcome additions but are not necessary to ensure basic aerobic fitness, muscle strength, or flexibility. In some cases, multipurpose rooms can be used for aerobics as well as educational activities.

Health centers are expanded versions of off-site medical care facilities. They can include traditional examination or treatment rooms as well as fitness-testing and on-site laboratories using dry chemistry or other similar techniques. Such centers maximize cost-effectiveness by providing primary care for simple illnesses, monitoring of chronic diseases, counseling at the point of need, a focus for wise-use, self-care and health promotion training, and triage and referral for more serious problems (Dalton and Harris, 1992).

Education facilities are important as well. They can be combined with the other facilities or be freestanding. They can house lending libraries with print and video materials and be a focus for hotlines and point-of-need information services. Integrating medical information, prevention information, and benefits information increases their impact.

Building healthier work cultures is important, too. There is evidence that specific stressors embedded in work-site cultures and management of work flow and human resources may provoke a stress reaction that contributes to lower productivity (Harris, 1984b). The National Institute of Occupational Health has done a series of studies on stress in the workplace and has isolated specific occupations and measurable conditions that increase stress and physical symptoms and possibly medical care expenditures. While it is not completely clear that any but the most extreme work-site conditions can result in disease or disability, it *is* clear that repeated provocation of the stress reactions over a long enough period of time will lead to physical illness. But before stressors cause objective disease, work-related stressors may impair productivity and availability for work (Harris and Dewey, 1984). Table 9.6 summarizes some ways of counteracting stress in the workplace.

Evaluating and Improving the Program. Ideally, each program should be structured from its inception to collect the data needed to periodically reassess the program from both management and scientific standpoints. Parameters to evaluate might include the following:

- Behavior changes by specific behavior
- Individual and population health risks
- Program expenses
- Medical care costs for specific target diagnoses and diagnostic categories
- Rates and costs of injuries
- Rates and costs of low-birthweight infants
- Aggravation of preexisting heart disease

Data elements to track are shown in Table 9.7.

This type of evaluation is useful to track individual and population health status information, to support continuous improvement in program effectiveness, and to research the most effective communications, counseling, and other techniques. Survey research may be valuable to assess program acceptance, communication effectiveness, and desire for new activities or elements (Harris and Theriault, 1993).

The data system used to track the health promotion program should collect information about encounters with the in-house health system and be linked to the benefits claim system so that all information can be collected for each individual in a common data-base format. This can be done on a large personal computer or workstation using a relational database; the process can be carried out either by employer personnel or by vendors used by employers.

Cost-effectiveness analysis may be able to show the relative effectiveness of different interventions or levels of prevention in reducing morbidity and/or mortality. For example, in comparing various methods of reducing coronary disease, the cost per year of potential life saved was projected statistically and ranged from $4,500 for the aggregate benefit in terms of years of life saved by smoking cessation to $95,000 for coronary bypass surgery (Kinosian and Eisenberg, 1988).

Table 9.6. Approaches for Modifying Organizational Stressors.

Stressor	Changing the individual	Changing the stressor
Power, authority, and responsibility		
Responsibility pressure	Counseling Behavior modification Supervisory training Selection, placement, and transfer	Participative management Quality circles Acknowledgment
Control rewards/participation	Supervisory training	Participatory management
Change	Counseling	Participative planning
Anticipatory pressure	Counseling	Information exchange Participatory management
Boundary role	Counseling	Decrease the number of boundaries Develop a social support system
Rewards		
Extrinsic	Placement or extrusion	Profit sharing Stock options Employee ownership

Intrinsic	Counseling	Role elaboration Participatory management
Importance	Counseling Sensitivity training	Participatory management
Punishment system		Substitute positive reinforcement
Relations with other people	Counseling	Flextime Job redesign
Promotion	Selection, placement, and transfer	Performance appraisal
Division of labor		
Role conflict	Role definition	Role analysis
Role ambiguity	Role definition	Role analysis and role elaboration
Qualitative overload	Skills training	Role analysis
Quantitative overload	Job redesign	Role analysis

Source: Harris and Dewey, 1984, p. 340. Reprinted with permission.

Table 9.7. Benefits and Costs of Health Promotion Activities.

Benefits	Costs
Reductions in costs of preventable illnesses: Medical costs Wage loss Replacement costs Decreased production due to disability Reduction in quality Reduction in service Turnover	Employee time lost to production during screening, treatment, and participation Amortized facilities costs Amortized equipment costs Staff salaries and benefits Contractor costs Laboratory and testing fees Integration into organization Communications packages Supplies
Reduction in costs of postponable deaths: Life insurance premiums or payouts Wage loss Production loss Value of life Workers' compensation Supervisory time	Opportunity cost of use of funds Maintenance Utilities Insurance Risk
Increase in Morale Productivity Image Work-force quality	

Source: In J. S. Harris, H. D. Belk, and L. W. Wood (eds.), *Managing Employee Health Care Costs.* Beverly, Mass.: OEM Press, 1992. Reprinted with permission.

Whether or not the benefits of health promotion accrue to the employer depends on whether the benefits program is self-insured, experience modified, or fully insured. If high turnover exists, the benefits may accrue to the new employer. Benefits may also accrue over a long period of time. For example, a reevaluation of the Multiple Risk Factor Intervention Trial (a comprehensive clinical intervention to lower cardiac risk among high-risk middle-aged men) showed, in ten years, a significant difference in cardiac mortality, whereas a seven-year evaluation did not (Multiple Risk Factor Intervention Trial Research Group, 1990). Similar results were noted in the North Karelia study in Finland (Puska and others, 1985). Data must also be adjusted for a variety of confounding factors, such as the discount rate, selection bias, medical plan choice, socioeconomic level of participants, benefits inflation, geographic differences in benefits inflation, and medical service use, as well as medical practice patterns, age, gender, and the migration to managed care plans (Harris and Theriault, 1993).

Conclusion

Since life-style and environmental factors are associated with the majority of illnesses and injuries today, it makes sense for employers, who ultimately pay for the consequences, to address these behaviors and other issues in the workplace. The organized structure there can improve the success of health promotion efforts. Further, as medical care costs, and the adverse economic effects of absence from work, continue to escalate, it makes sense to emphasize cost-effective programs that prevent illness and injury. Employees are increasingly demanding health promotion, which follows logically from growing employee involvement and responsibility, wise-use training, and self-care. Prevention and promotion activities would logically be part of a total compensation package as well. As health promotion develops as a discipline, key issues will include the following:

- Integration of all health-related programs at the work site, including health promotion
- Risk-rated benefits
- Improvement in behavioral technologies
- Improvement in communications and media technologies to trigger or support behavior change
- Improvement in data collection and analysis
- More comprehensive planning for prevention and promotion programs

The health promotion approach should be wide ranging, incorporating many or all of the elements discussed here. It should also integrate the focus of the organization and its intended mission, use the social structure of the workplace to reinforce messages and actions, utilize the communications vehicles already present in the workplace, and utilize existing or improved reward systems to encourage healthier life-styles. If health promotion at the work site is to be maximally effective, incentives, verbal and other communication, management support, and the work environment must be aligned to provide a consistent set of messages that support health. If a synergistic program spanning wellness through illness to rehabilitation and reintegration into the work force is effective, it will manage costs and health much more cost-effectively than a medical financing program alone.

CHAPTER TEN

Total Compensation:
Megaflex

The primary impact of benefits cost escalation has been a drop in employees' standards of living as cash wage increases have been constrained and resources have been transferred to the medical sector of the economy (V. R. Fuchs, 1993; Starr, 1992). However, employers have tended to look at benefits, wages, and salaries separately. In fact they are part of a total compensation budget that employers can devote to labor costs. Therefore, an approach that looks at the entire package and allows each employee or family to elect the most appropriate combination package makes sense to optimize both satisfaction and cost control (Abbott, 1993).

Benefits costs are functionally invisible and sometimes incorrectly estimated (see Chapter Eight). However, workers often understand the relationship, or at least the trade-offs. They may realistically attach more value to benefits they already have than to wage increases they may or may not get. They may also understand that benefits costs can rise much faster than wages, so that a preference for benefits is a rational means of financial protection. Benefits constitute a disproportionately large part of total compensation for lower-income employees (who, as a group, may also have higher health risks than usual). Older workers, on the other hand, tend to have both higher wages and higher health risks. It is unlikely, however, that employees completely appreciate the degree to which medical benefits cost increases are suppressing wage gains. Medical benefits do greatly increase total compensation for those who use them, but they have little positive benefit for those who do not. (About 20 percent

241

of employees account for about 80 percent of medical care costs. The 20 percent have much greater collective life-style risks; see Lynch, Teitelbaum, and Main, 1992).

Some employees are aware of this unequal distribution and have responded by asking for greater choice and risk-rated benefits. These demands for choice and economic equity are two of the foundations of the *megaflex* or total compensation approach. The others are based on economic theory. Utility theory posits that if employees are able to select benefits levels and types that they personally regard as most valuable, they should be more satisfied and use the benefits most optimally. In particular, overinsurance should decrease. In addition, the "price tags" used in a flexible compensation system should make employees more aware of the true costs of medical care if structured to reflect actual costs. The information needed to administer this type of plan (derived from employee preferences) provides much clearer and more detailed data on preferred utility, which can be used for strategic health management.

The rationale for a total compensation budget and an individual selection approach might be to:

- Increase available choices of benefits levels and types
- Increase the utility of benefits to each employee
- Use a total compensation approach to labor costs
- Increase data capture and use
- Increase the net value of benefits by using pretax dollars
- Reduce payroll taxes

Flexible benefits plans have multiple goals. Primary among them is to "maximize utility," or increase the personal value of the choices made to employees. By purchasing the best personal combination of benefits, employees would tend not to over- or underinsure and would therefore not over- or underuse medical services.

A related intent is to offer more choice. Paradoxically, this may defeat the purpose of reducing the number of suppliers to better manage care (see Chapter Eleven), but it certainly supports individual customization of benefits. According to this theory, the 16 percent of companies that are not currently offering HMO plans will make one available to employees in the next two years, and many of those that do not offer a PPO plan would make one available. About 20 percent of employers already offering these plans would add more options to those that employees already have (Taylor and Leitman, 1989).

The progress toward "Work Force 2000" continues apace. With changing demographics and a shortage of experienced employees in certain occupations, employers may be competing in a seller's market for labor for key occupations. Yet there has been little overt progress to adapt work-site conditions and benefits packages to older workers, female workers with multiple responsibilities, untrained younger workers, speakers of English as a second language, and immigrants with other specific needs and cultural values. Flexible benefits plans should be able to offer options that meet the needs of these diverse groups.

Flexible benefits plans also provide the opportunity for dual-wage-earner families to eliminate duplication of coverage by using their benefits dollars for options other than duplicate health insurance, increasing price sensitivity by exposing these families to copayments and deductibles. This has in fact happened ("Strategies in Section 125," 1991).

Employees prefer choice. In a survey by the Employers' Council on Flexible Compensation, 93 percent of women and 80 percent of men who had been involved in a flexible benefits plan did not want to go back to standard benefits plans. These plans clearly meet employee needs.

A recent survey revealed that 27 percent of firms with more than a thousand workers prefer full flex plans — that is, all benefits are in the menu (Hewitt Associates, 1992). Forty-five percent of those with union employees were already offering flex plans, while 15 percent more intend to add them.

Flexible Benefits Plan Structure and Mechanics

Several types of flexible benefits plans are permitted under Section 125 of the Internal Revenue Service Code. These plans offer a choice between taxable and nontaxable benefits.

244 Strategic Health Management

Flexible Spending Accounts

In a *flexible spending account* (FSA), employees can choose cash, health care coverage, or dependent care. A subtype of an FSA is a *premium conversion account,* in which contributions for health insurance can be made pretax. This decreases the employee's taxable income and the employer's payroll taxes.

Health Care Spending Accounts

Another type of flexible benefits plan for health care is a standalone *health care spending account.* Employees with this plan can set aside pretax dollars for medical expenses not covered by medical insurance.

Cafeteria Plans

Full flex benefits, otherwise known as *cafeteria plans,* allow a wide variety of choices. Employees are given "credits" or a personal budget they can allocate among a number of options such as day care, life insurance, legal insurance, and in some cases additional vacation or direct compensation. Examples are shown in Table 10.1.

Elder care is becoming particularly important. A third of families are involved in the care of an elderly relative. Most of the caregivers are female, and many are in the work force. Elder care benefits have been shown to increase productivity and decrease absenteeism, tardiness, and telephone use by these people, who are increasingly torn between work and family responsibilities.

Megaflex

The trend is now toward *megaflex,* or the total compensation approach, in which trade-offs are allowed between a wide variety of benefits as well as cash wages. This overt, priced exchange makes very explicit the trade-offs the employees are making be-

Table 10.1. Typical Cafeteria Plan Options.

Nontaxable benefits	Taxable benefits
Medical insurance	Vacation benefits
Child care	Deferred compensation
Life insurance	Long-term care
Dental insurance	
Day care	
Eye care	
Life-style programs	
Education and training	
Retirement programs (401K)	
Elder care	
Family assistance	

tween various levels of benefits, between managed and unmanaged care (which typically have different price tags), and between benefits and cash wages.

Shaping the Flexible Benefits Program

The flexible benefits strategy must be grounded in the desire to manage all compensation as a single line item, in order to take the "big-picture" approach. It is almost imperative to use strategic planning to clarify the goals for flex programs and then to plan a multiyear implementation. Because of their complex nature, flexible benefits require planning, a timetable, and a clear budget. In fact, overt design of delivery systems using a flexible approach has been advocated by the Employers' Council on Flexible Compensation as almost mandatory. Part of the strategic planning process includes participation by employees in the design phase for various options.

A strategic plan is also needed because a paradigm shift is involved in moving to a flexible compensation scheme. Flexible benefits are complicated multiyear endeavors that, while they can save a good deal of money by various means and increase morale, satisfaction, and the perceived value of benefits, require top management support to "stay the course" and to make the necessary initial investment. They also require a shift from paternalism to empowerment, as employees become more aware of their options, explore the reasons for pricing differences, and even exercise some control over plan design. Open and effective employee education, a new enrollment and information system, and interactive communications are required. Possible goals for the plan might include any or all of the following:

Meeting Employee Demands

- To increase information gathered about employee preferences
- To increase employee choice
- To decrease taxable income for employees
- To adapt to work-force diversity
- To vary contributions according to preferences
- To allow variety by location

Improving Financial Performance

- To decrease state payroll taxes and social security levies
- To meet competitive pressure
- To contain costs through defined contribution options and caps
- To unify benefits programs under one umbrella

Restoring Market Forces to Medical Care

- To educate employees about benefits value and cost
- To increase employee involvement
- To make the wage-benefit trade-off clear to employees
- To restore price sensitivity by increasing potential out-of-pocket expenses
- To control costs by increasing the utility of benefits design choices
- To provide a framework for new benefits

Design Data

A key source of data that should inform management and help shape the flex package is a detailed analysis of claims history (see the discussion of claims data analysis in Chapter Six). This analysis can also be used to gain knowledge of relative prices paid for various procedures and diagnoses under the current plan. Using techniques to project service use in the future, price tags can be assigned for various coverage options to keep the plan cost-neutral. Simulations can be used to determine what would happen to plan costs under various employee participation scenarios. This is high-level sensitivity analysis in business terms.

The mechanics of the flex plan should allow monitoring of utilization and the quality of care. This means that data from various optional plans should be available and integrated into a common data base to allow evaluation of overall utilization, quality, and costs.

Comment and Test Marketing

It is helpful for employee groups to make suggestions and review proposed flex packages, including communications. This is a critical role, since it is quite possible to make flexible benefits plans so abstruse that the average employee cannot understand them.

One could test market plans using statistical techniques such as conjoint analysis and technology such as interactive voice response to conduct a mock enrollment or to poll employees about their preferences and utilities. While a model including information on previous use, health status (gained through surveys or Health Risk Appraisals), and mock delivery option selections would tend to be complex, the more variables that are introduced the more accurate the model would tend to be, at least in theory. This information would shape the options that are selected and the way they are priced.

Risk-Rating Flex Plan Options

One interesting possible design option for flexible plans is to include incentives for positive life-style changes or low–health risk behaviors. It is now well known that employees and dependents who have higher levels of health risk such as smoking, lack of exercise, heavy alcohol use, driving without seatbelts, and overweight have significantly higher benefits costs and utilization (Brink, 1987). This finding has been replicated in a number of other studies. It would therefore make sense to "level the playing field" by having employees pay for services they are likely to use, given voluntary life-style choices. One study, for example, showed that smokers can cost at least $1,000 more on average than nonsmokers. Employers have often chosen not to collect the entire differential. For example, one major food manufacturer capped the differential at $600. These programs often provide incentives for employees to change their life-style, but they are not intended to be coercive. They are intended to meet objections from those who lead healthy lives that they should not be subsidizing others' dangerous habits. Including family members in the choice of benefits plan and helping them become wiser users of medical care is crucial.

Managed Care Integration

One critical issue is how to integrate flexible benefits with managed care. This can be clarified during the strategic planning process. Business decisions that would have to be made include selecting an incentive or penalty structure for the use of various networks and the type of managed care plan to be included. A multiple-option plan is often a good place to start if one is attempting to use flexible benefits to move toward a system of managed care. Another option might be a PPO. It would be very important to include elements of managed care in high-option plans, which have the most comprehensive coverage. As previously noted, 70 percent of costs are generated by 10 percent of employees due to ill health or other psychosocial factors. These are the very employees who would overtly select a high-option plan in order to reduce personal financial exposure (Sperling, 1993).

It would be equally important to ensure that utilization management is included with nonmanaged plans, because employees and dependents with chronic or catastrophic illnesses — who typically have a long-term relationship with a physician — will select indemnity plans since they do not wish to change providers. It is worth noting again that there is no cost sensitivity as soon as the out-of-pocket maximum is reached, which happens sooner rather than later with individuals who use major medical services, so that utilization management is imperative.

Plan sponsors often intend to implement more stringent managed care in the long term but use a flexible benefits or total compensation strategy as a transition. The two are not entirely compatible philosophically, since managed care restrict choice to some extent. (The "choice," of course, is choice of providers within the health plan, not choice of all benefits options within the flex plan.) Point-of-service plans are a good interim design as long as incentives of at least 20 to 30 percent between in- and out-of-plan costs are used. With this level of differential, the extra out-of-plan cost to the employee should compensate for higher price and volume, allowing the plan to break even. Use of large copayments is also a good point-of-need deterrent to leaving the network. Another alternative might be an open-ended HMO with a gatekeeper function. If PPOs are used, varying the deductible, copayment, and out-of-pocket maximum could also steer employees to in-plan providers, who presumably are more efficient or at least have lower unit prices.

In pricing and financing managed care plans as flexible benefits options, then, it is important to look at the following factors:

- Total expense of claims
- Enrollment patterns anticipated
- Any adverse selection that might result
- Utilization differences
- Effectiveness of gatekeepers
- Discounts that might be gained in managed care plans
- Administrative expenses
- Network design
- Geographic coverage
- Contract terms
- Initial costs, including administrative systems and communications

Better information systems for enrollment and tracking will be needed to manage individual choice and to have a better grasp of what costs are being accrued and how to manage them. That in itself is an advantage for strategic management. Individual benefit communications, interactive voice response, and video can all be used for education purposes and to help with informed choice. One important maxim to keep in mind is "keep it simple," since flexible benefits are already fairly complex. If they become so complex as to become incomprehensible, the advantages of employee choice are lost.

Conclusion

Flexible benefits plans, as part of a total compensation strategy, require a greater initial expense and are more complex than indemnity plans. However, they increase utility by allowing flexibility and choice and are well accepted by employees and dependents. More complete information collection improves the ability to manage the plan and total expenses. Flex plans can also provide a platform for risk-rating benefits and introducing managed care. Finally, they help to accommodate the needs of an increasingly diverse work force.

Reconciling the philosophical differences between flexible benefits and managed care requires careful thought and presentation to employees. It may be that, with well-educated consumers, the two choices are alternatives rather than points along the continuum. This is still a subject of debate.

CHAPTER ELEVEN

Alliances
with Managed Care

Managing care is a more active and involved method of managing benefits costs and medical quality than simply defining a plan and managing the financing of care. It is an operations management approach rather than a financial one, looking "inside the box" rather than accepting an "intact product" from insurers or providers. It therefore affords a greater opportunity to increase the value of purchased care. It also requires added expertise and involvement, provided by the strategic health management team.

A number of methods are currently in use to manage care (Iglehart, 1992b). There is some confusion about the different activities that are currently being designated as "managed care." To completely manage care, one must manage price, volume, technology, and quality. This can be done either by oversight management through third-party organizations, by economic incentives and contracting, or by active management of practice and processes by health providers themselves.

Employers might therefore have objectives to manage care in the following ways, for the reasons given:

- To manage the volume of medical care — to reduce or eliminate medically unnecessary diagnostic measures and treatment
- To manage the price of care — to avoid becoming a victim of cost shifting and to pay more nearly market-appropriate prices

251

- To manage technology—so that only cost-effective pharmaceutical, medical, and surgical technology is used
- To manage quality—to increase the appropriateness, efficiency, and effectiveness of care; if improved, it should have
  a major impact on the first three points

Managed care of various sorts is taking an increasing share
of the medical care market. According to the Health Insurance
Association of America, only 18 percent of plans were traditional
fee for service in 1989 (Standard and Poor, 1991a). Managed fee-
for-service plans accounted for 49 percent of total health care benefits in 1990, HMOs accounted for 17 percent, and PPOs accounted for 16 percent. (It is not clear whether these statistics
referred to fully paid plans or whether they included self-insured
plans, since Standard and Poor surveys commercial organizations.) The proportion of employers offering HMOs has risen
from 54 percent in 1986 to 63 percent in 1990, and the proportion
offering PPOs has risen at a much faster rate—from 15 percent
in 1986 to 32 percent in 1990 (Piacentini and Foley, 1992).

In another survey of the largest 2,500 companies in the
United States, by 1992, even with multiple plans available, only
22 percent offered traditional fee-for-service alternatives. Managed fee-for-service plans increased from 57 to 69 percent. Fifty-
six percent offered staff or group-model HMOs, 50 percent
offered IPAs, and 22 percent offered point-of-service plans.
Thirty-five percent offered PPOs. The most rapid growth was
in point-of-service plans, which more than quadrupled, and in
PPOs, which more than doubled. The largest companies offered
managed care somewhat more often than the full group. In particular, IPAs were offered by 9 percent more companies than
the previous survey by the same organization showed, and point-
of-service plans were offered by 34 percent more. The respondents also felt that PPOs were not particularly tough in excluding physicians with high costs (Taylor and Leitman, 1989, 1990).
The role of HMOs is considerably larger in some employer
groups, particularly large ones. The largest employers appear
to have about one-third of their employees enrolled in HMOs
(Gold, 1992).

Utilization review of high-cost outpatient services has now been included in 75 percent of plans. Slightly over half restricted the types of procedures or technologies covered. Presumably this meant excluding experimental technology. Slightly less than half offered mail order drugs to obtain discounts. Only 34 percent had primary care physicians serving as gatekeepers for referrals. Only one-third recorded generic substitution drugs, 26 percent contracted with centers of excellence, and 18 percent provided rewards for efficient high-quality providers (Taylor and Leitman, 1989, 1990; Field and Shapiro, 1993).

The conclusion seems to be that while large companies are moving away from traditional fee-for-service plans to more restrictive managed indemnity, they offer a wide range of options and seem to be reluctant to move employees into tightly managed plans. Proven effective methods such as gatekeepers, generic substitutions, centers of excellence, and restriction of questionable procedures are not used that often.

The success of managed care in attracting members is related to potential enrollees' knowledge of the options, how they work, and how cost effective they are. Employees in general are not well informed about managed care plans. For example, 31 percent of the public were unaware that one generally must choose a primary care physician in HMOs; 44 percent were unaware that HMOs provided more preventive care. Forty percent were unaware of whether it was more difficult to see a physician in an HMO than in fee-for-service medicine, and 46 percent did not know whether HMOs were more expensive than other options (Employee Benefits Research Institute, 1990).

The public was also ignorant about PPOs, which are often (mistakenly) regarded as more liberal HMO lookalikes. (Admittedly, some of the confusion exists because PPO design is highly variable, with a few requiring a gatekeeper physician and some using utilization review.) Fifty-two percent did not know whether one must choose a primary care physician in a PPO panel. Fifty-eight percent were unaware of whether PPOs provide more preventive care; 55 percent were unaware of the difficulty or lack of it in seeing a physician in a PPO, and 61 percent were unaware of the relative expense of PPOs compared to other options (and presumably in or out of network) (Employee Benefits Research Institute, 1990).

Employers who wish to persuade employees to move into more managed environments would do well to charge contribution rates in proportion to the actual cost of the plan rather than following the usual tack of trying to equalize the total out-of-pocket amount paid by the employees. Better yet, they could offer a fixed risk-adjusted contribution toward all plans and let any remaining expense be out of pocket (H. S. Luft, personal communication, Aug. 1993). Some recent studies indicate that the choice of plan is highly sensitive to relative out-of-pocket price to the individual or the family (Long, Settle, and Wrightson, 1988).

While widely used, the distinctions between the various types of management of the price, volume, and appropriateness of care are not well understood. Further, their relative effectiveness and effects on providers and employees bear discussion.

Externally Imposed Management of Care

Management, or active intervention in the broader medical care delivery and financing process, takes a number of forms and can be classified in several ways. While the mechanics of "medical management" are intuitively understood by those who deal with it routinely, the potential and actual effects of each intervention are different. It is therefore important to understand the similarities and differences and the expected and actual outcomes of each technique to fit the method to the intended effect.

Management may be agreed to or externally imposed on providers without agreement in advance, usually through a contract between the managing organization and individuals or groups of providers. Management may be retrospective, concurrent, or prospective. It may be implicit, using "professional expertise," or it may be explicit, using carefully considered, agreed-on definitions, methods, guidelines, and standards. Prospective and explicit management is generally more effective, as well as more reproducible, than retrospective or implicit techniques. Some highly successful managed care organizations have used implicit approaches. These have tended to be staff or group-model HMOs with enough daily contact among careful providers to have developed standard yet unwritten processes of care. There are still opportunities for quality improvement even in these organizations, ranging from better customer service (a primary need) to better production efficiency (see Chapter Three) to fine-tuning clinical care.

Any type of management has the potential to antagonize patients and providers and can complicate rather than improve the situation. Therefore, both the relationships with all "customers" of the management process and the efficiency of the process must be carefully considered and executed.

Retrospective Techniques

A number of retrospective techniques are in common use to manage the price of care, either per unit or on an aggregate basis. The latter involves repackaging separated charges that are customarily paid as a global or single fee.

Bill Review. Bill review, a reasonable activity in most business relationships, is sometimes marketed as a form of managed care. While this does not involve managing care per se, the financial aspects of medical care are now commonly managed by *retrospective* review of bills. In the unmanaged, or indemnity, situation there is no agreement on the services to be provided or the price. (There is also no agreement on quality of care, even if that could be agreed on or measured.) As a result, providers are free in nonmanaged situations to increase prices as they see fit, driving up the usual, customary, and reasonable profiles in the community. Bill review is an action by the reviewer without prior agreement by providers that they will abide by payment decisions. This may result in conflict and ill will if employees receive bills for the balance.

Bills are most frequently reviewed for charge levels and adherence to standard billing practices. Typically, practitioner bills will be reviewed against a statistical average of fees for each procedural code in their geographic area and paid at a given percentile. This is known as usual, customary, and reasonable payment. The percentile used is an employer decision; it may range from the 50th to the 95th depending on the payer. At percentiles above about the 75th percentile, virtually all charges are paid and the exercise is relatively futile in net, considering the administrative expense and aggravation for all parties concerned. This form of control is only relative, since the usual, customary, and reasonable level rises as each practitioner raises charges and the percentiles therefore move up, creating a moving target.

A number of providers have now started to charge for every segment of a procedure using separate procedure codes. This process, known as *unbundling,* can increase fees by several fold. It is not justified by any additional labor or supply expense but is typically used as a method of increasing fees to the full-pay sector to compensate for Medicare or managed care discounts or caps. If providers "unbundle" surgical procedures, for example, the bill can be several times higher than it would be once rebundled. Bill review software is supposed to detect and reverse unbundling of surgical and other procedures.

Some practitioners also now routinely engage in "upcoding," in which, for example, they will charge for an extended visit even when a limited one was performed. This practice is recommended by some practice management consultants under the label *revenue enhancement.* Providers can and do "balance bill" patients, sending a bill to patients for amounts not paid by the funding organization. These amounts can be significant.

In addition, software has been developed to "profile" providers and look at the relative percentages of brief, limited, intermediate, and extended provider visits. If the profile is skewed toward the upper end of the curve, visits may be recoded with or without medical records.

Partly because it is not agreed to in advance, retrospective review has engendered a good deal of paperwork, animosity, and administrative complexity in the appeals and resubmission process. It also increases expenses for providers by reducing immediate cash flow and creating the need for financing of working capital. The situation is exacerbated by the fact that many providers submit incomplete, inconsistent, redundant, or late bills, so that the payment cycle is stretched out for months. This then engenders a cycle of repeat billing (especially if it triggers an automated billing cycle), appeal, record submission, and carping to physicians. It clearly drives up administrative costs.

Many hospitals, which are now paid in some states and by Medicare on a *diagnostic related group* (DRG) basis, have installed sophisticated software that will find the most remunerative DRG supported by the medical record and bill accordingly. This in turn has spawned a counterindustry of DRG downcoding run by payers or third parties. In many cases, hospitals then load all charges that were not paid by Medicare, Medicaid, and managed care organizations onto "full payers," and may double or triple the charge. (If this charge is reduced by a review organization, or care is denied as inappropriate and a bill for the balance is sent, it can easily amount to half or more of an average family's yearly income.)

Retrospective File Review. Many review organizations state that they review medical records, either as a quality assurance exercise or to ensure payment only for medically necessary diagnostic tests and treatments. This is one way of managing the volume of care on a forward basis, albeit using financial tools. In some cases, the review organizations will deny payment or at least send warning letters for procedures that appear to be medically unnecessary based on the diagnosis.

Retrospective appropriateness review is a complicated undertaking because many providers will not submit a diagnosis with their bill, causing "suspension" of the bill and then demands for medical records. This is one way to detect, although with a rather wide net, medically unnecessary care. Warning letters sometimes have a sentinel effect that causes providers to think more carefully about what they are doing, but they often do not have this effect because many different providers are used by a given group of workers. The letters have no force, and again there is no contract between the provider and the payer.

There has been little published to quantify savings from bill review or retrospective chart audits. One should therefore carefully reanalyze any claims of savings made by vendors. Based on empirical examinations of billing practices, savings should be considerable, but one should always understand the methodology used and demand frequent usable reports.

Prospective and Concurrent Techniques

Several prospective and concurrent approaches deserve mention.

Prospective Payment. Paying for care on a per case basis is one form of price management. While this has been instituted in a number of states and by some employers, the only well-designed evidence on its effect comes from the Medicare Prospective Payment System, which was adopted in 1985. According to one study, a drop in admission rates of 10.3 percent occurred in two years when Medicare put in a prospective payment system that reimbursed on a case-by-case basis by diagnostic group (Feldstein, 1988). While hospital occupancy rates dropped, outpatient care rose significantly — particularly outpatient surgery. Several other studies show increases in outpatient costs offset drops in inpatient costs (Holahan, Dor, and Zuckerman, 1990; Russell and Manning, 1989).

Volume Management

Most prospective and concurrent techniques are intended to manage the volume of care. Aspects of these programs can be used to manage the appropriate application of technology and medical quality, although the latter two areas are not generally explicitly structured or widely applied.

Second Surgical Opinions. Second surgical opinions, or independent assessments of the need for surgery, were pioneered at Cornell/New York Hospital Medical Center in the mid 1970s. They were initially quite effective, demonstrating that over 30 percent of surgeries were inappropriate. However, this was true only when the opinion was obtained by practitioners not associated with the person proposing to do the procedure. For reasons that are not entirely clear, the number of disallowed procedures from second surgical opinions has decreased markedly.

One might think that the spread of utilization review and managed care would have created de facto standards of care. Documentation is improving and in some cases can actually be obtained to check its rigor and accuracy. However, it is not clear, especially in light of the data on inappropriate admissions and procedures from the RAND studies (see Chapter Three), that the prevalence of inappropriate surgery is decreasing. In addition, in many areas the second opinion comes from someone associated with the proposed surgeon, blunting the incentive to be accurate.

Many review companies now use target lists of specific procedures, which does improve the yield but may miss uncommon but not well-thought-out procedures. If one were to focus on commonly misapplied procedures such as hysterectomy and Caesarean section using rigorous diagnostic replication and stringent and logical therapeutic criteria during a telephonic or preauthorization records review, as the author has observed in a few managed care organizations, the yield might well be increased.

Precertification. Utilization review, or its expanded version, utilization management, was developed in the 1980s to manage the volume and appropriateness of medical care as costs rose rapidly and it became apparent that many hospital stays and days were medically unnecessary. That is, the procedures or treatments either should not have been performed or could have been done safely in a less intensive setting. Hospital precertification was the first form of utilization review. One might think that this technique would screen proposed admissions for appropriateness, but in fact precertification as actually practiced focused instead on reducing inpatient lengths of stay to statistical averages by certifying payment for only that number of days. These programs have been faulted for failing to halt inappropriate admissions and inappropriate surgeries; only 1 to 2 percent of admissions are typically denied (Grey and Field, 1989).

Initially reviewers used the United States averages, which blended a wide spectrum of dissimilar practice patterns and variable practices, at a relatively high percentile. Judging by present knowledge, which reveals that the aggregate number of bed-days per 1,000 people can be reduced to the low 100s in the

best-managed care organizations, that "standard" and the practice of allowing virtually all admissions resulted in two to five
times the number of hospital days that were necessary under
the best conditions.

The state of the art has gradually changed; better utilization review programs now use the lengths of stay for the
Western region of the United States at the 25th percentile. As
more structured practice guidelines are introduced, some inappropriate admissions are being denied or rerouted to other
settings. Even though the decisions are framed as being made
for payment and not medical management, to avoid legal issues of practicing medicine without actual knowledge of the patient, and even though there is no contract, the best-managed
indemnity programs have reduced the hospital utilization rate
by half or more. Programs this effective are not common, however, and the quality of utilization management varies widely.

Concurrent Review. Precertification programs have been expanded to include *concurrent review* of records during hospitalization for both appropriateness and length of stay. Unfortunately,
uniform criteria for appropriateness, which are available to reviewers, are rarely used. *Discharge planning* is typically sold as
a separate activity but in fact is part of the continuum of care
for hospital stays.

Outpatient Review. As treatment is shifted to the outpatient setting and the cost of outpatient diagnostic treatment procedures
have increased, a focus on the ambulatory environment is clearly
warranted. However, outpatient review has been implemented
very slowly. A number of problems, such as the cost-effectiveness
of requiring certification for a multitude of relatively low-cost
procedures, have slowed its development.

Providers also regard precertification for referrals and for
imaging and other diagnostic procedures as excessively intrusive, although judging from the proportion of medically inappropriate referrals and procedures detected in a typical review
program, this is hardly a defensible position. Practice parameters
for ambulatory care against which proposed diagnostic testing

and treatment can be evaluated are badly needed. It would clearly be preferable for provider organizations to take over these functions, but to date they have not done so effectively except in capitated and a few other HMOs.

Prescription Drug Utilization Management. Managed care networks, employers, and hospitals have taken steps to manage the cost and volume of prescription medication use. This is an important area in which to reduce variance and inappropriate use, since medication reactions are common. The elderly in particular often are the subject of unneeded polypharmacy and may become impaired because of overmedication. Pharmaceutical management efforts have included the following interventions:

- Generic substitution for high-cost but equivalent drugs
- Use of formularies that restrict the use of therapeutic options to those that are most cost effective
- Prior authorization programs for expensive and possibly unproven medications
- Therapeutic substitution programs, primarily in hospitals
- Step therapy
- Information systems to review drug use

One problem is that without a contract, there is no obligation to comply with utilization management. When utilization management or bill review organizations reduce fees or refuse to pay for medically unnecessary care, providers in the unmanaged situation (and even sometimes in the managed situation) often vent their frustration in front of the patient, neutralizing any positive employee relations benefits and even creating a negative effect for the plan.

How Well Does Utilization Management Work?

It is not clear how well utilization management has worked. In 1989, the Institute of Medicine convened a group of experts to evaluate utilization management activities to determine their effectiveness and their effect on the quality of care (Grey and

Field, 1989). The conclusions were not encouraging. The panel determined that a wide variation in the effectiveness of the programs existed. There seemed to be some effect on reducing the number of bed-days per thousand but almost no effect on admission rates for hospital care. The panel did not comment on the effectiveness of outpatient review. The impact of utilization management on total cost was less clear, because savings were offset by increased spending for outpatient care and administration of the utilization management program. The committee found that systematic evidence of the impact of utilization management on quality was virtually nonexistent.

In one case that the author is familiar with, there was a gradual decline in adjusted bed-days per thousand from over 600 to below 400 with increasingly stringent benchmarks. The utilization management company had switched from the regional 50th percentile to the national 50th percentile to the Western regional 50th to the Western regional 25th (Harris, 1985b, 1986, 1987, 1988a). Each time this happened, the number of bed-days per thousand decreased. Anecdotally, stringent managed care can reduce both inpatient and outpatient utilization by 20 to 40 percent, but these results are derived from audits or studies of utilization programs rather than published studies.

The only well-controlled and peer reviewed utilization review study showed that an early generation private review reduced inpatient days by 11 percent, with a 7 percent reduction in hospital expenditures and a total reduction in expenses to about 6 percent. The study also showed that admissions fell by about 13 percent. The results remained the same after adjusting for illness, age, gender, coordination of benefits, HMO impact, number of physicians in the area, geographic region, deductibles, and coinsurance (Feldstein, Wickizer, and Wheeler, 1988; Wickizer, Wheeler, and Feldstein, 1989).

In a study pooling data from eight Houston-area employers, utilization review significantly reduced total inpatient charges per insured and significantly increased total outpatient charges per insured. The result was a net increase in cost of 9.6 percent in that particular market (Custer, 1989).

In fairness to utilization management organizations, many

employers have told them not to be very aggressive in order not to upset providers or employees. However, a good part of the observed lack of effectiveness is due, at least empirically, to lack of explicit or stringent standards of care, particularly for the medical necessity of admission. The standards used in utilization review organizations may be sketchy or may rely on the clinical experience of the reviewer. This has led to wide variance in the process and effectiveness of utilization management. Absence or lack of rigor of utilization standards is an invitation both to disputes and legal actions.

Utilization management was supposed to stabilize the process of medical care, but if this approach itself is a variable process, it will not accomplish that goal. A good way to start standardizing the process of utilization management might be to have practice protocols on line and to have collection and use of those data elements be mandatory. Utilization management works in theory, but the proof is in the execution. Only with a standardized, effective process, with adequate systems support and continuous improvement, will utilization management realize its potential (Harris, 1992c).

Inpatient care now accounts for less than half of all costs, so focusing on inpatient management is only a partial solution. Even though outpatient care has accounted for the bulk of medical care costs for several years, few utilization management programs provide effective management for outpatient care.

Bilateral or Agreed-to Management of Care

In indemnity insurance, there is no contract between buyers and sellers of medical care and no operational management of that care. Managed care, on the other hand, is a group of financing and organizational methods and entities based on agreements between providers and buyers of medical care specifying price and in some instances volume and quality. One of the main advantages of the managed care plans discussed below — including PPOs, HMOs, and newer hybrids such as dual or triple options and open-ended HMOs — is the contract and therefore explicit agreement between the provider and the financing organization on the services to be provided, at least in general terms, and the price.

A number of managed care structures have developed. The distinctions are blurring as PPOs add utilization management and as HMOs add less restrictive options. Nevertheless, a review of the pure types of management agreements is useful to understand their features and effectiveness.

Preferred Provider Organizations

According to the Commerce Department (Francis, 1993), there were about 27 million people enrolled in about 650 PPOs at the end of 1991. This number may be significantly higher, depending on one's definition. Total membership is lower than HMO membership but has grown much more rapidly in the recent past. Public knowledge about PPOs is somewhat limited. Nonenrollees therefore do not express a great deal of interest in joining (Taylor and Leitman, 1991a).

PPOs are essentially arrangements between providers and payers to reduce fees by some mechanism. In some cases, PPO providers will agree to a defined fee schedule. The most common form of preferred provider arrangement, however, is one in which there is a discount from retail charges. Because charges are typically loaded to compensate for discounts to Medicare, Medicaid, and HMO beneficiaries, what appears to be retail is actually inflated by a significant amount. The question then is, discounts from what? For example, if the mean charge for an office visit should be $50 but Medicare and other similar organizations are paying only $30, full-pay patients may encounter charges of $70 or higher if there are more reduced-fee patients than full-pay patients. While reducing this by 20 percent is protecting the payer to some extent, it is not reducing the charge toward a reasonable level determined by market forces. Further, discount arrangements typically do not prevent providers from raising their charges periodically.

Some hospitals have agreed to per diem charges in PPO arrangements. These are typically in the thousand-dollar range, which can be anywhere from 20 to 80 to 90 percent of fully loaded charges. In other words, the fully loaded charges may be anywhere from the per diem amount to $10,000 a day for intensive care. One problem with hospital per diem contracts is that they have frequently been negotiated to include an "escape hatch." In these arrangements, unless per diems equal some percentage of charges (anywhere from 60 to 80 percent), total payments will be increased to that percentage. Thus, as charges are raised or loaded through cost shifting, the savings effect is significantly reduced.

In many PPOs, the arrangement is nonexclusive. It is possible to use any provider at a higher copayment or those in a PPO network with a reduced copayment. Some employers have reduced the copayment to 10 percent or 0 in an attempt to "steer" people into the PPO. This low level of copayment is such that there is little disincentive not to use the system. Fairly wide splits, in the range of 20 to 40 percent, are probably needed to ensure high in-network use rates in PPOs, although this also seems to depend on customer satisfaction and employee communications.

In the pure form of PPOs, no management of utilization exists. A significant copayment should probably be retained to deter medically unnecessary use if there is no utilization management. Many PPOs are now combined with utilization review to increase their impact. In this form, they resemble network-model HMOs without fixed prepayment.

Prepaid Care

The earliest attempt at managing care used both financial incentives and the organization of medical care to ensure access and payment. These *prepaid health plans,* in which providers were paid a specific amount per employee (or per capita, thus "capitation"), included what became the Kaiser Foundation Health Plans and the Ross-Loos Medical Plan in Southern California. These plans agreed to provide all necessary care for a fixed amount. Other prepaid plans arose in the Midwest during the Depression. Blue Cross and Blue Shield plans were prepaid service benefit plans that were formed during that time to ensure payment to physicians and hospitals while guaranteeing access to

employed groups (Starr, 1982). Prepayment was simply an economic measure to attempt to match resource use with a fixed
budget. The Blues, in contrast to HMOs, agreed to pay for what
the patient could find and use within the service benefit definitions. They did not facilitate access or coordination of care. It
did not necessarily guarantee the most efficacious management
of price, volume, or quality but did force attention to those issues.

Health Maintenance Organizations

HMOs are comprehensive prepaid plans that are the descen-
dants of these early organizations. HMO enrollment grew from
six million in 1976 to over forty million in 1991, or 18 percent
of all Americans. Enrollment growth decelerated in the late
1980s, from 21 percent per year in 1987 to about 5 percent in
1991 (Standard and Poor, 1992).

The biggest increases in HMO enrollment were among
people between forty and sixty-four; this group enrolled at a
faster rate than younger individuals. An increase among upper-
income people has also occurred. The rate of HMO membership among people with household incomes of more than $50,000
increased from 7 percent in 1987 to 18 percent in 1991. College graduates continue to join HMOs at a slightly greater rate
than those with lower education levels (from 11 percent in 1987
to 18 percent in 1991).

The decrease in the HMO growth rate reflects increasing
market saturation, employer and employee dissatisfaction over
cost savings versus expectations, and questions about quality of
care (generally speculative and unproven). Some observers think
that a good deal of this dissatisfaction has to do with poor perceived customer service and interpersonal issues rather than the
quality of clearly needed care, because satisfaction surveys of
HMO enrollees typically show that enrollees are more satisfied
with the quality of urgent or emergency care (that is, situations
where the diagnosis or need for intervention was not in dispute)
than those in fee-for-service systems (Taylor and Leitman, 1991a).

Dissatisfaction could also reflect "shadow pricing," in
which many HMOs have prices only slightly lower than the in-

demnity pricing in their market. Thus they appear to be less expensive, but they were not pricing close to their achievable cost figures. However, HMOs, particularly those qualified under the Federal HMO Act, provide preventive services as well as diagnostic and curative services. There are some mental health benefits, but they are typically more restrictive than any indemnity plans. There is considerable debate about the cost-effectiveness of much inpatient mental health and substance abuse care and some outpatient care, and this difference does affect the value of the package. Many managed care plans do not have deductibles and did not have copayments. (Recently, however, a number of plans have added copayments to deter medically unnecessary use as an alternative to queuing.) Thus while the cost to the employer may appear to be close to indemnity levels, the total out-of-pocket cost to the employee, especially including preventive services, is often much lower. This provides some incentive for employees to sign up for managed care plans. The comparison is therefore "apples to oranges," but the perception that HMOs are shadow pricing persists, particularly on the part of employers.

There are several types of HMO, with varying degrees of management control. The original prepaid care was delivered by a closed panel of physicians. This model was introduced at about the same time by the Health Insurance Plan of Greater New York, Kaiser, and the Ross-Loos Group. Prepayment introduced incentives for efficient care that could frequently only be delivered through organized practice. More recent models of managed care include Independent Practice Associations (IPAs), in which individual physicians contract with a financing organization, and networks, which may be groups of group practices or individuals who contract with a fiscal intermediary. Despite the managed care label, overt standards of care or utilization management may not exist, particularly in IPAs or some group models.

In staff-model HMOs, the clinicians are paid a salary and perhaps a bonus by the organization — for example, the Group Health Cooperative of Puget Sound. In group models, a group practice contracts with one or more fiscal intermediaries. The

Permanente Medical Group, for instance, contracts with Kaiser Foundation Health Plan, the financing vehicle. A network model is a combination of groups and independent practitioners. Simply defining an HMO's organizational model does not define the method by which the providers are paid within the fixed payment made by employers or individuals to the financing organization. Provider payment in models other than the staff model may range from discounted fees for service to a fee schedule to capitation (fixed prepayment per person). One reason for the popularity of nonstaff models among providers is that they escape the risk element of capitation. Providers in general do not like capitation because they are afraid of having one or two very expensive patients in their practice and running a deficit. In fact, they also do not wish to deal with the economic aspects of practice. Another is that some states, such as California, have statutes prohibiting the "corporate practice of medicine," necessitating the use of group models to avoid violating the law.

Group and staff models predominate in the West and Mountain regions. HMOs are most numerous on the West Coast and in Minnesota, Massachusetts, and the District of Columbia, all of which have more than 25 percent of the population enrolled in such organizations. Oregon, Arizona, Wisconsin, Connecticut, Michigan, and Utah have between 15 and 25 percent of their populations enrolled in HMOs. These all tend to be states with concentrations of large industries. In 1990, 12.3 percent of the plans with 12.4 percent of enrollees were staff models, 13.5 percent of plans with 29.9 percent of the enrollees were group models, 15.1 percent of plans with 14.9 percent of enrollees were network models, and 61.1 percent of the plans with 42.8 percent of the enrollees were independent practice associations (Louis Harris and Associates, 1990). Two-thirds of HMOs are for profit, but over half the members are enrolled in nonprofit plans (Group Health Association of America, 1991).

One key to the effectiveness of these organizations is their initial selection of providers. In many instances, physician-initiated networks and some commercial networks have accepted most of the providers in the community. There is wide variation in efficiency and effectiveness of care (at this point) in any medical population. Therefore, costs would tend to be much higher and quality much lower than desired. There is also no assurance of the quality that one will receive when one selects a network.

Network developers then intend to remove inefficient providers as data are collected. However, data systems in the past have been inadequate to determine who is efficient, and significant political uproar is often caused in attempting to remove popular but ineffective or inefficient providers. This also creates a perception of instability in the network that antagonizes employers. As a result, a number of managed care plans are still far from optimally effective.

Open-Ended Plans

To combine employees' desire for choice and all parties' desire to manage price and perhaps volume and quality, commercial insurers pioneered the combination of their indemnity products with managed care plans. The indemnity portion may or may not be managed through utilization management. This situation is similar to PPO design. Employees can use the network at a reduced copayment and perhaps reduced deductible, or they can use any provider in the community under terms more nearly equal to those of an indemnity plan. Considerable savings can accrue to the employer because of penalties for nonnetwork use. Plans are typically designed to provide a slight net cost advantage to the plan for network use and effective deterrents for out-of-network use. Options may range from simple in-network/out-of-network dual options to triple options in which employees may use a managed care plan, a PPO option, or open indemnity.

The "platform," or insurance licensing vehicle, that can be used can either be a PPO platform (typically licensed by the state insurance department), an open-ended HMO (typically licensed by some other department, such as the Department of Commerce in many states), or an indemnity platform with an alliance with one or more managed care plans. These plans obviously introduce an additional element of administrative complexity and require sophisticated data systems to be properly administered, but they do create choices for employees. If the plans are structured properly, 70 to 90 percent of encounters will occur within the network.

Management by Providers

Providers have repeatedly stated that they would rather run managed care networks themselves, thereby removing the financing organizations. In theory, this structure should have a number of advantages, including a flattened administrative structure, control by those doing the work, and by extension, a foundation for continuous quality improvement. However, very few examples of successful provider-run organizations exist (Eisenberg and Williams, 1981).

Providers do not seem to understand that networks must maintain financial viability. There are many examples of IPAs started by physicians that encountered serious financial difficulties and either went out of business or were sold to commercial organizations. During these sales, the physicians believed that there was significant value to their assets, but in fact, because the networks had lost so much money and owed so much money to providers, they possessed *negative* value. This resulted in fairly unrealistic disputes between the purchasers and sellers.

Does Managed Care Work?
It Depends on Whom You Ask

The typical "evaluation" of managed care effectiveness or quality in the lay and benefits literature consists of surveys of opinions, often without statistical studies to quantify or validate the opinions.

Financial Results

In one recent article, benefits officers were quoted as saying that managed care plans save 3 to 4 percent per year per employee. In addition, they felt that there were lower annual percentages of increases. However, in another study, only about one-third of employers surveyed felt that HMOs were effective in controlling costs, and half of employers in one survey felt that HMOs attracted the better risks, increasing costs in their indemnity plans (A. Foster Higgins & Co., 1989). Most data available on PPO effectiveness also consist of surveys of employers and benefits officers asking whether they felt that the PPO was effective in saving money.

In a more carefully designed probability study of employers, employer satisfaction with cost was higher for HMO plans than for conventional and PPO options. Despite this, employers still express higher overall satisfaction levels for alternatives other than HMOs. The authors of this study speculate that concerns about service and selection may explain the results (Gabel, DiCarlo, Fink, and DiLissavoy, 1989).

Adverse selection and shadow pricing are legitimate issues to be concerned about, but the evidence does not seem to support fears that they are causing excessive profit taking. Many employers are concerned that, in multiple-option situations, their healthy employees would join HMOs and their indemnity rates would therefore go up as a sicker group was left in the fee-for-service plan. HMO rates, however, are set on a communitywide basis, and it is impossible for every employer to have a healthier mix of HMO enrollees than the HMO average (there may, however, be high-risk small employers and lower-risk larger groups, a consequence of who works for whom). If there is favorable selection in the HMO as a whole, then the rates should be lower than comparable fee-for-service costs for its standard set of benefits. As noted, HMOs tend to have a broader base of benefits except for mental health, and so any studies would have to be adjusted to make the package comparable for all options.

The evidence on selection in HMOs is mixed. It appears to follow a curve in which there is an initial upsurge of enrollment in HMOs that tends to level out over time, with approximately half of the population ultimately selecting HMOs under the present less-than-supportive atmosphere.

Little empirical evidence exists with regard to shadow pricing, but what is available does not suggest that HMOs are achieving exorbitant profits at the expense of employers. What is more likely is that they simply have not achieved maximal operating efficiencies by eliminating unnecessary steps in care. In addition, HMOs—particularly those complying with federal "qualification" requirements—offer a broader array of preventive services than other plans. Most studies show considerable losses in parts of the HMO market. This analysis does not deal with the relative internal efficiency of HMOs or other managed care systems (Gold, 1992).

It is unlikely that HMOs would be able to retain excessive earnings and still remain competitive. Further, the repeal of the equal-dollar contribution requirement under the Federal HMO Act gives employers more flexibility to negotiate contributions to better reflect expected savings. It is more likely that a number of HMOs, particularly the commercial ones that were created by insurance companies without necessarily having the expertise or the will to aggressively manage care, are in fact losing money due to ineffective management of both price and volume. A number of these programs have made the mistake of paying fee-for-service physicians; allowing escape hatches in hospital per diem contracts; paying retail for pharmaceuticals, durable medical equipment, and ancillary services; and having ineffective utilization management programs.

Some HMOs have taken steps to use adjusted community rating, which approximates or approaches experience rating. This could work for or against an employer, depending on whether the employees are young or older and how sick they are.

According to a survey by the newsletter *Managing Employee Benefits,* the actual cost to the employer was $2,683 per employee for HMOs, $2,952 for PPOs, and $3,214 for indemnity plans as of September 1991. It should be noted that HMO members in many surveys have 2.7 members per family, as opposed to 2.4 for indemnity plans, so that the per capita cost is lower. The real savings were clearly larger than the estimates or the qualitative opinions.

On the basis of statistical evaluation of cost structures across many studies, Luft concluded that HMOs experience 10 to 40 percent lower costs than individuals in conventional plans. The primary source of savings was the much lower rate of hospital use, due primarily to lower admission rates (Luft, 1981). For example, in 1990, IPAs experienced 393 bed-days per thousand, staff or group-model prepaid plans experienced 372 bed-days per thousand, and the population at large experienced 710 bed-days per thousand (Camerlo, Giffin, Hodges, and Palsbo, 1992). Anecdotal information now indicates that many HMOs, particularly on the West Coast and in the Rocky Mountain area, have reduced bed-days to 180 per thousand or less and some well-managed plans have decreased hospital use to below 130 bed-days per thousand (A. M. Wiesenthal, personal communication, Jan. 1993; Doyle, 1990).

In the RAND National Health Insurance experiment, individuals assigned to HMO options had 25 percent lower costs than the individuals in the fee-for-service sector, with a 40 percent reduction in hospital use (Manning and others, 1984). A disproportionate reduction in discretionary admissions occurred, particularly for surgical care.

Repeated reviews of HMOs have not revealed any difference in health outcomes. In fact, in the RAND experiment, outcomes were generally equal to or better than fee-for-service care (Newhouse, 1991).

Quality

Employer beliefs are sometimes at odds with the facts about managed care. One survey showed that about 40 percent of employers assumed there was a difference in quality among indemnity plans, point-of-service plans, IPA or networks, and staff-model HMOs. A narrow majority indicated that no difference existed (Blendon and Hyams, 1992). The same survey showed that 22 percent of employers felt that staff or group-model HMOs provided better-quality care. Among those who thought there was a difference in plans, 27 percent felt that managed fee-for-service approaches provided higher quality of care, and 28 percent felt that traditional fee-for-service plans provided better quality care. PPOs gathered 20 percent and IPAs or networks 20 percent. On the other hand, when the question was reversed, 41 percent felt that staff or group-model HMOs provided lower-quality service, and 22 percent thought that IPAs or networks provided lower quality of service. Both may in fact be true, since people tend to identify HMOs or PPOs with specific entities, while "fee-for-service" medicine is amorphous.

In 1989, the primary source of information on "quality" was feedback from employees in 74 percent of the cases. General reputation in the community was the source of "data" in 56 percent of cases, and information from brokers and consultants was used in 48 percent. Formal statistical measures of quality were used in only 45 percent of the cases (Taylor and Leitman, 1989). The way employers evaluate quality is changing rapidly, however.

Interestingly, when evaluating the success of managed care programs, 76 percent of respondents in that survey stated that quality of care was most important, and only 66 percent said the dollars saved were important. Sixty-one percent stated that employee satisfaction was very important. Only 2 percent said that each dimension was not really important.

Satisfaction

Satisfaction is another indicator of success in any economic endeavor. A number of studies have examined satisfaction levels for individuals in HMOs and fee-for-service settings. In general, these studies show that consumers voluntarily enrolling in HMOs are equally satisfied with both systems (Davis and others, 1986; Rositter, Langwell, Want, and Rivnyak, 1989). HMOs do better among consumers on the cost of care, paperwork demands, and office waiting time. Fee-for-service systems do better on continuity of care and interpersonal aspects of care. In one Louis Harris and Associates survey, 90 percent of HMO members were satisfied with their doctors and 76 percent were satisfied with the quality of hospital care, slightly exceeding satisfaction levels in the fee-for-service sector (Taylor and Kagay, 1986).

Employees want a choice of providers, regardless of how good or bad they are. In a national survey, being a member of a health plan that limits members to the most cost-effective providers and excludes those who are not cost effective gathered only 42 percent support (Taylor and Leitman, 1991a). Keep in mind that this is a national survey and is not specific to one employer or to employees after they have been educated about the trade-offs.

The Current Situation:
Data Analysis to Shape Tactics

To develop a full managed care strategy, an employer should first assess the cost, deliverables, and quality of current managed care programs. The total price of fully managed care options should be calculated, including employee and employer contributions. Both contributions should be evaluated—employees often pay less for managed care plans, since deductibles and copayments are often lower and ambulatory care is more fully covered. This can then be compared to the cost of the other benefits options offered. When making this comparison, it is important to price plans for equivalent features and out-of-pocket expenses so that an accurate comparison can be made. As noted, managed care plans may include more preventive and fewer mental health services.

In evaluating the efficiency of current and proposed managed care programs, one should also benchmark utilization against the best possible practices in managed care. This of course is only part of the equation, with price, technology, and quality being the other elements. However, particularly with HMOs, the intent of the organization—aside from prevention and comprehensiveness of services—is to manage utilization. Therefore, evaluating inpatient bed-days per thousand, admission rates, and rates of outpatient visits, referrals, diagnostic testing, procedures, and surgery is key to determining how well the organization is managing care. Of course, these figures must be corrected for the age and gender of the employee and dependent population. Depending on the mechanics of management, presence or absence of internal utilization review, and other factors, managed care organizations range from being totally ineffective to providing well-managed care. Targets for plans are shown in Table 11.1 (Harris, 1992d).

Price can be monitored as well. If managed care organizations are willing to forward the data (they frequently either have not collected them or will not do so), the cost per visit and procedure can be compared to benchmarks and to the contract

Table 11.1. Benchmarks: What Is Appropriate or Necessary?

Indicator (Annual)	Managed Care Target Level
Admissions/1000 persons	50–80
ALOS[a]	3.5
LOS for routine vaginal deliveries	1.0
Bed-days/1000 persons	100–300
Primary care visits/person	3.5
Outpatient surgeries/1000 persons	35–65
Specialist visits/1000 persons	450–600
Prescriptions/1000 persons	4–5

[a]ALOS = average length of stay.

Source: In J. S. Harris, H. D. Belk, and L. W. Wood (eds.), *Managing Health Care Costs.* Beverly, Mass.: OEM Press, 1992. Reprinted with permission.

terms. This is an oversight exercise as long as the managed care organization is paid on a fixed price per person. However, if there are overrides or risk sharing or if the organization is based on discounted fee-for-service arrangements, then monitoring prices paid is critical. It is typically easier to obtain this information from an IPA or a network model because in these models, claims forms are submitted by providers, and tapes of payments should exist somewhere in the organization. Again, the cost must be adjusted for the age and gender of the employee and dependent population.

If the intent is to improve medical care or to increase its use, employee satisfaction can be monitored as well. This is an important area, since one of the major dissatisfiers of managed care is customer service — lack of information, inability to get through on telephone lines, and so on. Member satisfaction also determines the rate of enrollment. If employers move to the extreme of a single managed care plan, monitoring customer satisfaction becomes critical to fulfill the objectives of the benefits program.

Employee preferences can also be surveyed. When an employer offers a variety of managed care and other options — for example, in a flexible benefits plan — but there is a clear preference to steer employees toward more management in order to improve quality and manage costs, it is important to repeatedly do this type of market research to understand preferences for choices and preferences for attributes of the delivery system.

Quality indicators that can be analyzed can include conventional sentinels for rare adverse events such as returns to the operating room, readmissions within thirty days, and adverse drug reactions. It should be noted that the system to detect adverse drug reactions typically is not very sensitive, because many of them are seen in physicians' offices. Many managed care programs do not have an organized system to assess the quality of care or collect the data needed to do so. More advanced quality indicators that allow improvement of the quality of care include variance from group mean levels of resource use per person; ratios of medical to surgical therapy for diseases with multiple treatment options such as heart disease; total resources used for admissions for chronic diseases such as high blood pressure, asthma, diabetes, and other entities that should be able to be managed on the outpatient basis; and so on. Other dimensions of quality can include customer satisfaction and customer judgment of quality of care.

Shaping a Managed Care Strategy

The mission of an employer's health management program would determine the extent to which managed care is offered or relied on. However, if the mission encompasses any of the attributes expressed by employers as being key drivers of their programs, including cost or quality management, managed care should be a clear and perhaps a major portion of the program. If the mission statement contains any phrases about cooperation with providers or use of operational parameters, then that may determine intent to offer a certain managed care plan. If cost is clearly a driver, the most stringent management of utilization and price should be instituted. Employers should clearly understand the operational and employee relations implications of these statements and perhaps modify them over time as employee knowledge and preferences change and the offerings available in the market shift.

The shape of the program will be determined by a combination of financial targets, employee perception, employee preferences for various degrees of management, quality, access, freedom from paperwork, and easy guidance into a complete system. This latter may be important to the large number of employees who do not have a personal physician and who find navigating the "system" or nonsystem difficult. Goals should be framed to move from the current shape of the benefits program to some combination of managed care options that will achieve cost goals, quality goals, and goals for employee satisfaction and preference.

Projections of enrollment can be made based on both out-of-pocket costs and preferences. If focus groups are available to rank relative trade-offs between cost and other attributes, they can be used to project relative rates of enrollment and therefore predictable costs in these plans. If one is dealing with a PPO, mathematical models can be used to project costs given certain enrollment and network-use assumptions. Objectives can then be framed to reach measurable targets for each one of these goals.

Xerox provides one interesting example of an overarching managed care strategy. Since the late 1980s, the company has been building its strategy based on HMOs to create a national network of managed high-quality care. The company has created six regional networks with one manager for each region. This is called the Health Link HMO. In each region, a different managed care plan serves as an overall manager under which utilization reporting will be consolidated. There is an accreditation process to admit local HMOs into each regional group. The plan adds another layer of administration of management. Xerox states that it is using a quality improvement approach to increase the value of what it is purchasing. It will be interesting to see if the quality improvement approach reduces the multiple layers of management inherent in the current situation (Darling, 1991). These managers tend to be more expert about quality management than the typical benefits manager or consultant, which could affect the outcome of the effort.

Vendor Selection

In framing the managed care program, employers may rely on existing options offered in the commercial market, may put together detailed specifications in requests for proposals to steer vendors of managed care programs toward their desired objectives and price, or may choose to put together their own managed care network (see Chapter Twelve).

Rather than frame the objective as choosing the "best managed care program," it would make more sense to determine whether an employer is interested in managing price, volume, quality, or technology. Then when assembling a request for proposals to determine which managed care programs should be offered, each of these issues can be addressed and target objectives set. Employers should demand the statistical data on the effectiveness of the various managed care plans listed below and compare them with targets shown in Table 11.1. While costs and administrative overhead, which are internal financial data, may seem intrusive, the same type of information is often asked of other vendors.

- Bed-days per thousand
- Outpatient procedure and diagnostic utilization
- Testing rates
- Referral rates
- Visit rates
- Price per covered individual
- Variance and other key quality indicators
- Costs for the provision of various services
- Administrative overhead

The employer should also ask for a detailed explanation of how utilization management is conducted. How contracts with providers are framed, including reimbursement mechanisms for both facilities and professionals, is important as well.

The employer should inquire about data collection, quality management systems, and customer service, too. In particular, it is important to ask for a complete explanation of quality improvement programs that might be in place to improve on any of the statistics presented.

The standard technique to assess managed care has been matching of employee zip codes and the locations of providers. However, it should be noted that this tells you absolutely nothing about any of the attributes outlined above. It is only a first approximation for access.

   In general, employers offer far too many managed care plans. This presents an administrative problem and is an effective barrier to any sort of targeted negotiation and to quality improvement efforts (see Chapter Twelve). On the other hand, use of some specialty managed care vendors — for mental health, for example — may prove quite valuable (Whittington, 1992; Mason, 1992).

Conclusion

Once the managed care approach has been agreed on, by combining the various dimensions of price, quality, volume, employee satisfaction, and employee demands, employers can find networks that can best provide this combination of attributes. Attention should be devoted to the structure and process excellence of volume management (through utilization management), price management (through contract administration), and data feedback. Perhaps the best approach would be to start collecting data on variance of resource use and quality indicators and then continually improve the system in a joint venture with the vendors offering the network.

CHAPTER TWELVE

Direct Contracting
for Medical Care

This chapter begins with a caveat. Many employers are dissatisfied with the customer service, quality of care, or cost of services they are obtaining from provider organizations. They are beginning to question the value added by the financial intermediaries they work with, either in paying claims, managing financial risk, or managing care. In many other purchasing areas, employers of all sizes have begun to forge closer relationships with suppliers. While this movement started with large employers, it has spread to other employers, either as purchasing cooperatives or simply as an important strategic approach.

Some employers have begun to work directly with provider organizations. There are several reasons for this. Some employers are dissatisfied with the performance of insurers and managed care organizations relative to achievable benchmarks. Some are interested in more directly controlling the services delivered, holding suppliers accountable for measurable performance. The latter is common with almost all other purchases but has not been in medical care so far. Some seek to reduce layers of administration and the associated costs. And some want to reduce the number of suppliers of care, enter into long-term relationships, and continuously improve the process and outcome of care.

Direct contracting can enable employers and coalitions of employers to more directly control their medical microenvironment. Benefits inflation has ranged from a few percent per year for the most aggressive large employers to rates in excess of 30 percent for some unwitting larger employers and many small ones.

Words probably cannot change the health care industry, particularly given fragmented market power and the fragmentation of the industry itself, but they can exert pressure to produce better products through contact specifications and closer relationships with a small number of vendors. Coalitions or pools of employers may do even better than individual employers because they have increased size and therefore leverage with providers and fiscal intermediaries.

Dealing with a large number of plan options is administratively complex. It also decreases any leverage purchasers may have and diffuses attempts to manage the quality of care purchased. Therefore, reducing the number of suppliers—a cornerstone of supplier improvement in other industries—makes sense here.

Medical provider organizations are quite interested in developing closer and more direct relationships with employers as well. They see this approach as a way of solidifying their patient base, which might change if employers change plans for any reason. When hospitals were asked if they contracted directly with employers, only 15 percent said yes in 1988 and only 16 percent thought it was highly likely that they might in the future (Louis Harris and Associates, 1988). This situation is changing rapidly, however. Many hospitals and physician-hospital organizations (PHOs) are now actively marketing to employers to fill excess capacity and improve their market position. They may need to think out their willingness to manage and finance risk, because some who are party to such a relationship must bear the risk of illness and injury and the risk of effective or ineffective provision of care. Supplier partnerships are much less adversarial than the current situation as well. Again, this is a key element of many quality improvement strategies, which hold the promise of reducing administrative and clinical costs while improving the quality of care.

Direct contracting can also lay the foundation for a quality improvement program under which suppliers would fix problems with price, volume, and appropriateness themselves, perhaps with the assistance of industry groups that understand quality improvement theory and practice.

Some desirable outcomes to be achieved from direct contracting and supplier improvement therefore include:

- Obtaining the terms that each employer wants based on the strategic direction of its benefits plan
- Reducing layers of overhead
- Reducing layers of management
- Improving customer service
- Obtaining a system of care that comes close to fulfilling specific key quality characteristics and criteria
- Making both parties — particularly providers — more aware of and responsible for the risk of operational ineffectiveness
- Keeping the health care system private by achieving improvement before public or financial pressure forces more drastic changes

Economic Rationale for Direct Contracting

Employers so far have been price takers rather than price makers. To become price makers, they must increase their market power or in some other way obtain specific contractual terms with providers. A few employers have attempted to solve the problems with the current medical care system by managing their microenvironment through direct contracting. The core condition employers would want to include contractually would be to change the price base or the rate of increase to a more realistic scheme that reflects value relative to other products and services, or at the least the best prices agreed to with other consumers (since pricing from the same provider varies widely from consumer to consumer).

In the first instance, employers would want to be sure that they paid no more than the best to average price for the local market rather than a high percentile of a retail statistical profile. In the second instance, employers would not use the usual, customary, and reasonable fee system but would return to fee schedules that are somehow pegged to market situations for other goods and services. The price basis for hospitals should be more reflective of undiluted costs plus some reasonable margin without cost shifting and without support of the 35 percent excess capacity and significant level of redundant technology inherent in the current system. It clearly makes sense to change financing from ex post facto, reactive financing to prospective agreements of various sorts. These could be capitated agreements for practitioners, per diems for facilities, or global capitation arrangements for what amount to vertically integrated systems.

Another area that should be governed by contract is the introduction of new technology prior to proof of efficacy. There should also be some mechanism for removing redundant older, less effective technology so that testing and treatment are not duplicated, as they are, for example, with CT, MRI, and myelography. Many other examples could be cited as well.

As other industries have clearly demonstrated, quality cannot be managed without clearly specifying the type of quality. For example, the quality of supplies in the semiconductor and auto industries improved only after buyers specifically stated in contracts with a reduced number of suppliers exactly what they wished to receive in terms of performance and number of defects. While it may be more obvious how to do this in those industries, a start could clearly be made in the medical care industry.

Contract Terms

Contracts with medical care providers should cover the scope of services expected, the types and models of services desired, access standards, provider selection, management, utilization management effectiveness, willingness to share risk, and data management and reporting. Providers may be selected based on geographic coverage, efficiency, structural or process quality, and financial stability. The desired model will probably be based on access through primary care physicians, use of mid-level providers, and comprehensive services. Services in a comprehensive model include the following:

Inpatient Care

- Acute care through community hospitals
- Tertiary care in a small number of special centers

- Skilled and intermediate nursing facilities
- Alcohol and substance abuse services
- Hospice care
- Birthing facilities

Outpatient Care

- Primary care
- Specialty care by referral
- Diagnostic laboratory services
- Imaging services
- Urgent and emergency care
- Geriatric care
- Home health care
- Outpatient surgery
- Physical, occupational, and rehabilitative therapy
- Alcohol and substance abuse treatment
- Dental care
- Hospice care
- Psychological and psychiatric care
- Vision care

Preventive Services

- Immunizations
- Preventive screening according to protocols
- Health risk appraisals
- Health promotion activities
- Wise-use and self-care programs
- Prenatal care
- Genetic screening on request

The following are desirable system characteristics:

- Continuity of care, starting with prevention and primary care
- Network selection, composition, and coverage
- Effective utilization management, as reflected in performance statistics
- Incentives for efficiency
- Reporting systems that produce information on case-mix-adjusted utilization, cost, and quality by provider and by employee group

- An effective quality improvement program
- Attention to customer service and satisfaction
- Outcome information
- Risk sharing for employees and providers
- Claims processing
- Administrative performance
- Ability to implement successfully

Examples and Precedents

The Health Action Coalition of northern Ohio offers one example of creating direct contractual, data-based relationships with providers of medical care. This business alliance is applying the *buy-right strategy* developed by Walter McCure at the Center for Health Policy Studies in Minneapolis, Minnesota (Traska, 1990). This approach emphasizes restructuring health care purchasing methods to give providers incentives to maximize efficiency and effectiveness by rewarding them with increased market share. The strategy emphasizes quality as well as cost. Market share on the purchaser side is increased by cooperative purchasing. It has also required the commitment of corporate chief executive officers to "stay the course" and not change strategy in midstream. In this project, physicians and hospitals are reaching consensus with providers on quality measurements and parameters. The initial part of the project included information collection, interpretation, and dissemination.

The Coalition used the Olmstead County benchmarks to compare the utilization and expenditure patterns for Cleveland employers with a comparable population in Rochester, Minnesota, served by the Mayo Clinic and an analysis of Medicare mortality data for the Cleveland area (Shaller and Ballard, 1992). The strategy was supported by Cleveland Tomorrow, an association of the chief executive officers of fifty of the largest companies in the city. The Cleveland Hospital Association developed a plan for community-based quality-of-care evaluation. A patient satisfaction survey was conducted using a quality judgment system developed by Hospital Corporation of America, the RAND Corporation, and the University of California at Los

Angeles. Risk-adjusted outcome indicators are being evaluated using the Apache III system and a customized risk-adjustment system. Several large employers, including BP America and Parker Hannifin, have instituted selective contracting for hospital care as part of this program.

Honeywell has pursued direct contracting for several years to develop more responsive networks (Burns, 1992). Its contracting framework resembles that outlined in the lists above. Honeywell is actually contracting with a network management organization, much the way Xerox and several other large employers have. In this model, an employer or group of employers — an example of a group is the Central Florida coalition — specifies the characteristics and measurements that the network should have. It is then the responsibility of the management organization to provide a delivery system that meets those specifications, either through direct provision of services or subcontracting. Examples are shown below. Other mid-sized to large employers, as well as a number of coalitions, are moving in this direction, sometimes through an intermediary organization (Darling, 1991).

Sample Specifications
for a Health Management Organization

Scope of Services

- Comprehensive, *coordinated* services
- Geographically accessible but nonredundant, primary, secondary, and tertiary inpatient services
- Geographically accessible but nonredundant preventive and primary midlevel care and physician services and specialty physician services, including psychosocial, maternal and child, medical, and surgical care
- Outpatient (presumably higher-value) diagnostic and therapeutic facilities
- Outpatient care and rehabilitative services as alternatives to inpatient care
- Coordinated or provided occupational health services, including emergency care, disability management, environmental health, and industrial hygiene and safety services

Service Model

- Immediately available information on access to the system
- Primary care entry to the system
- Shared-risk preventive services
- Immediate access to appropriate urgent and emergency care
- Prompt access for acute conditions
- Coordinated care for chronic conditions
- A prearranged system for out-of-area care and transfer
- Use of the highest-value level of care in each instance
- Management of nonnetwork providers

Provider Selection (Institutions and Health Professionals)

- Commitment to prevention, wise use, and health promotion
- Commitment to and selection on the basis of quality
- Commitment to coordination of care
- Meets accessibility criteria
- Licensed and accredited
- Commitment to and provision of outpatient rather than inpatient services when medically appropriate
- Efficient services as judged by minimal excess capacity, appropriate admissions, length of stay and service rates, and lower cost
- Effective services as judged by an appropriate volume of specific services, minimal rework, and excellent functional outcomes
- Information system and records quality and efficiency
- Effective quality assurance and improvement protocols and programs
- Financial strength
- Effective provider relations and assistance programs

Management Programs

- Health promotion
- Health, wise-use, and self-care education
- Employee assistance (broadly based, with brief interventions and gatekeeper functions)
- Inpatient and outpatient utilization management
- Program evaluation and improvement
- Management information systems

Monitoring and Reporting System

- Provider selection and deselection
- Provider performance
- Program quality
- Employee needs
- Employee satisfaction
- Inpatient utilization rates measured against benchmarks
- Outpatient utilization rates measured against benchmarks
- Appropriateness of admissions and service use
- Outcomes (adverse, functional, and positive)
- Cost rates

Incentives and Risk Sharing

- Minimal cost for use of appropriate services
- Access to additional benefits if services are used appropriately
- Access to additional benefits for positive life-style or change
- Provider reward based on risk accepted, efficiency of service, and effectiveness of health management
- Payment based on prospective, risk-adjusted budget targets
- Control or decrease of costs to employer
- Development of an advanced model for marketing to other payers

Management and Service Provision Experience

- Previous system management experience
- Client experience/references
- Legal structure, appropriate licensing
- Conflict of interest and antitrust issues excluded
- Community responsibility
- Claims payment experience and performance
- Customer service excellence
- Appeals and grievance procedure
- Communications system
- Satisfaction monitoring system
- Problem identification and resolution

A number of companies have expanded direct contracting to specialized services such as mental health and substance abuse treatment, wellness, occupational health services, rehabilitation, and maternal care and cardiology in a few cases (Kenkel, 1993b). Centers of excellence — high-volume, high-quality places of treatment for specific diseases or surgical procedures, usually at significantly lower costs — have been a particular focus of "carve-out" programs that are directly arranged (Christiansen, 1991). A Medicare demonstration project for coronary artery bypass surgery is an interesting new example (Kretz, 1991).

The Process of Value Improvement

The key to better value in health care is the creation of an environment for constructive change based on a structured dialogue between providers, consumers, and payers. Cooperation is an essential element of this process. All sides come to better understand the needs and expectations of the others and seek to design systems that will meet those needs and expectations. The approach is data driven and process focused. This type of partnership can use simple statistical tools such as Pareto diagrams or 80/20 analysis to decide which problems to attack.

It can be easily argued that inefficiency in medical care is not the providers' problem but that both providers and purchasers are at once the cause and solution for inefficient health care (McEachern, Makens, Buchanan, and Schiff, 1992). Chapters Two, Three, and Seven illustrated the point that actions taken on both the demand and the supply side have resulted in wide variance in the provision of care. Demand for results beyond the capabilities of the system and cost-generating behavior built into the way the system is structured are partly responsible. One answer to these problems is a new supplier-customer partnership.

Supplier improvement presupposes or rests on this partnership. It implies that the two sides are interested in cooperating to improve the quality and perhaps the price of the product or service delivered. The intent to form such a partnership can be included in contract terms in direct contracting, but in this particular instance, the objective is to form an alliance between purchasers and organizations that can manage medical care. The creation of an alliance also implies a joint agreement to use quality improvement principles, including careful and accurate measurement of the process and outcome of care, resources used, and accurate costing. All of these at the moment are unusual in medical care.

One of the main tactics of supplier improvement efforts in other industries has been to reduce the number of suppliers to a key few who will work carefully with the purchasers to meet detailed specifications. In this case, the specifications may have more to do with customer service and with outcomes and perhaps efficiency than with the specifics of the process of medical care. If there are medical professionals on the strategic health management team for the employer, then more technical details may be included.

Employer's Role

In many instances, the employer's most valuable contribution may be to offer process improvement expertise rather than technical content. Many employers have already gained a tremendous amount of expertise and knowledge in quality improvement and may contribute that knowledge and perhaps training materials to joint efforts (Laffel and Blumenthal, 1989). Provider organizations in turn can contribute knowledge of the process and flow of care to individual improvement projects.

The other area in which employers can assume the leadership role is in the specification of key quality characteristics. These are attributes that "delight the customer." (See Chapter Three for a potential list.) They may involve quality of care as perceived by the end consumer, customer satisfaction, administrative simplicity or outcome as measured by complication rates, return-to-work rates, absence durations, or time to return to full function. It would make more sense to focus on positive outcomes than on avoidance of negative ones. After key quality characteristics of care and system organization and performance are specified, measurable criteria for monitoring and outcomes of various improvement projects can be matched against them (see below).

A simple way to describe the quality management paradigm that has evolved over the last thirty to forty years is that it involves delivering the best value to the customer that the producer can afford at a price the customer is willing to pay (Makens and McEachern, 1992). In medical care, employers and other consumers have not often specified, but instead have assumed, the best value. It is clear that prices of medical care at the present time are not prices the customer is willing to pay, but since the end customer does not pay them, this usual market constraint does not effectively apply.

Paradigm Shift for Medical Care Organizations

Adopting quality improvement techniques requires a paradigm shift. Paradigms have been described as "any set of rules and regulations that describes boundaries and tells us what to do to be successful with those boundaries" (Makens and McEachern, 1992, p. 23). A number of paradigms in medical care must be changed, including the emphasis on implicit professional judgment of quality rather than explicit measurement and improvement and the fixation on individual performance rather than process improvement to prevent errors and increase efficiency and effectiveness. Medical and administrative professionals will also have to be willing to widen their vision and to commit to researching, using, and improving best practices rather than the usual way they have done things (which was assumed but never documented to involve best practices).

As one useful approach, medical organizations might start to think about models that involve the *four pillars of quality*. The four pillars are reducing management-induced waste (process inefficiency), emphasizing involved and eager employees, meeting customer needs and expectations, and using statistical thinking (Makens and McEachern, 1992). Statistical thinking should be familiar to providers as the basis of epidemiology. The pillar of "involved and eager employees" is one that is often not achieved in medical care because of its vertical and parallel hierarchies (Starr, 1992). This results in an unfortunate waste of the contributions of all "team" members other than a few key administrators or physicians. This may be one of the reasons that turnover is so high in medical care and that almost a million nurses refuse to practice.

The supporting pillars are "the voice of the customer" and "the voice of the process." These adapt rather nicely to medical care. The "voice of the customer" is clearly seeking key quality characteristics, which may or may not have been specified but which include reasonable cost and high quality. The "voice of the process"—which refers to how medical care is conducted—introduces the professional dimension of clinical care and the process by which it is delivered. The processes used in medical care are complex, numerous, and surprisingly variable. That variation is an a priori definition of low quality in many contexts.

To adopt this approach, those working in the process must be able to understand and listen to what their customers are saying. This is not as common as it could be in medical care or with fiscal intermediaries, which are rapidly attempting to transform themselves from financers to managers of care. Listening to the voice of the customer is not the same thing as pouring more marketing resources into attempts to persuade people to buy a product that may or may not be well developed and may or may not have intrinsic management capability or quality.

Voice of the Customer: Key Quality Characteristics

To understand how to bring the needs and expectations of all parties into alignment, one must understand the nature of customer needs. From the viewpoint of customers, many types of quality may exist. In one three-level model, the first level entails the basic needs of customers that must be met, the next level encompasses the needs and expectations that they have come to expect will be met, and the final level involves those things that are unexpected but that delight them when they occur. Every time customers come in contact with the organization's processes and outputs, their needs and expectations change. Over time, level 3 delights become level 2 needs and expectations. Level 2 expectations tend to become "must" needs and so on (Kano, Seraku, and Tsuji, 1982).

This is precisely what appears to be happening as employers and employees become more knowledgeable about what the medical care system can reasonably be expected to do and what it should not be doing. If employers follow the employee involvement strategy suggested earlier, this process will surely be accelerated, probably to the benefit of employees and employers.

By identifying and listening to customers at each step in a

process of care, the ownership of the process can be returned
to the professionals, eliminating layers of overhead and regulation. This should be satisfying to both the professional community and the employer/customer. Part of the advantage gained
is by internalizing the inspectors, or making each practitioner
an "inspector" responsible for ensuring that his or her actions
are carried out according to the standard process and that there
are no defects. Thus, an extra layer of bureaucracy can be eliminated and professional control can be regained (Roper, 1989).

While some health professionals assert that consumers
are not in a position to be accurate judges of quality, one of
the definitions of quality is a subjective side dealing with a person's preferences or desires (known as *utility*). In previous discussions (Chapters Seven and Ten), we have noted that if benefits plans are most closely approximated to each individual's
utility, unnecessary services probably will be reduced (Makens
and McEachern, 1992).

Understanding the Process of Medical Care

As noted in Chapter Three, medical care can be conceptual-
ized as a process with a number of dimensions or as a series
of parallel processes. The production processes include scheduling, customer service, supply, housekeeping, food, testing,
and record keeping. Clinical processes are more intellectual than
physical, covering the decision making needed to make a diagnosis, understand the patient's situation, and select (hopefully
cooperatively) one of a series of treatment alternatives, along
a specified time continuum.

Each of these processes can be mapped to graphically
depict actions, decision points, and endpoints. Flow mapping
is one of the best ways for all involved parties to understand
how things are done, how decisions are made, and when actions are not taken. Process maps often expose redundant pathways, lack of coordination, missed decision points, and "blind
alleys." They are also useful tools to raise questions about why
things are done a certain way. They are a basic starting point
to understand processes and to start improvement efforts.

Another important element of process understanding is a survey of the literature studying the relative effectiveness of various clinical processes. Many of these have not been subject to controlled or comparative evaluation. At the least, this search will make it clear that the best alternative is not known. One can then select measurements to monitor the stabilization and the improvement of the process one is concerned with. Information systems are therefore also quite important, since manual tracking of these variables is possible but not optimal.

Key Process Variables

After key quality characteristics are defined, process improvement groups should then identify the key process variables that are the major sources of variability in the key quality characteristics. These variables are upstream from key quality characteristics and are embedded in the process itself. For example, the amount of time involved and the accuracy of services provided can be identified as key quality characteristics without precise knowledge of the internal attributes in the process, but these characteristics are unlikely to be achieved without standardizing and improving the key variables, or drivers, in the process. That knowledge comes from those who do the work — the providers. However, employer representatives outside the process may be more effective as facilitators and may be able to ask why things are done a certain way.

A Data-Driven Process

Statistical thinking focuses on the concept that there is variation in everything we do. This approach provides a deeper knowledge of how the variation that we observe and react to happens. It provides a set of criteria for detecting key information and separating it from "noise in the process." This is similar to shifting from a case-by-case clinical viewpoint to a population-based epidemiological viewpoint (Makens and McEachern, 1992). Deming (1986) has pointed out that if one reduces variation, one improves quality. The first step in reducing variation is removing unusual reasons for variation known as *special causes*. Variation that results from a less-than-optimal process then remains. This is known as *common cause variation.*

Medical care has traditionally been inspection oriented and focused on the individual practitioner. The response to any detected adverse event was to view it as the result of a special cause; this might involve a person who was not doing a job correctly and would be sent back for more education. That approach is adversarial, causes fear among health workers, and is ineffective. The goal is not to find someone who needs to be "regrooved"; emphasis should be placed on removing special causes and then addressing common cause variation by designing a process that does not permit error as easily. The question is not "Who made a mistake?" but "How did the process permit the mistake to be made?" This does not mean creating a number of redundancies or failsafe measures, but simply designing a process that can be replicated time after time. Steps that can be used in improving a process to reduce common cause variation include the following:

1. Find a process to improve.
2. Organize a team of knowledgeable workers.
3. Clarify the process of making any obvious improvements.
4. Find the key quality characteristics.
5. Understand the extent of their variation.
6. Define key process variables.
7. Understand their variation.
8. Select improvements for the process.
9. Perform the plan-do-check-act (PDCA) cycle: plan the change, do it, check it, and act again.

In checking, one would ask whether the variation has been reduced and whether the process is moving closer to customer values. Then one would act to institutionalize the change or abandon it (Makens and McEachern, 1992).

Finding processes to improve can be done in a number of ways, including brainstorming and what is known as *nominal group process.* In the latter, groups of involved workers identify a number of perceived problems and rank order them. They use data in comparison to benchmarks described above to identify probable causes, ranked in order of greatest effect on outcomes and in order of business necessity or total costs (Scholtes, 1988).

Targets to be attacked could include high-cost diagnoses or specific procedures that cause large numbers of complaints or irritation in the system. Another effective tactic is to find "easy wins," in order to start out with a win and ensure that this new form of thinking is endorsed and built on.

Total costs can be modeled through a *total burden of illness* model that looks at both direct and indirect costs (Parsons and others, 1986). Extending the analysis to the total burden of illness multiplies the apparent direct cost to an employer by several fold, making the true cost of illness—including disability, lost wages by others in the family for caregiving, and so on—much larger (McEachern, Makens, Buchanan, and Schiff, 1992).

Infrastructure for Quality Improvement

For continuous process improvement to be successful, an organizational structure for quality improvement must be in place. This would include a conducive environment and widespread knowledge of the tools for process improvement, such as statistical and meeting tools. It can be argued that there is no such thing as a purely "clinical system" in medical care. Contiguous support systems influence clinical behavior and clinical demands on internal supply organizations such as laboratory, supply, housekeeping, and others, making them almost inseparable (McEachern, Makens, Buchanan, and Schiff, 1992).

Figure 12.1 portrays a cooperative process among a group of providers and both clinical and operational elements of a health care institution. The model is one its authors have commonly used that has been very successful as a framework for improving organizational effectiveness in many contexts. As the diagram illustrates, many corporations—including Kodak, Xerox, and Hewlett-Packard—participated in a quality improvement cooperative initiative with HCA West Pace's Ferry

Figure 12.1. Purchaser-Provider Model; Purchaser-Payer Interaction.

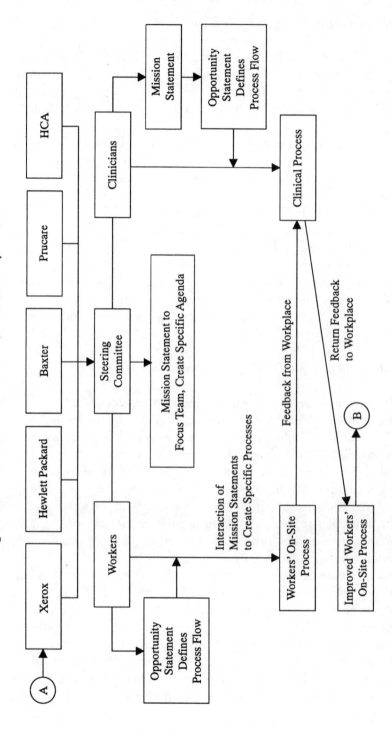

Source: In J. S. Harris, H. D. Belk, and L. W. Wood (eds.), *Managing Employee Health Care Costs.* Beverly, Mass.: OEM Press, 1992. Reprinted with permission.

Hospital. In one of the initial projects, the proportion of repeat Caesarean sections was reduced from 22 percent to less than 15 percent (McEachern, Hallum, and Schiff, 1992).

Effectiveness of Quality Improvement in Medical Care

A number of quality improvement projects are now under way in organizations such as Kaiser Permanente, Harvard Community Health Plan, Intermountain Health System, Alliant Health Systems, Hospital Corporation of America, and others, but quantified evidence of success has not yet been published (with a few exceptions cited above). There are anecdotal reports from sources such as the National Demonstration Project on quality in health care (Berwick, Godfrey, and Roessner, 1990).

Structuring a Supplier Improvement Program

The mission of the health management program should include statements calling for continuous quality improvement to direct it to partnership with suppliers for both acute care and prevention. If this is not an intrinsic focus of the program, its focus and targets will not be considered in the quality improvement context. A paradigm shift is truly necessary to move from "shopping the program" of benefits or periodic battles between customers and marketing representatives to a continuous, ongoing, and intensive quality improvement engagement.

Goals can be framed either in terms of criteria that operationalize key quality characteristics or in terms of improvements in diagnostic or procedural areas identified in the data analysis. Projections of improvement can be made once data on sample projects have been published by the organizations currently doing similar improvement projects in those diagnostic or procedural areas. Objectives can be set calling for changes in the process, reductions in certain costs, or completion of intermediate activities such as mapping and standardizing a small number of processes as an initial step.

The parties to a supplier improvement program must initially agree on the dimensions of quality to be improved. At a general level, these could be customer service functions of managed care organizations, "hotel functions" such as registration, schedules, and housekeeping, and support functions such as laboratory and radiology services. Clinical quality should also be addressed. Defining exactly what that is may take some time and may take a good deal of discussion between providers and several levels of consumers.

Support from both the health care organization and the employer is critical to the success of this effort. Management support, as in any organizational development effort, is central to the success of quality improvement. One key point is that these are ongoing efforts that require constancy of purpose over a long period of time. Without consistent management support, this will not happen and the efforts will fail, to the detriment of all parties.

It is unlikely that an organization will understand how to use quality improvement techniques if it has not transformed itself to use these techniques in its ongoing business. Again, if the employer has undertaken this transformation and the health care provider has not, the employer can use its quality improvement staff to assist the health care organization in changing its viewpoint.

Training for quality improvement teams and those who work with them must be done to support the process. Training requires an investment in time and money that will be recaptured in increased efficiency. A number of packaged quality improvement training programs are available, but at this point none specifically addresses medical care within its own paradigm so that it would be likely to be accepted and used.

One other critical point about implementation and tactics is that data currently collected in medical care may well be lacking sufficient detail to make it possible to quantify and track process changes. At a minimum, the current random state of medical record keeping and frequent absence of recorded data must be corrected in order to support the quality improvement effort (Winslow, 1992).

Conclusion

Direct contracting and supplier improvement hold great promise for moderating medical care costs, focusing on management of the total burden of illness, including preventing that burden, dealing with associated human resource issues, and removing layers of administration regulation and adversarial attitude that are not serving any of the parties in the medical care dialogue.

CHAPTER THIRTEEN

Managing
Health Through Internal
Organizations

An even more direct strategy than contracting with provider organizations is to build an internal health promotion and medical organization to provide integrated services. Building an employer-based or employer pool medical care system affords an opportunity for better control of design and execution of that system. Such organizations typically have better integration of prevention and health promotion with primary, secondary, and tertiary care. Because there is no profit built into this type of system, it may be the least expensive delivery option. Quality improvement can be incorporated if the host organization is already dedicated to quality improvement.

There are distinct advantages to locating health care delivery systems at the work site. Lost time for travel back and forth to providers for initial care, monitoring, and reevaluation is reduced if the site of delivery is the workplace. The workplace can also be an excellent milieu for behavior change in favor of health through peer influence and environmental support. This is particularly true of health promotion, but it can also be true for efficient use of medical care and self-care of chronic diseases. A conflict of interest may be built in that can be guarded against through rigorous adherence to standards of professional ethics such as the American College of Occupational and Environmental Medicine Code of Ethical Conduct. There must be no appearance of nonneutrality, particularly if there is distrust of the employer for other reasons.

Care has been provided at the work site since before the turn of the century, primarily in remote locations. Some industries have had a history of company medical care, some in a paternalistic vein; precedent clearly exists. A number of companies now provide services at the work site ranging from primary care to laboratory and radiological testing.

Planning In-House Medical Systems

One of the key pieces of information needed to determine whether services should be provided internally or contracted out through the benefits program or through direct contracting would be a make/buy analysis of the costs of each option. One such analysis was conducted at Eastman Kodak and documented a much lower unit cost for a number of services (Anstadt, Lester, Powell, and Tsunaitas, 1992). A similar analysis at J. P. Morgan Bank showed that services could be provided or contracted for at a fraction of the "retail" cost (Schneider, 1992).

Some effort at evaluating the quality of care provided by the two alternatives would be useful. In addition, the management capabilities of the internal unit should be assessed to determine whether it can be run as efficiently and with as high quality as external providers. Arguably, few benchmarks in the external community exist, since quality is not widely measured and management capability is varied across multiple areas of administration. However, assurances that the internal unit could be run in a businesslike and high-quality way are important. In fact, because of resistance from the private medical community, the internal option would need to be above reproach and very well documented against objective standards for quality of care and customer service.

Implementation

In many cases, providers have initially been opposed to on-site programs. However, if careful groundwork is laid, such resistance may disappear, particularly if a well-known local physician becomes the medical director of the program. The basic concern seems to be that patients will use the in-house facility rather than their current source of medical care. A compromise is to have the in-house program deal with health promotion, disease prevention, and chronic disease maintenance, which are typically not areas of focus in private practice. A number of very successful programs have used midlevel practitioners for health promotion, primary care, and chronic disease maintenance such as monitoring and counseling of people with diabetes, hypertension, asthma, and allergies in close consultation with their private physicians. This "integrated system" actually improves health and is generally well accepted by private practitioners. Provider reaction could be gauged by quiet discussions with local providers or with local medical societies or through some sort of formal survey.

There are a number of successful programs at the work site, some of which have existed for decades. The general principle is that through the use of standards of practice, contracting for ancillary services, a focus on prevention, counseling, and empowerment of employees, overall health care costs can be reduced. In addition, one critical variable is the provision of services at the work site, so that hours to days spent in travel and waiting rooms are recovered.

The Gillette Company has run on-site clinics for years that have included radiology and laboratory services. The company believes that it has experienced significant savings as a result. It estimates that it is saving more than $700,000 a year by reducing overhead for reimbursement, its ability to formulate and use practice protocols, and the reduction and elimination of the profit of outside vendors (Bryant, 1991; Tomsho and Milbank, 1993). Similar full-service programs have been installed at Coors, Quadgraphics, and GTE (Tomsho and Milbank, 1993).

Morgan Guaranty Trust Company provides a number of on-site services, particularly targeted at high-risk groups who have not sought care, such as lower-income pregnant women. The program includes targeted periodic screening examinations and imaging facilities to obtain tests at a rate far below normal. Medical care is provided at any facility with 1,000 or more employees. Services are directed at minor complaints and monitoring of chronic diseases as well as health promotion. The company uses on-site physicians and contract consultants who are paid an hourly salary that is less than the cost of a single patient encounter in Manhattan. (Of course, the costs of administration and overhead would have to be added for the in-house option for a truly comparable comparison.) The staff serves special needs populations such as HIV-positive employees through direct services, support laboratory services, and referral to specialists. One surprisingly useful service is offering Pap smears to the large number of older women who have never had one. The facility also provides emergency response and triage. Laboratory and radiology studies are done on-site at 25 to 35 percent of the prevailing charge in New York. There seems to be no problem with private practitioners using this source of laboratory and x-ray testing. The department also manages disability and provides case management.

An interface exists between the medical department and the insurance carrier that refers cases for management. This type of case management corrects both over- and underutilization. The medical department also conducts precertification, bill review, and concurrent review. The department counsels employees about their medical bills as well. The director of this program has also worked closely with the director of benefits to design a benefits package that includes preventive services and utilization management (Schneider, 1992).

Targeted programs are one focus at the First Chicago National Bank. A women's health program has found wide acceptance and has decreased the cost of low-birthweight and premature infants, among other entities. This program includes on-site gynecological examinations, self-care seminars, low-birthweight and prematurity prevention programs, and second opinions on surgery (Burton, Erickson, and Briones, 1992). Caesarean sections, hysterectomies, and D&Cs are among the ten most common surgical procedures in the country and at First Chicago. Significant evidence exists that a large number of these procedures are inappropriate or do not contribute to the ultimate improvement of women's health. First Chicago also has an active Employee Assistance Program focusing on identification and early intervention for mental health and social problems (Burton and Conte, 1992).

In addition, First Chicago has pioneered a data system that integrates data from the on-site clinics with claims data and data from the Employee Assistance Program so that a complete profile of each employee can be obtained, aggregated, and analyzed on a population basis to determine the effects of on-site care, the Employee Assistance Program, benefits changes, and so on (Burton, Hoy, and Stephens, 1992).

The Southern California Edison Company has also instituted an extensive on-site program encompassing health promotion, disease prevention, screening, and some primary care. Moreover, the company has implemented its own PPO in the Los Angeles basin that includes physicians and hospitals as well as centers of excellence for specific high-cost, high-risk procedures (Kenkel, 1993a). The company is now considering adding a gatekeeper function to the PPO. The Southern California Edison program is unique in that it also includes an in-house claims processing organization. The claims organization makes it possible to control data collection and quality and therefore analyze the impact of the various facets of the health management program (Schmitz and Courtright, 1992). Prior to 1988, cost increases were averaging more than 20 percent year over year. Between 1988 and 1989, costs dropped slightly.

The department provides primary care services on site, prevention, pharmacy services, and referral. There is an internal utilization review function as well. Preventive health rebates are offered to those who participate in preventive services. There is an aggressive quality assurance monitoring and evaluation program, which includes an occurrence monitoring system.

Northern Telecom, Inc., has provided a multifaceted health management program that integrates on-site and community delivery systems. The object was to provide continuous, preventively oriented information, services, and financing. The components include the following:

- An age-, gender-, and risk-targeted screening program
- Health promotion incentives
- Learning centers in some facilities

- An extensive health promotion program supervised by nurse practitioners
- Organizational stress interventions linked to the management development program
- An integrated, preventive safety program covering both on-job and off-job safety
- Ergonomics programs at workstations
- Preventive services provided through the benefits package
- Self-care materials and courses
- On-site primary care
- Point-of-need preventive counseling and behavioral contracting
- An Employee Assistance Program integrated with on-site services and the benefits program
- Wise-use materials and courses integrated with new employee orientation
- A single point-of-service managed care option provided through the benefits program
- Referral to high-quality practitioners

The corporate medical staff has worked with the claims processing and utilization management vendor to continuously improve the process of utilization management through the use of tighter standards and information management. Results, while not designed as a controlled trial, appear to demonstrate a continuous reduction in inpatient utilization, high-cost mental health cases, frequency and per case cost of targeted diagnoses affected in the short term by health behavior change and in nonspecific complaints (believed to be affected by the wise-use program). The impact on work-related injuries and illnesses was demonstrated by both a sharp drop in frequency and a halving of workers' compensation cost in the first three years of the program. Employees reacted very positively to these programs (Dalton and Harris, 1992).

Goodyear has taken the direct provision of medical care a step further, opening clinics in Oklahoma, Alabama, and Ohio, after local physicians refused to work with the company to manage health care costs. The clinics are open to employees, dependents, and retirees, offering low-cost medical care and free pharmacy services. They also perform minor surgery and deliver babies. Nestle Foods is opening an on-site clinic that will offer similar services.

The trend toward on-site care is accelerating somewhat among large employers. J. C. Penney has recently opened a large day-care and urgent care facility operated by Presbyterian Health Systems at its headquarters in Texas. USX is opening a $1.2 million clinic at its Merrillville, Indiana, facility, again run by a contractor. The Mayo Clinic has opened primary care facilities, linked to its referral network, for Deere & Co. at Waterloo, Iowa, and Moline, Illinois. General Electric, Union Camp, and GTE are involved in some form of on-site care as well (Kenkel, 1993a).

Program Design

The shape and extent of on-site programs will be dictated by the level of intent to provide comprehensive health management to the work force and dependents. This in turn depends on the willingness of management to undertake activities that, while they may not be directly related to the core business, clearly support it. These activities are often not well executed or are highly variable in the outside community. To the extent that these various options have not been well executed or are not integrated well, the in-house option probably makes sense.

The scope of in-house programs is then dictated by available funds for investment and the availability of management talent to effectively run program options ranging from health promotion to claims management to network selection and management. Professional medical managers may be required. The reason that on-site care, private network development, and claims management are uncommon is probably a combination of the lack of critical mass in most companies, which are not large enough to support these operations, an unwillingness to get into unfamiliar business activities, intensive marketing by carriers and claims processors, and a potential fear of lack of objectivity in the program if the program is run in-house.

There has also been significant resistance from the provider community, which fears erosion of its client base. These fears may be, but do not have to be, realistic. If providers can adopt the desired standards of care and become part of an integrated system, they could provide primary and specialist care on referral from the health promotion and screening program on site. However, making rather than buying clearly reduces the amount of profit made on medical care. It may well reduce the amount of medically unnecessary care and may add a preventive dimension effectively. There is certainly a potential advantage in terms of data management. It is possible that consortia of companies could provide a number of these services with more cost-effective economies of scale.

Goals and Objectives

The goals of the program will typically be framed in terms of the efficiency and effectiveness of care and health management. Objectives to follow those goals can then focus on the specific delivery system desired. There might be series of sets of objectives, framed in terms of implementation of different components of the system, reductions in morbidity and mortality, cross management, and integration. The integration objectives are particularly important. Many of the advantages of on-site services will be lost if they are not carefully integrated with community medical resources to provide continuity of care, continuity of information, and improvement in customer satisfaction. In fact, one of the key dimensions of on-site services is that they must satisfy the customer to a greater extent than off-site options, if those are offered, in order to capture the greatest number of encounters within the system.

One often neglected but critical question is how to extend these services to dependents who typically live in a widely scattered area. When employee populations were concentrated around the immediate vicinity of a manufacturing operation or a transportation center, this was not as much of an issue. However, a good deal of the benefit of an on-site system would be lost if dependents could not use it. Telephone counseling and sending materials home might provide some outreach for health promotion, self-care, and wise-use activities. Of course, in-house claims and utilization management are not dependent on the location of the users. With day-care centers being opened on site, better access for dependents may exist.

Implementation

Once the shape of the program has been determined and objectives quantified, so that it is clear to employers what the various activities are, the basic tactical issue is carefully mapping out all of the steps necessary to design, budget, staff, train, and execute each of these components. In a sense, each of these is similar to the corresponding step in starting a new business. The components could include data analysis, health promotion, disease prevention, on-site care, utilization review, claims processing, and proprietary managed care organizations or an owned medical system. The components of a comprehensive, integrated system are presented in the following list (Dalton and Harris, 1992):

Primary Prevention

AIDS education
Back injury prevention
Blood pressure control
Cancer awareness
   Breast, testicular, skin,
   colon, cervical
Cholesterol control
Ergonomics
Fitness
Health fairs
Incentive programs
Nutrition
Prenatal care and education
Safety
Screening

Seatbelts/child safety
   restraints
Smoking control
Social support
Stress management
Substance abuse education
Travel wellness
Weight management

Secondary Prevention

Chronic disease monitoring
CPR/first aid
Emergency response
Employee assistance
Primary care

Self-care/discharge
instructions
Self-care
Wise use of health services

Tertiary Prevention

Disability management
Rehabilitation
Return to work/modified duty

Many of these functions can be performed well by nurse practitioners and perhaps physicians' assistants, reserving serious cases and perhaps data analysis and program oversight for physicians. Team members can come from many disciplines, but being multiskilled is often useful to increase productivity.

One key decision is what management information will be tracked to determine program effectiveness and efficiency. I would recommend capturing, at a minimum, diagnostic codes, procedural codes, expenses or costs, and a minimum data set necessary to document and validate the diagnosis and link it to appropriateness of treatment. All this should be stored in a relational data base for easy monitoring and analysis.

In most cases, the in-house option will be a start-up activity the employer may be building on one or more existing components. These might include a preexisting low level of on-site care and/or some health promotion activities. In a few instances, there are in-house claims processing operations, either in the workers' compensation area or group health. Typically, these are not automated, and therefore implementation of automated information systems becomes a key objective.

As an example, on-site claims processing has a number of theoretical advantages. The gains in data accuracy and availability should be substantial, and the ability to manage the process should be increased. The advantages must be tempered by the ability to use state-of-the-art computer systems and maintain confidentiality and to process claims in a very efficient and effective manner. One caveat is that those running the program must resist the temptation to make exceptions to the benefits plan at the behest of management or employees. This will subject the plan to possible disqualification or other adverse action under the ERISA Act or create an atmosphere of inequity. It may also reduce the ability to manage costs.

Conclusion

A number of employers have opened on-site facilities to reduce costs and improve quality. These goals have been met, at least anecdotally. There may be a substantial initial investment, but these units hold the promise of more manageable care and less variability. It is critical to provide care in a neutral manner and to have a user-friendly organization, while building self-efficacy among employees and dependents. Preventive activities can be built into in-house programs more easily than they can be in the community. Access for dependents remains a problem except in smaller communities.

CHAPTER FOURTEEN

Opportunities and Barriers to Strategic Health Management

This book started with a description of the U.S. medical industry, as financed by employee benefits. The first few chapters outlined how the "system" evolved and what employees and employers wanted from it. I explored the structural and process issues leading to some present outcomes of the medical care industry and its processes: some excellent acute care, but also high-tech solutions in search of problems to solve; an overabundance of resources; geographic, specialty, and acuity maldistribution of resources; access problems in several senses; inefficient and highly variable clinical and operational processes; compensation and benefits programs that do not maximize personal benefit (utility); and a lack of shared information and responsibility for health and care.

The book then explored the nature of quality and value in medical care, the current business structure of the medical industry, and a strategic management process for health and the downstream costs when health fails. The points that one is led to through this analysis are that the "system" is not functioning in a manner that is responsive to consumer preferences or financial constraints, that costs are increasing geometrically, taking resources from other sectors of the public and private economy, and that the best solution might well be to avoid having to engage with the system as much as possible. In summation, we will reverse the order of our analysis, starting with the less expensive, more logical, and chronologically primary alternative — promoting health and preventing disease. We will then progress through the strategies employers can use to manage

313

health and medically related costs, from less intensive and expensive strategies onward and upward.

The Strategic Health Management Process

As long as employers retain responsibility for total compensation and employee well-being, it would be to their advantage to take an informed, proactive, data-driven strategic approach to those issues. National "health" care reform or not, the health of the work force, in its broad sense, including motivation and bonding to the employer, strongly influences the quality and quantity of the work product, employee health status, and satisfaction with work and life. Nasty surprises in managing total compensation will continue to bedevil employers unless they can understand cost drivers and manage them. Passivity prevents reaching goals, be they profit, market share, or human resource targets.

The strategic health management process is not so different from any business strategic management. It starts with gaining a clear understanding of the current problems and opportunities one faces, in the context of the particular environment. Current problems are based on economics and expectations. There is a significant opportunity to use the collective ingenuity of managers, employees and dependents, medical personnel, and perhaps community resources to cooperatively improve all aspects of health and medical care: customer service, operational efficiency, clinical effectiveness, appropriate application, and utility maximization. The environmental forces affecting current and future results include the suppliers and end users of health and medical care, the government, and private financing programs that have created a unique set of economic rules for medical services. As was discussed in Chapter Five, the strategic health management process is a structured, data-based way of cost effectively addressing the major health issues in an employed population. It starts with a thorough understanding of the current health problems and future health risks in that group of employees and dependents. That information can be gained from analysis of health insurance claims data, adjusting for the age, gender, and insurance plan types of the population, and comparing the data with several benchmarks. This analysis will also tell the strategic health management team how efficient currently purchased care is, after adjusting the data for the mix of cases paid for. The former information will allow the strategic health management team to design programs to promote health and prevent disease, and the latter will lay the groundwork for better management of acute and chronic medical care.

Promoting health, and in fact more cost-effective management of medical care, require selling and promoting new ideas of involvement, self-responsibility, positive life-styles, shared decision making, and parsimonious care. As with any successful marketing effort, marketing health and cost-effective care should be based at least in part on consumer needs, demands, and preferences. Thus, objective data should be combined with survey data to understand employees' and dependents' knowledge, preferences, and wants about health, health promotion, and medical care. Matching the two will probably yield some high-risk, high-demand areas (for example, family substance abuse prevention, cholesterol and blood pressure management), some high-risk, low-demand areas (vehicle restraint programs, safety, smoking cessation), and some low-need/yield, high-demand areas (weight management, nutrition).

Using the information described above, the strategic health management team, under the direction of top management, can select appropriate goals, strategies, and tactics to manage the health of their particular groups. There are advantages to involving employee representatives in this planning process. In companies that have embraced the continuous quality improvement approach, employee involvement would be an integral part of the improvement of health management.

Employee Involvement

Employees and dependents are integrally involved in health management now, but not in the most effective ways possible. They engage in activities that may lead to disease and disability, as well as healthy behaviors, and purchase medical care, often without understanding the risks, benefits, and alternatives. These actions translate into productivity or lack of it and costs to both employers and employees. It would therefore make good business, as well as behavioral, sense for those paying the bills to involve employees in design and to sponsor self-efficacy, self-care, wise-use, skill-building, and health education classes and activities. These were discussed in Chapter Seven, along with logic and evidence supporting their effectiveness.

Involving employees in a broad range of health-related areas as the basis for a series of needed changes is long overdue. It represents a shift in both the responsibility and accountability for health, as well as a change in the balance of power in the medical interchange.

Promoting Health

In general, prevention has proven to be more cost effective than care or cure after disease or injury has developed. In this volume, I have outlined the causes of ill or suboptimal health. Many of them are amenable to health promotive or preventive efforts, but are much more expensive and difficult to deal with by means of acute or chronic medical interventions.

Health, Disease, Prevention, and Recovery

Many of the determinants of health and disease are outside the scope of the current medical delivery system. They include lifestyle risks, work climate, work exposures, socioeconomic level, and psychological factors. And the determinants of medical service use are not entirely related to health status. Factors influencing the decision to seek medical services include individual symptom sensitivity and knowledge about symptoms, disease, and the effectiveness of tests and treatments. Once treatment is sought, the course of treatment can be highly variable, depending on the decisions of one or more practitioners and, in some cases, the preferences of the patient and the family, if the practitioner spends the time to explore alternatives and reach a consensus based on the patient's values.

The multiple factors affecting health and service use suggest that there is an interest and role for employers and employees in the management of health and of medical service use as long as employers continue to fund care or bear the consequences of absence from work. The strategies suggested here will improve health and productivity by attacking the many facets leading to medical service use.

I would suggest intervening far earlier than is common in most benefits programs: at the beginning of the wellness cycle (Chapter Eight). This cycle posits that there is a continuum of health, from wellness at the positive end to neutral or "okay" health at the midpoint, through symptoms to disease at the other (O'Donnell and Harris, 1993). A continuum of care parallels this spectrum (or cycle, as one becomes ill and then recovers). Ideally, health care should be prevention focused, and when care is needed, centered around the restoration of function rather than the simple care or cure of disease or injury. (These foci, interestingly enough, are some of the mainstays of occupational medicine.) Again, I would argue that employers, as well as employees, would have an interest in "being the best they can be" by staying well, feeling their best, and achieving meaningful goals (all dimensions of wellness).

Promoting Health

Promoting health is most effective when approached in an organized, consistent manner that directly addresses the specific risks in an employee and dependent population (Chapter Nine). Health promotion programs run the risk of being perceived as fads or "nice-to-have" extras. In reality, while there can be a faddish element to some of the programs' elements that have been used, careful attention to the scientific basis of each activity, and program design as a whole will keep the program focused and cost effective.

Prevention has been shown repeatedly to be more cost effective than later salvage and repair (Leaf, 1993). The analysis and cost-effectiveness ratio may vary depending on the breadth of the costs and effects considered, but the direction of the results is the same. Further, there is strong employee demand for preventive and health promotive activities. Health promotion programs are much more likely to be net satisfiers than benefits programs in today's environment of perceived takeaways.

Total Compensation

A total compensation perspective is critical, if for no other reason than that benefits costs are eroding cash wages at an alarming rate. By considering the entire package as one, both managers and employees can determine the optimal and affordable contribution to each area (see Chapter Ten). On an individual level, each employee can select options that most nearly match his or her preferences for insurance, wages, and other benefits. People work for compensation of various types, including a package of benefits. But the usefulness of the package depends on how it meets each individual or family's needs. The total reimbursement from the package depends on how much medical care one uses: a family with a serious illness could receive, or be protected from, thousands of dollars in expense. Those who are not ill may pay thousands of dollars for insurance coverage, presumably for the security of protection from possible medical expenses.

Allowing employees to choose their own options of cash wages, medical insurance, pension, time off, and other forms of compensation and benefits should reverse the decline in satisfaction with benefits that has occurred in the last few years. It should also decrease inefficient use of resources by matching needs with coverage. The total compensation approach is needed to make employers more competitive in labor markets as well as end-product markets.

Managing Care

It is clear that there is, at the least, tremendous variance in the utilization and appropriateness of acute and chronic medical services among small areas and providers, and even between instances of care by the same provider. To a great extent, this occurs because the infrastructure of medical care does not support efficiency or quality through peer interaction, information exchange, and efficient processes. Both clinical and support processes are fragmented and inefficient, by and large. There are few explicit guidelines for care in use, and little exists in the way of feedback to providers to understand and improve their practices.

While there is clearly a deficiency in research on outcomes and relative efficacy and efficiency of alternative diagnostic pathways and treatments, this variance is not supported by the existing medical literature. Thus, the divergence in practices appears to occur after training (although it is also true that standards of practice, evaluation, and continuous improvement are not taught in medical school or many residencies either).

Managed care, in its best form, provides the structure for efficient, effective care. It is effective because it is based on specific agreements between buyers and managers of medical care, and between financiers or managers of care and providers. It is unreasonable to expect any complex system to function without management. That management should be directed to improving the quality of clinical care and support and hotel processes. Management that views medical care as a process or a series of processes should be able to stabilize and improve those processes through information automation and feedback, clinical process standardization, administrative simplification, and process streamlining. Management starts with a foundation of primary care, with specialists being used carefully and parsimoniously in areas in which they are really needed.

Managed care has achieved lower utilization, lower costs, and lower rates of cost increase than unmanaged alternatives with equal or better quality. Management is necessary because of a great potential surplus of suppliers, tests, and treatments. Use of fewer blind alleys and unnecessary care will result in improved quality accompanied by improved efficiency.

Beyond managing care, managing health is important as well. Health promotion, disease prevention, employee involvement, and wise use of the medical care system are key to preventing the causes of these growing costs and to reducing outlays. These elements of health management improve the quality of life as well.

Buying, Improving, and Building Health Systems

The currently available medical care plans and systems are not, by and large, the most efficient or effective ways of delivering care. They are specialist based, administratively cumbersome, geographically remote, and perhaps most important, not based on agreed-on specifications or standards. Better options can be created by specification-based contract or systems set up by employers that are better managed.

Some pioneering employers have started to create their own systems built on quality-based contracting. They have reduced the rate of cost increases by up to half. Quality measurements are not yet available, but employee satisfaction appears to be the same as under previous plans. In the best case, these agreements form the basis for quality improvement projects to improve care.

Other employers have built part or all of a comprehensive health management system. These efforts range from wellness activities to integrated health management programs at the work site. The latter provide a continuum of prevention and care ranging from preventive screening to primary care to rehabilitation. These programs are more manageable than outside programs and can reflect the employer's culture and internal dynamics. They can tap social support for behavior change as well. They also can be run for less than purchased services in many cases. Internal systems can also interface well with external referral sources and can provide management expertise and guidelines to community practitioners. A certain size of employer or group of employers is required for these efforts, but the payoff has been worth it.

Political Solutions

Driven mainly by a concern about rising costs, affordable medical care has become a major issue on the public agenda. The American public has consistently opined that the "health" system needs a major overhaul. However, a much smaller proportion has actually experienced a problem with their own care.

Thus, there may be a problem gaining broad support for dramatic changes in the way care is perceived to be available and delivered. Issues like the decrease in real wages caused by rapidly increasing benefits costs, which are real negatives for all wage earners, do not seem to be taken into account; they are infrequently addressed directly by polling questions, and therefore are probably not considered as factors in other answers about medical care.

It is not entirely clear how much the public, or employees as a substantial subset of the public, are dissatisfied with the prescriptive relationships that typically exist with medical providers. When asked if they are satisfied with the amount of information and time they obtain from *their* physicians, people are generally satisfied but believe that physicians in general do not inform patients adequately. Polls that ask about relative decision making are rare to nonexistent. This is a key issue, because unequal relationships without adequate information exchange cannot take patient preferences and utility into account and therefore lead to suboptimal care.

These polls also have not asked about beliefs about the relationship of life-style to disease or demand for preventive or health promoting programs. In surveys conducted by employers, employees have seemed to understand the relationship and to be quite interested in health promotion activities. They may express preferences for activities with marginal return, such as weight management, and not appear to be interested in leading causes of disability such as injuries and substance abuse, but in general, employees seem to prefer prevention. Polls that assess preferences for preventive activities in comparison to curative ones might yield some interesting results.

Some preventive services are included in many of the reform packages that have been proposed, but health promotion activities, either direct or credited if paid for by employers, have not been included. No current proposal explicitly addresses, reimburses, or requires health education, skill building, self-efficacy training, or training in wise use of medical care. Their inclusion is needed to manage the full spectrum of health and to control the costs of acute care.

Many efforts at changing the financing and delivery of medical care have been opposed by organized medicine, academic medicine, and facilities associations. One would expect such defense of one's interests, but perhaps not quite so cloaked in an allegedly altruistic concern for quality and patient relationships. In some cases, such as Medicaid and Medicare, opposition has been neutralized by reimbursement schemes that ultimately proved very inflationary. As in many areas of American politics, action may be questionable when concentrated interests are arrayed against diffuse ones. As President Clinton has recognized, concentrated support in favor of change will be needed to ensure its passage. Even so, it is likely that change will be incremental and phased in over a period of time.

Conclusion

Strategic health management is a logical, data-based, continuously improving process of actively and mutually managing health in its broadest sense. It involves employees and many members of the management team to produce effective, broadly based results. Over time, this approach has led to improved productivity, if for no other reason than greater availability for work and decreased cost trends. It is compatible with continuous improvement in other areas and harnesses the creativity and energy of many employees and even dependents. If structured properly, at the least the process may stop the slide in employee satisfaction with benefits and by extension the employment relationship. At best, strategic health management can become a core program for human resource and business development, under any but the most comprehensive scheme of acute care financing.

International Benchmarks and Competitive Challenges

In considering changes to the medical care financing and delivery "system," it may be useful to examine the structure, process, and outputs (including customer satisfaction) of the medical care systems in other major industrialized countries. All of them have lower expenditures per capita (see Chapter One) and yet do better than the United States on most, if not all, population indicators of health status. The correlations between delivery system and financing designs, costs, and cost growth rates may provide ideas for both political and managerial strategies to manage costs and quality. Customer satisfaction and other measures of quality will allow us to determine whether these differences affect the value of the outcomes, allowing for historical and cultural differences. The reason for examining other systems is not primarily that the U.S. industrial cost structure is handicapped by medical care costs, but that we might learn from other systems that are less specialized and technologically intensive and that have fewer payers and operate with budgets.

Funding and Design

The Canadian system is a provincial government health insurance model. Each province runs its own health system under general federal rules, with a fixed federal contribution financed by general taxes. Seventy-three percent of all expenditures are financed by the public system, and 20 percent are paid by citizens out of pocket. The fact that the government is essentially the only buyer of services controls the budget available to hospitals

and physicians. Provincial governments negotiate a global budget with a consortium of individual hospitals and a fee schedule
with the provincial medical society (Schieber, Poullier, and
Greenwald, 1992).

The Canadian provincial plan designs typically cover 100
percent of hospital care, outpatient care, and prescription drugs
for the elderly. Prescription drug coverage for others varies
province by province. Private insurance is permitted only for
items not covered by public insurance such as private hospital
rooms, prescription drugs in some provinces, ambulance services, and nursing home care. More than 60 percent of Canadians are covered by complementary private policies.

The German health system is also based on the social insurance model (that is, social insurance provides extensive cross
subsidization among different risk groups and ignores economic
loss and allocating costs). By contrast, casualty insurance, which
is commonly one of the bases for insurance in the United States,
contains the premise that premiums should be set according to
expected risk or loss.

Virtually the entire German population is covered by
statutory sickness funds, which do not compete with each other,
being targeted at specific groups, and by private insurance.
About 1,200 sickness funds cover an estimated 88 percent of
the population. They are financed through payroll contributions
by the employer and the employee. About 9 percent of sickness
fund members purchase complementary private insurance, and
another 10 percent of the population opt out of the public system and are fully covered by private insurance. Seventy-three
percent of all health expenditures are paid by the sickness funds,
and about 11 percent are direct out-of-pocket payment.

The sickness fund plan design in Germany covers hospital care at 100 percent, with a small copayment for the first two
weeks. Outpatient care is also covered at 100 percent, and
prescription drugs require a $2 copayment.

Japan's health care financing is based on the German social insurance model. The whole population is covered by one
of three plans: the Employee Health Insurance Plan, the Community Insurance Plan, and Health and Medical Services for

the Aged. About 62 percent of the population is covered by 1,800 employer-sponsored plans, which are part of the Employee Health Insurance Plan. Small businesses, the self-employed, and farmers are covered through the Community Health Insurance Plan, which is administered by a conglomeration of local government and private bodies. The elderly are covered by the Health and Medical Services for the Aged Plan, which pools funds from the other plans. The system is financed through employer and employee income-related premiums. Limited private insurance exists for supplemental coverage. Public expenditures accounted for 72 percent of total health care spending, and out-of-pocket expenses accounted for 12 percent (Schieber, Poullier, and Greenwald, 1992).

Fifty-two percent of the Japanese population is covered through Health Insurance for Employees and 48 percent through the other two plans. All employers of more than 700 employees may contract out of the government plan and establish an independent plan.

In the Japanese plan design, hospital care is covered at 90 percent for employees and 80 percent for dependents, with an out-of-pocket maximum of $392 per month. In the Community Plan, only 70 percent of hospitalization is covered. Outpatient care is covered at 90 percent for employees and 70 percent for dependents in the Employee Health Insurance Plan and at 70 percent in the Community Insurance Plan. The elderly are covered at 100 percent, with a $6 per month copayment. Prescription drugs are similarly covered at 90 percent for employee health insurance and 70 percent for national health insurance. The elderly are covered at 100 percent.

Health Insurance for Employees is financed through payroll taxes. The National Insurance Plan is funded 50 percent through federal and local government taxes and income-adjusted premiums, which can be as high as $2,543 a year (as of 1991).

The French health care model is also based on the social insurance or Bismarck model, similar to that of Germany. The entire population is covered by a compulsory health insurance plan financed through the social security system but channeled through organizations similar to the German sickness funds.

There are three major plans and several smaller ones that are quasi-autonomous nongovernmental bodies. The system is financed through employer and employee payroll taxes. Seventy-four percent of the total health care expenditures are public, and 17 percent are out of pocket. More than 80 percent of the population purchases private insurance from nonprofit mutual organizations. About 2 percent of the population has private commercial insurance.

In the United Kingdom, virtually the entire population is covered under a system that is financed by general taxes. Eighty-five percent of costs is paid by the government, and the remaining 15 percent is paid by employer and employee payroll tax contributions to the national insurance fund. There is minimal cost sharing. There is a private market outside of the government market, but it is fairly small. Nine percent of the population have supplemental coverage, often used for elective surgery. Much of the private coverage is financed by employers. The plan design in Great Britain covers hospital care, prescription drugs, and outpatient care at 100 percent, with a nominal copayment for prescription drugs.

The entire Swedish population is covered through a public system with automatic coverage for all residents. The national plan is funded 10 percent by employer payroll tax, 65 percent by local taxes, and 6.5 percent by another federal tax. Seven percent of the population's supplemental insurance is paid for by private employers. This insurance is provided mainly to business executives and covers private rooms and nonemergency surgery.

The Swedish plan design covers 100 percent of hospital fees, with a $10 copayment per day with a maximum of $150 per year. Outpatient care is covered at 100 percent, with a $10 per visit copayment and again a $150 per year maximum. Prescription drugs are covered at 100 percent for "essential drugs."

Delivery System/Industry

The Canadian delivery system is composed largely of nonprofit community hospitals and self-employed physicians. Only about

5 percent of Canadian hospital beds are for profit and privately owned. Private hospitals do not participate in the public insurance program. The public financing systems are funded about two-thirds by the provinces and a third by the federal government.

Ambulatory and inpatient care are completely separate in the German system. Ambulatory care physicians are paid according to negotiated fee schedules for sickness fund payers and a separate fixed fee schedule for private patients. Hospitals are paid negotiated per diems for sickness fund patients. Hospital per diems include physicians' remuneration for public patients, with a separate fee-for-service payment for physician services under private insurance.

About 50 percent of the hospitals are public, 35 percent are private voluntary hospitals, and 14 percent are private for-profits generally owned by physicians. Most hospital physicians are salaried employees of hospitals, and ambulatory physicians are self-employed.

Japanese physicians and hospitals are paid on the basis of nationally negotiated fee schedules. Physicians in public hospitals are salaried, and those in private practice are reimbursed on a fee-for-service basis. Interestingly, physicians prescribe and dispense pharmaceuticals, a major source of their income.

About 80 percent of Japan's hospitals are privately operated and often physican owned. There are no other for-profit hospitals (Ikegami, 1991; Iglehart, 1988a, 1988b).

In France, public hospitals are paid under global prospective budgets. Private hospitals are paid on negotiated per diems. About 65 percent of the hospital beds are public, and 35 percent (equally divided between profit and nonprofit) are private. Physicians in public hospitals are salaried, but physicians in private hospitals are paid on a negotiated fee-for-service basis. Many ambulatory care physicians and those in private hospitals are self-employed, while those in municipal health centers and public hospitals are salaried.

In the United Kingdom, there are 190 local health districts in charge of paying doctors and running hospitals. Ninety percent of the U.K. hospital beds are public or voluntary and are generally owned by the National Health Service. A recent reform act will separate the hospital districts' funding from provision of care. Hospitals will become self-governing, while the districts will pay for care on a fee-for-service basis. It is not clear whether this will be simple fee-for-service or negotiated per diem or fee schedules. Interestingly, British physicians are not particularly interested in the introduction of market principles.

Outpatient physicians are reimbursed by capitation and negotiated in binding fees. Hospital physicians are generally on salary. The National Health Service currently owns most hospitals, which receive an annual prospective budget. General practitioners serve as gatekeepers (Schieber, Poullier, and Greenwald, 1992). As of 1991, it became possible for large physician practices to become "budget holders" receiving larger capitation payments and being placed at risk for a defined risk of inpatient and outpatient services (Schneider, 1992; Day and Klein, 1991).

The Swedish health care system is administered by twenty-three county councils and three municipalities. County councils own or operate regional hospitals, which are reimbursed on a perspective annual budget. Most outpatient care is provided by regional primary care clinics. Physicians in hospitals are salaried.

The government is now implementing a system based on the U.S. DRG system, in which hospitals will be paid on a per operation or per diagnosis basis. There are waiting lists for certain procedures, such as coronary artery bypass, lens replacements, and hip joint replacements.

Practice Patterns and Other Outcomes

While Canadians had longer hospital stays, American physicians and hospitals used more inputs and paid significantly higher prices for those inputs (Newhouse, Anderson, and Roos, 1988; Fuchs and Hahn, 1990; Devin, 1988).

Germany is the only one of major industrial countries to experience a decline in its health costs-to-gross domestic product ratio, which declined from 8.4 percent of GDP to 8.1 percent in 1980 to 8.1 percent in 1990. This is probably due to the fact that German nominal GDP grew faster than nominal health spending because of a rapidly growing economy. The ratio also holds on a per capita basis. In terms of rank for per capita spending, Germany dropped from second to fourth between 1980 and 1990 (Schieber, Poullier, and Greenwald, 1992).

Japan's health care spending–to–GDP ratio has been the second lowest after the United Kingdom over the ten-year period examined. Japan's health care prices increased 0.7 percent per year faster than the GDP deflated. This to some extent reflects the relatively low inflation in that country. Interestingly, Japan has the second lowest spending per capita, at about 50 percent of the U.S. level.

France's spending on health unadjusted for inflation or population growth outstrips the growth of the economy. This may well be correlated with the very high proportion of the population covered by private insurance, even though the funding comes from the government.

The United Kingdom devotes the smallest percentage of its GDP to health care of any country. This has been true since the early 1980s. Health care spending grew only slightly faster than the growth rate of the GDP.

Satisfaction

Satisfaction with out-of-pocket costs in Canada is reasonably high. According to a Louis Harris survey commissioned by the Harvard Community Health Plan, over half of those covered by the provincial plans were satisfied with control, waiting time, out-of-pocket expenses, and the quality of care (Harvard Community Health Plan, 1990).

In a six-nation comparison, the Germans are the most satisfied with their level of health care costs. The areas of greatest dissatisfaction are access to elective services and the ability to keep personal costs low.

Despite the structural similarities to the German system, the majority of Japanese feel that too much money is spent on hospitalization, advanced technology, and treating people who are terminally ill. They also find spending on physicians too

high. The Japanese are most likely to feel they have been discouraged from seeking medical treatment. The length of stay
in Japan is quite long, and there is significant duplication of
service and equipment because of rivalries between clinics and
hospitals (Harvard Community Health Plan, 1990).

Britons are least likely to feel they have been denied
needed care. They are most satisfied with not waiting too long
to see a doctor and receiving what they perceive to be high-
quality care.

Only 29 percent of Swedes are satisfied with their country's success in providing top-quality care. However, they do
not feel that they have personally been denied access to care,
and they rank lowest in the feeling that they have been discouraged from seeking medical care (Harvard Community
Health Plan, 1990). Most Swedes feel that about the right
amount of money is being spent on physicians and hospitals.

Observations

There is virtually no correlation between expenditures (regardless of how measured) and indicators such as life expectancy
and infant mortality. Satisfaction appears not to be well correlated with expenditure either (Tables A.1 and A.2).

Table A.1. Satisfaction with Health Care.

	Very satisfied (%)	Somewhat satisfied (%)	Not very satisfied (%)	Not at all satisfied (%)
Canada	60	34	5	1
Germany	45	47	7	1
Great Britain	39	48	9	3
Japan	12	55	24	3
Sweden	28	54	14	3
United States	55	33	7	3

Source: Adapted from Harvard Community Health Plan, 1990.

Table A.2. Reasons for Dissatisfaction with Health Care.

	Discouraged from seeking medical treatment (%)	Unable to see a specialist (%)	Unable to get all the tests needed (%)
Canada	22	28	24
Germany	12	19	21
Great Britain	12	16	16
Japan	26	21	14
Sweden	6	16	18
United States	21	18	20

Source: Adapted from Harvard Community Health Plan, 1990.

References

Abbott, R. K. *Redefining Flexibility in a Total Compensation Environment*. Lyndhurst, N.J.: Alexander Consulting Group, 1993.

Abramowitz, K. S. *The Future of Health Care Delivery in America*. New York: Sanford C. Bernstein & Co., Inc., 1993.

A. Foster Higgins & Co., Inc. *Foster Higgins Health Care Benefits Survey, 1989. Report 1: Managed Care Plans*. Princeton, N.J.: A. Foster Higgins & Co., Inc., 1989.

A. Foster Higgins & Co., Inc. *Foster Higgins Health Care Benefits Survey, 1991. Report 1: Indemnity Plans: Cost, Design, and Funding*. Princeton, N.J.: A. Foster Higgins & Co., Inc., 1992.

American Hospital Association. *Panel Survey*. Chicago: American Hospital Association, 1990.

American Hospital Association. *Hospital Statistics, 1990–1991*. Chicago: American Hospital Association, 1991.

American Hospital Association. *Hospital Statistics, 1991–1992*. Chicago: American Hospital Association, 1992.

American Medical Association. *Physician and Public Opinion on Health Care Issues, 1992*. Chicago: American Medical Association, May 1992.

Amler, R. W., and Dull, H. B. (eds.). *Closing the Gap: The Burden of Unnecessary Illness*. New York: Oxford University Press, 1987.

Anders, G., and Winslow, R. "Health Care Industry Is Now Restructuring: With It Comes Pain." *Wall Street Journal*, June 16, 1993, pp. A1, A7.

333

Anderson, K., and Woottom, B. "Changes in Hospital Staffing Patterns." *Monthly Labor Review,* 1991, *114,* 3–9.

Angell, M. "How Much Will Health Care Reform Cost?" *New England Journal of Medicine,* 1993, *328,* 1778–1779.

Anstadt, G., Lester, D. L., Powell, B. A., and Tsunaitas, E. M. "The Business Planning Process Supply to an In-House Corporate Occupational Medical Unit." In J. S. Harris, H. D. Belk, and L. W. Wood (eds.), *Managing Employee Health Care Costs: Assuring Quality and Value.* Beverly, Mass.: OEM Press, 1992.

"As Outpatient Care Gains, Communities Need to Trim Their Excess Hospital Beds." *Wall Street Journal,* Feb. 22, 1993, pp. B1, B6.

Avorn, J., and Soumerai, S. B. "A New Approach to Reducing Suboptimal Drug Use." *Journal of the American Medical Association,* 1983, *250,* 1752–1753.

Bandura, A. "Self-Efficacy Mechanism in Physiological Activation and Health-Promoting Behavior." Paper presented at the National Health Management Conference, San Francisco, Sept. 1991.

Barge, B. N., and Carlson, J. G. *The Executive's Guide to Controlling Health Care and Disability Costs.* New York: Wiley, 1993.

Barker, J. *Breaking Out of the Box.* New York: Benchmark Press, 1989.

Bartlett, E. E. "Eight Principles for Patient Education Research." *Postgraduate Medicine,* 1985, pp. 667–669.

Barton, M. D., and Schoenbaum, S. C. "Improving Influenza Vaccination Performance in an HMO Setting: The Use of Computer Generated Reminders and Peer Comparison Feedback." *American Journal of Public Health,* 1990, *80,* 534–536.

Benham, L., and Benham, A. "The Impact of Incremental Medical Services on Health Status, 1963–1970." In R. Anderson, J. Crabits, and O. Anderson (eds.), *Equity and Health Services: An Empirical Analysis of Social Policy.* New York: Ballinger, 1975.

Berlin, L. "Does Misradiography Constitute Malpractice?" *Radiology,* 1977, *123,* 523.

Bernstein, S. J., and others. "The Appropriateness of Hysterectomy: A Comparison of Care in Seven Health Plans." *Journal of the American Medical Association,* 1993, *269,* 2398–2402.

Berwick, D. M. "Continuous Improvement as an Ideal in Health Care." *New England Journal of Medicine,* 1989, *320,* 53–56.

Berwick, D. M. "The Clinical Process and the Quality Process." *Quality Management in Health Care,* 1992, *1*(1), 1–8.

Berwick, D. M., and Coltin, K. L. "Feedback Reduces Test Use in an HMO." *Journal of the American Medical Association,* 1986, *255,* 1450–1454.

Berwick, D. M., Godfrey, A. B., and Roessner, J. *Curing Health Care: New Strategies for Quality Improvement.* San Francisco: Jossey-Bass, 1990.

Blackburn, H., and Luepker, R. "Heart Disease." In J. E. Last and R. B. Wallace (eds.), *Maxcy-Rosenau-Last Public Health and Preventive Medicine.* (13th ed.) East Norwalk, Conn.: Appleton & Lange, 1992.

Blanchfield, B. B. "Hospital Capital in the 1990s: Competition Versus Global Budgets." In R. J. Blendon and T. S. Hyams (eds.), *The Future of American Health Care.* Vol. 2: *Reforming the System: Containing Health Care Costs in an Era of Universal Coverage.* Washington, D.C.: Faulkner and Grey, 1992.

Blendon, R. J., and Edwards, J. N. "Looking Back at Hospital Forecasts." In R. J. Blendon and J. N. Edwards (eds.), *The Future of American Health Care.* Vol. 1: *System in Crisis: The Case for Health Care Reform.* Washington, D.C.: Faulkner and Grey, 1991a.

Blendon, R. J., and Edwards, J. N. (eds.). *The Future of American Health Care.* Vol. 1: *System in Crisis: The Case for Health Care Reform.* Washington, D.C.: Faulkner and Grey, 1991b.

Blendon, R. J., Edwards, J. N., and Hyams, T. S. "Making the Critical Choices." *Journal of the American Medical Association,* 1992, *267*(18), 2509–2520.

Blendon, R. J., and Hyams, T. S. (eds.). *The Future of American Health Care.* Vol. 2: *Reforming the System: Containing Health Care Costs in an Era of Universal Coverage.* Washington, D.C.: Faulkner and Grey, 1992.

Blumberg, M. S. "Physicians' Fees as Incentives in Changing the Behavior of the Physician: A Management Perspective."

Proceedings of the 21st Annual Symposium on Hospital Affairs.
Chicago: Graduate and Hospital Administration, Graduate
School of Business, University of Chicago, June 1979.

Blumenthal, D. "Administrative Issues in Health Care Reform."
New England Journal of Medicine, 1993a, *329,* 428–429.

Blumenthal, D. "Total Quality Management and Physicians'
Clinical Decisions." *Journal of the American Medical Association,*
1993b, *269,* 2775–2778.

Bly, J. L., Jones, R. C., and Richardson, J. E. "Impact of Work-
Site Health Promotion on Health Care Cost and Utilization:
Evaluation of Johnson & Johnson's Live for Life Program."
Journal of the American Medical Association, 1986, *256,* 3235–3240.

Borenstein, D. G., and Wiesel, S. *Low Back Pain: Medical Diagnosis
and Comprehensive Management.* Philadelphia: Saunders, 1989.

Brailler, D. T., and Van Horn, L. "Health and the Welfare
of U.S. Business." *Harvard Business Review,* 1993, *71,* 125–132.

Brand, D. "An X-Ray Screening Protocol for Extremity Injuries." *Research Report Series,* Department of Health and Human Services, Publication 84-3347, 1984.

Breslow, L., Fielding, J. E., Hermann, A. A., and Wilbur,
C. S. "Worksite Health Promotion: Its Evolution and the
Johnson & Johnson Experience." *Preventive Medicine,* 1990, *19,*
13–21.

Brink, S. D. *Health Risks and Behavior: The Impact on Medical Care
Costs.* Milwaukee, Wis.: Milliman and Robertson, 1987.

Brook, R. L. "Practice Guidelines and Practicing Medicine: Are
They Compatible?" *Journal of the American Medical Association,*
1989, *262,* 3027–3030.

Brown, L. D. "Commissions, Clubs, and Consensus: Reform
in Florida." *Health Affairs,* 1993, *12,* 7–26.

Bryant, M. "Comeback for the Company Doctor?" *Business and
Health,* Feb. 1991, pp. 44–50.

Bureau of the Census. *1989 Service Annual Survey.* Washington,
D.C.: U.S. Government Printing Office, 1991.

Bureau of Labor Statistics, U.S. Department of Labor. *Employee
Benefits in Medium and Large Firms.* Washington, D.C.: U.S.
Government Printing Office, 1982.

Bureau of Labor Statistics, U.S. Department of Labor. *Employee Benefits in Medium and Large Firms.* Washington, D.C.: U.S. Government Printing Office, 1984.

Bureau of Labor Statistics, U.S. Department of Labor. *Employee Benefits in Medium and Large Firms.* Washington, D.C.: U.S. Government Printing Office, 1986.

Bureau of Labor Statistics, U.S. Department of Labor. *Employee Benefits in Medium and Large Firms.* Washington, D.C.: U.S. Government Printing Office, 1988.

Bureau of Labor Statistics, U.S. Department of Labor. *Employee Benefits in Medium and Large Firms, 1989.* Washington, D.C.: U.S. Government Printing Office, 1990.

Bureau of Labor Statistics, U.S. Department of Labor. *Employee Benefits in Small Private Establishments, 1990.* Washington, D.C.: U.S. Government Printing Office, 1991.

Bureau of Labor Statistics, U.S. Department of Labor. *Employee Benefits in Medium and Large Firms.* Washington, D.C.: U.S. Government Printing Office, 1980.

Burns, A. "Reinventing the Detailer." *American Medical News,* May 17, 1993, pp. 13–15.

Burns, J. "The Corporate Physician as a Health Management Leader." In J. S. Harris, H. D. Belk, and L. W. Wood (eds.), *Managing Employee Health Care Costs: Assuring Quality and Value.* Beverly, Mass.: OEM Press, 1992.

Burns, J. "Outpatient Care Providers Notch Another Year of Robust Growth." *Modern Healthcare,* May 24, 1993, pp. 76–80.

Burton, W. N., and Conte, D. "Value-Managed Mental Health Benefits." In J. S. Harris, H. D. Belk, and L. W. Wood (eds.), *Managing Employee Health Care Costs: Assuring Quality and Value.* Beverly, Mass.: OEM Press, 1992.

Burton, W. N., Erickson, D., and Briones, J. "Women's Health Programs at the Workplace." In J. S. Harris, H. D. Belk, and L. W. Wood (eds.), *Managing Employee Health Care Costs: Assuring Quality and Value.* Beverly, Mass.: OEM Press, 1992.

Burton, W. N., Hoy, D. A., and Stephens, M. "A Computer Assisted Health Care Cost Management System." In J. S. Harris, H. D. Belk, and L. W. Wood (eds.), *Managing Em-*

ployee Health Care Costs: Assuring Quality and Value. Beverly, Mass.: OEM Press, 1992.

Business and Health, 1990, *8,* 24–38.

Caldwell, C. "Mentoring: The Evolving Role of Senior Leaders in a TQM Environment." *Quality Management in Health Care,* 1993, *1*(2), 13–21.

Camerlo, K., Giffin, R., Hodges, D., and Palsbo, S. *HMO Industry Profile, 1992.* Washington, D.C.: Group Health Association of America, Inc., 1992.

Caper, P. "Approaches to the Measurement of Effectiveness and Efficiency in Medical Care: The Use by Employers of Community Wide Population Based Patterns of Care." In J. S. Harris, H. D. Belk, and L. W. Wood (eds.), *Managing Employee Health Care Costs: Assuring Quality and Value.* Beverly, Mass.: OEM Press, 1992.

Carey, J., and others. "A Bitter Tonic for Drug Makers?" *Business Week,* Mar. 8, 1993, pp. 84–86.

Cates, W., Jr., and Holmes, K. K. "Sexually Transmitted Diseases." In J. M. Last and R. B. Wallace, *Maxcy-Rosenau-Last Public Health and Preventive Medicine.* East Norwalk, Conn.: Appleton & Lange, 1992.

Chassin, M. R. "Practice Guidelines: Best Hope for Quality Improvement in the 1990s." In J. S. Harris, H. D. Belk, and L. W. Wood (eds.), *Managing Employee Health Care Costs: Assuring Quality and Value.* Beverly, Mass.: OEM Press, 1992.

Chassin, M. R., and others. "Does Inappropriate Use Explain Geographic Variations and Use of Health Services? The Study of Three Procedures." *Journal of the American Medical Association,* 1987a, *253,* 2533–2537.

Chassin, M. R., and others. "How Coronary Angiography Is Used: Clinical Determinants of Appropriateness." *Journal of the American Medical Association,* 1987b, *258,* 2543–2547.

Chassin, M. R., and others. *The Appropriateness of Selected Medical and Surgical Procedures: Relationship to Geographic Variations.* Ann Arbor, Mich.: Health Administration Press, 1989.

Chorba, T. L. "Assessing Technologies for Preventing Injuries in Motor Vehicle Crashes." *International Journal of Technology Assessment in Health Care,* 1991, *7,* 296–314.

Christiansen, L. "Change of Hearts." *Business and Health,* June 1991, pp. 18–22.

Clements, M. "What Worries Voters Most?" *Parade Magazine,* May 4, 1992, pp. 4–5.

Collen, M. F. "The Institute of Medicine Computer Based Patient Record Project." In J. S. Harris, H. D. Belk, and L. W. Wood (eds.), *Managing Employee Health Care Costs: Assuring Quality and Value.* Beverly, Mass.: OEM Press, 1992.

Congressional Research Service, House Ways and Means Committee. *Cost and Effects of Extending Health Insurance Coverage.* Education and Labor serial no. 100-EE. Washington, D.C.: U.S. Government Printing Office, 1988.

Congressional Research Service, House Ways and Means Committee. *1991 Greenbook.* Publication no. 39-759. Washington, D.C.: U.S. Government Printing Office, 1991.

Connell, F. A., Blide, L. A., and Hanken, M. A. "Clinical Correlations of Small Area Variations and Population Based Admission Rates for Diabetes." *Medical Care,* 1984, *22,* 939–949.

Connell, F. A., Day, R. W., and LoGerfo, J. P. "Hospitalization and Medicaid Children: Analysis of Small Variations and Admission Rates." *American Journal of Public Health,* 1981, *71,* 606–613.

Cooper, H. "Next Generation Arrives in Gallbladder Surgery." *Wall Street Journal,* Aug. 20, 1993, p. B1.

Cooper, J. B., Newbauer, R. S., and Kiz, R. J. "An Analysis of Major Errors and Equipment Failures in Anesthesia Management: Consideration for Prevention and Detection," *Anesthesiology,* 1984, *60,* 34–42.

Cowan, C. A., and others. "Health Care Indicators." *Health Care Financing Review,* 1992, *13*(3), 111–131.

Crittenden, R. A. "Managed Competition and Premium Caps in Washington State." *Health Affairs, 12,* 1993, 82–88.

Custer, W. S. *Employer Health Care Plan Design, Plan Costs, and Health Care Delivery.* Washington, D.C.: Employee Benefits Research Institute, 1989.

Dalton, B. A., and Harris, J. S. "A Comprehensive Approach to Corporate Health Management." In J. S. Harris, H. D. Belk, and L. W. Wood (eds.), *Managing Employee Health Care*

Costs: Assuring Quality and Value. Beverly, Mass.: OEM Press, 1992.

Darby, M. "Low Rate of Inappropriate Cataract Surgery Identified in Academic Centers." *Report on Medical Guidelines and Outcomes Research,* 1993a, *4*(14), 6.

Darby, M. "New Patient Preference Tools Force Tough Choices." *Report on Medical Guidelines and Outcomes Research,* 1993b, *4*(14), 1, 5.

Darling, H. "Employers and Managed Care: What Are the Early Returns?" *Health Affairs,* 1991, *10,* 147–160.

Darnay, A. J. *Manufacturing U.S.A.: Industry Analyses, Statistics, and Leading Companies.* Detroit, Mich.: Gale Research, Inc., 1992a.

Darnay, A. J. *Service U.S.A.: Industry Analyses, Statistics, and Leading Companies.* Detroit, Mich.: Gale Research, Inc., 1992b.

Davis, A. R., and others. "Consumer Acceptance of Prepaid and Fee for Service Care: Results from a Randomized Controlled Trial." *Health Services Research,* 1986, *21,* 429–452.

Day, P., and Klein, R. "Britain's Health Care Experiment." *Health Affairs,* 1991, *10,* 39–59.

De La Fuente, D. "California Groups Join for Survival." *Modern Healthcare,* June 21, 1993a, pp. 4–26.

De La Fuente, D. "Doctors' Orders: Integrate." *Modern Healthcare,* May 3, 1993b, pp. 23, 25–32.

De La Fuente, D. "For Profit Chains Growth Helps Boost Rehab Industry." *Modern Healthcare,* May 24, 1993c, p. 88.

De La Fuente, D. "Provider Groups Entice Independent Practices Through 'Clinics Without Walls.'" *Modern Healthcare,* May 31, 1993d, p. 31.

Deloitte and Touche. *U.S. Hospitals and the Future of Health Care.* Vol. 4. Boston: Deloitte and Touche, 1990.

Deming, W. E. *Out of the Crisis.* Cambridge, Mass.: MIT Press, 1986.

Devin, R. G. "Perspective: Canada." *Health Affairs,* 1988, *7,* 17–24.

Donabedian, A. "Quality and Cost: Choices and Responsibilities." In J. S. Harris, H. D. Belk, and L. W. Wood (eds.), *Managing Employee Health Care Costs: Assuring Quality and Value.* Beverly, Mass.: OEM Press, 1992.

Donabedian, A., Wheeler, J.R.C., and Wyszewianski, L. "Quality Cost and Health: An Integrated Model." *Medical Care,* 1982, *20,* 975–992.

Doubilet, P., and Abrams, H. L. "The Cost of Underutilization: Percutaneous Transluminal Angioplasty for Peripheral Vascular Disease." *New England Journal of Medicine,* 1984, *310,* 95–105.

Doyle, R. A. *Managed Care Guidelines.* New York: Milliman and Robertson, 1990.

Dunford, G. "Splinters in the Floorboards." *California Family Physician,* July-Aug. 1993, p. 5.

Durant, G. D. "Ambulatory Surgery Centers: Surviving, Thriving into the 1990s." *Medical Group Management Journal,* 1989, *36,* 14–20.

Dwyer, P., and Garland, S. "A Roar of Discontent." *Business Week,* Nov. 25, 1991.

Eagle, K. A. and others. "Length of Stay in the Intensive Care Unit: Effects of Practice Guidelines and Feedback." *Journal of the American Medical Association,* 1990, *264,* 992–997.

Eddy, D. M. "Variations in Physician Practice: The Role of Uncertainty." *Health Affairs,* 1984, *3*(2), pp. 75–89.

Eddy, D. M. "Clinical Decision Making: From Theory to Practice." *Journal of the American Medical Association,* 1990, *263,* 287–290.

Eddy, D. M. "The Challenge." *Journal of the American Medical Association,* 1992, *263,* 287–290.

Eichorn, C. H., and Eichorn, H. H. "Prevention of Intraoperative Anesthesia Accidents and Related Severe Injury Through Safety Monitoring." *Anesthesiology,* 1989, *70,* 572–577.

Eisenberg, J. M. *Doctors' Decisions and the Costs of Medical Care.* Ann Arbor, Mich.: Health Administration Press, 1986.

Eisenberg, J. M., and Williams, S. V. "Cost Containment and Changing Physicians' Practice Behavior: Can the Fox Learn to Guard the Chicken Coop?" *Journal of the American Medical Association,* 1981, *246,* 2195–2201.

Eisenberg, J. M., and others. "Substituting Diagnostic Services: New Tests Only Partially Replace Older Ones." *Journal of the American Medical Association,* 1989, *262,* 1196–1200.

Employee Benefits Research Institute. *Poll: Public Attitudes on HMO's and PPO's.* Washington, D.C.: Employee Benefits Research Institute, Apr. 1990.

Employee Benefits Research Institute. *Retiree Benefits.* Research brief no. 112. Washington, D.C.: Employee Benefits Research Institute, 1991.

Employee Benefits Research Institute. *Sources of Health Insurance and Characteristics of the Uninsured.* Research brief no. 133. Washington, D.C.: Employee Benefits Research Institute, 1992.

Employee Benefits Research Institute and the Gallup Organization, Inc. *Public Attitudes on the Value of Benefits.* Report no. G12. Washington, D.C.: Employee Benefits Research Institute, 1990.

Enthoven, A. C. "Health Tax Policy Mismatch." *Health Affairs,* 1985, *4,* 5–15.

Enthoven, A. C. "Management of Competition in the FEHBP." *Health Affairs,* 1989, *8,* 33–50.

Enthoven, A. C. "Health Care Costs: A Moral and Economic Problem." *California Management Review,* 1993, *35*(2), 134–151.

Enthoven, A. C., and Kronick, R. "A Consumer Choice Health Plan for the 1990s: Universal Health Insurance in a System Designed to Promote Quality and Economy." *New England Journal of Medicine,* 1989, *320,* 29–37, 99–107.

Ermann, D., and Gabel, J. "The Changing Face of American Health Care: Multihospital Systems, Emergency Centers, and Surgical Centers." *Medical Care,* 1985, *23,* 401–420.

Executive Learning, Inc. *Continual Improvement Handbook: A Quick Reference Guide for Tools and Concepts: Healthcare Version.* Brentwood, Tenn.: Executive Learning, Inc., 1993.

Falkson, J. L. *HMOs and the Politics of Health System Reform.* Bowie, Md.: Robert J. Brady, 1980.

Farquhar, J. W., and others. "The Effects of Community Wide Education on Cardiovascular Disease Risk Factors: The Stanford Five City Program." *Journal of the American Medical Association,* 1990, *264,* 359–365.

Feldstein, P. J. *Health Care Economics.* (3rd ed.) New York: Wiley, 1988.

Feldstein, P. J., Wickizer, T. M., and Wheeler, J.R.C. "Private Cost Containment: The Effects of Utilization Review Programs on Health Care Use and Expenditures." *New England Journal of Medicine,* 1988, *318,* 1310-1314.

Ferguson, S., Howell, T., and Batalden, P. B. "Knowledge and Skills Needed for Collaborative Work." *Quality Management in Health Care,* 1992, *1*(2), 1-11.

Field, M. J., and Shapiro, H. T. *Employment and Health Benefits: A Connection at Risk.* Washington, D.C.: National Academy Press, 1993.

Fielding, J. E. "Occupational Health Physicians and Prevention." In J. S. Harris, H. D. Belk, and L. W. Wood (eds.), *Managing Employee Health Care Costs: Assuring Quality and Value.* Boston: OEM Press, 1992.

Fielding, J. E., and Piserchia, P. V. "Frequency of Worksite Health Promotion Activities." *American Journal of Public Health,* 1989, *79,* 16-20.

Fowler, F. J., Jr., and others. "Symptom Status and Quality of Life Following Prostatectomy." *Journal of the American Medical Association,* 1988, *255,* 3018-3022.

Francis, S. "Health and Medical Services." In B. H. Franklin, T. J. Hauser, and J. D. Jameson (eds.), *U.S. Industrial Outlook 1993.* Washington, D.C.: International Trade Administration, U.S. Department of Commerce, 1993.

Fredrickson, L. W., Soloman, L., and Brehony, F. (eds.). *Marketing Health Behavior.* New York: Plenum, 1984.

Freimann, M. P. "The Rate of Adoption of New Procedures Among Physicians: The Impact of Specialty and Practice Characteristics." *Medical Care,* 1985, *23,* 939-945.

Friedson, E. *Profession of Medicine: A Study of the Sociology of Applied Knowledge.* New York: Dodd-Mead, 1970.

Fuchs, M. "Medical and Dental Instruments and Supplies." In B. H. Franklin, T. J. Hauser, and J. D. Jameson (eds.), *U.S. Industrial Outlook 1993.* Washington, D.C.: International Trade Administration, U.S. Department of Commerce, 1993.

Fuchs, V. R. "The Growing Demand for Medical Care." *New England Journal of Medicine,* 1968, *729,* 190-195.

Fuchs, V. R. *Who Shall Live.* New York: Basic Books, 1974.

Fuchs, V. R. "National Health Insurance Revisited." *Health Affairs,* 1991, *8,* 8–17.

Fuchs, V. R. "No Pain, No Gain: Perspectives on Cost Containment." *Journal of the American Medical Association,* 1993, *269,* 631–633.

Fuchs, V. R., and Hahn, J. S. "How Does Canada Do It? A Comparison of Expenditures for Physician Services in the United States and Canada." *New England Journal of Medicine,* 1990, *322,* 884–890.

Gabel, J., DiCarlo, S., Fink, S., and DiLissavoy, G. "Employer Sponsored Health Insurance in America." *Health Affairs,* 1989, *8,* 116–128.

Gallup Organization. *Public Attitudes on Health Insurance.* Fall report. Washington, D.C.: Employee Benefits Research Institute and the Gallup Organization, Inc., 1989.

Gardner, H. H., and Sneiderman, C. A. "Ensuring Value by Supporting Consumer Decisionmaking." In J. S. Harris, H. D. Belk, and L. W. Wood (eds.), *Managing Employee Health Care Costs: Assuring Quality and Value.* Beverly, Mass.: OEM Press, 1992.

Garfinkel, S., Riley, G. F., and Iannacchione, V. G. "High-Cost Users of Medical Care." *Health Care Financing Review,* 1988, *9*(4), 41–52.

Garland, S. "A Prescription for Reform." *Business Week,* Oct. 7, 1991.

Garvin, D. A. *Managing Quality: The Strategic and Competitive Edge.* New York: Free Press, 1988.

Geisel, J. "Health Benefits Cost Rose 'Only' 10% in 1992." *Business Insurance,* Mar. 1, 1993, p. 1.

Gibbs, J. O., Mulvaney, D., Henes, C., and Reed, R. W. "Work Site Health Promotion: Five Year Trend in Employee Health Care Costs." *Journal of Occupational Medicine,* 1985, *27,* 826–830.

Gibson, R. "National Health Expenditures." *Health Care Financing Review,* 1980, *2,* 21–22.

Ginzberg, E. "High-Tech Medicine and Rising Health Care Costs." *Journal of the American Medical Association,* 1990, *263,* 1820–1822.

Gleicher, N. "Caesarean Section Rates in the United States: The Short-Term Failure of the National Consensus Development Conference." *Journal of the American Medical Association,* 1984, *252,* 3273–3276.

Gold, M. "Health Maintenance Organizations: Structure, Performance, and Current Issues for Employee Benefits Design." In J. S. Harris, H. D. Belk, and L. W. Wood (eds.), *Managing Employee Health Care Costs: Assuring Quality and Value.* Beverly, Mass.: OEM Press, 1992.

Goldsmith, J. "Driving the Nitroglycerin Truck." *Healthcare Management Forum Journal.* Mar./Apr. 1993, pp. 36–42.

Goldstein, M. S. *Income of Physicians, Osteopaths, and Dentists from Professional Practice.* Washington, D.C.: Office of Research and Statistics, Social Security Administration, 1972.

Gonzales, M. L. (ed.). *Socioeconomic Characteristics of Medical Practice.* Chicago: American Medical Association, 1992.

Gould, J. B., Davey, B., and Stafford, R. S. "Socioeconomic Differences in Rates of Caesarean Section." *New England Journal of Medicine,* 1989, *321,* 233–239.

Goyert, G. L., Bottoms, S. F., Treadwell, M. C., and Nehra, P. C. "The Physician Factor in Caesarean Births." *New England Journal of Medicine,* 1989, *320,* 706–709.

Greene, J. "Towns Breathe New Life into Closed Hospitals." *Modern Healthcare,* Mar. 25, 1991, pp. 24–28, 30.

Greene, J. "Diversification, Take Two: Hospitals Are Assessing Non-Acute-Care Services to Broaden Their Marketability and Boost Their Appeal to Healthcare Buyers." *Modern Healthcare,* July 12, 1993a, 28–32.

Greene, J. "Systems Scurry to Find Partners for Networks." *Modern Healthcare,* June 28, 1993b, pp. 58–62.

Greenspan, A. M., and others. "Incidence of Unwarranted Implantation of Permanent Cardiac Pacemakers in a Large Medical Population." *New England Journal of Medicine,* 1988, *318,* 158–163.

Grey, B. H., and Field, M. J. *Controlling Costs and Changing Patient Care? The Role of Utilization Management.* Washington, D.C.: National Academy Press, 1989.

Grodin, M. A. "Informed Consent and Medical Benefit Selection." In J. S. Harris, H. D. Belk, and L. W. Wood (eds.), *Managing Employee Health Care Costs: Assuring Quality and Value.* Beverly, Mass.: OEM Press, 1992.

Grossman, M. "The Concept of Human Capital and the Demand for Health." *Journal of Political Economics,* 1972, *80,* 223–255.

Group Health Association of America. *National Directory of HMOs, 1991.* Washington, D.C.: Group Health Association of America, Inc., 1991.

Grumbach, K., and Lee, P. R. "How Many Physicians Can We Afford?" *Journal of the American Medical Association,* 1991, *265,* 2369–2372.

Hamilton, W. K. "Unexpected Deaths During Anesthesia." *Anesthesiology,* 1979, *50,* 381–383.

Hammett, T., and others. "Compensation vs. Productivity— Interest Continues to Soar: 1993 American Group Practice Association Survey Results." *Group Practice Journal,* 1993, *42,* 26–35.

Harder, W. D., Kletke, P. R., Silberger, A. B., and Willke, R. J. *Physician Supply and Utilization by Specialty: Trends and Projections.* Chicago: American Medical Association, 1988.

Harris, J. S. *Cost Effective Health Care.* Nashville, Tenn.: Northern Telecom, Inc., 1984a.

Harris, J. S. "Stress and Stressors in Critical Care." *Critical Care Nursing,* 1984b, *4,* 84–97.

Harris, J. S. "Corporate Values, Sex Distribution, Employee Age Guide Wellness Design." *Business and Health,* 1985a, *2,* 58–59.

Harris, J. S. *Cost Effective Health Care.* Nashville, Tenn.: Northern Telecom, Inc., 1985b.

Harris, J. S. *Cost Effective Health Care.* Nashville, Tenn.: Northern Telecom, Inc., 1986.

Harris, J. S. *Cost Effective Health Care.* Nashville, Tenn.: Northern Telecom, Inc., 1987.

Harris, J. S. *Cost Effective Health Care.* Nashville, Tenn.: Northern Telecom, Inc., 1988a.

Harris, J. S. "Mental Health Cost Trends and Utilization Management." *Journal of Occupational Medicine,* 1988b, *30,* 662–663.

Harris, J. S. "What Employers Can Do About Health Care Costs: Managing Health and Productivity." In K. McLennan and J. A. Meyer (eds.), *Cost and Care: Current Issues in Health Policy.* Boulder, Colo.: Westview Press, 1989.

Harris, J. S. "Is Health Care Cost Management Working?" *Occupational and Environmental Report,* 1991, *5,* 105–108.

Harris, J. S. "The Bridge from Quality Assurance to Quality Improvement." In J. S. Harris, H. D. Belk, and L. W. Wood (eds.), *Managing Employee Health Care Costs: Assuring Quality and Value.* Beverly, Mass.: OEM Press, 1992a.

Harris, J. S. "The Cost Effectiveness of Health Promotion Programs." In J. S. Harris, H. D. Belk, and L. W. Wood (eds.), *Managing Employee Health Care Costs: Assuring Quality and Value.* Beverly, Mass.: OEM Press, 1992b.

Harris, J. S. "Does Managed Care Manage Health Care Costs Effectively? It Depends." In J. S. Harris, H. D. Belk, and L. W. Wood (eds.), *Managing Employee Health Care Costs: Assuring Quality and Value.* Beverly, Mass.: OEM Press, 1992c.

Harris, J. S. "Watching the Numbers: Basic Data for Health Care Management." In J. S. Harris, H. D. Belk, and L. W. Wood (eds.), *Managing Employee Health Care Costs: Assuring Quality and Value.* Beverly, Mass.: OEM Press, 1992d.

Harris, J. S. "Why Doctors Do What They Do." In J. S. Harris, H. D. Belk, and L. W. Wood (eds.), *Managing Employee Health Care Costs: Assuring Quality and Value.* Beverly, Mass.: OEM Press, 1992e.

Harris, J. S. "The Future of Health Promotion." In M. P. O'Donnell and J. S. Harris (eds.), *Health Promotion in the Work Place.* (2nd ed.) Albany, N.Y.: Delmar, 1993a.

Harris, J. S. "The Health Benefits of Health Promotion." In M. P. O'Donnell and J. S. Harris (eds.), *Health Promotion in the Work Place.* (2nd ed.) Albany, N.Y.: Delmar, 1993b.

Harris, J. S. "Health Promotion in the Work Place." In C. Zenz, D. B. Dickerson, and E. Horvath (eds.), *Textbook of Occupational Medicine.* (3rd ed.) St. Louis: Mosby/Year Book, 1993c.

Harris, J. S., and Custer, W. S. "Health Care Economic Factors and the Effects of Benefit Plan Design Changes." In J. S. Harris, H. D. Belk, and L. W. Wood (eds.), *Managing*

Employee Health Care Costs: Assuring Quality and Value. Beverly, Mass.: OEM Press, 1992.

Harris, J. S., and Dewey, M. J. "Organizational Stress." In M. P. O'Donnell and T. Ainsworth (eds.), *Health Promotion in the Work Place.* New York: Wiley, 1984.

Harris, J. S., Goldstein, S. R., and Tager, M. J. *Wise Moves: Taking Charge of Your Health.* Chicago: Great Performance, Inc., 1986.

Harris, J. S., and Theriault, K. A. "Key Management Indicators: Using Insurance Claims and Employee Survey Data to Keep Health Promotion Programs on Course." In J. Opatz (ed.), *The Cost Effectiveness of Health Promotion Programs.* Champaign, Ill.: Human Kinetics Press, 1993.

Harris, J. S., and others. "The American College of Occupational and Environmental Medicine Position on National Health Care Reform." *Journal of Occupational Medicine,* 1993, *35,* 623–627.

Harris, S. S., Casperson, C. J., DeFriese, G. H., and Estes, E. H., Jr. "Physical Activity Counseling for Healthy Adults as a Primary Preventive Intervention in a Clinical Setting." *Journal of the American Medical Association,* 1991, *261,* 3590–3598.

Harvard Community Health Plan. *Annual Report.* Boston: Harvard Community Health Plan, 1990.

Harvard Medical Practice Study. *The Report of the Harvard Medical Practice Study to the State of New York, Patients, Doctors, and Lawyers: Medical Injury, Malpractice Litigation, and Patient Compensation in New York.* Cambridge, Mass.: President of Fellows of Harvard College, 1990.

Harvey, L. K. *AMA Survey of Public Opinion on Health Care Issues.* Chicago: American Medical Association, Mar. 1991.

Harvey, L. K., and Shubat, S. C. *Physicians' Decisions on Health Care Issues.* Chicago: American Medical Association, Apr. 1989.

Havlicek, P. L., Eiler, M. A., and Neblett, O. T. *Medical Groups in the U.S.: A Survey of Practice Characteristics.* Chicago: American Medical Association, 1993.

Health Insurance Association of America. *Source Book of Health Insurance Data, 1992.* Washington, D.C.: Health Insurance Association of America, 1992.

Helling, D. K., Norwood, G. J., and Donnor, J. D. "An Assessment of Prescribing Using Drug Utilization Review Criteria." *Drug Intelligence and Clinical Pharmacy,* 1982, *16,* 930–932.

Henry J. Kaiser Family Foundation and Louis Harris and Associates. *Americans and Their Health Insurance.* Commonwealth Poll. New York: Louis Harris and Associates, Mar. 1992a.

Henry J. Kaiser Family Foundation and Louis Harris and Associates. *Health Insurance Survey.* New York: Louis Harris and Associates, Apr. 1992b.

Hewitt Associates. *Flexible Compensation Programs and Practices, 1990–1991.* Lincolnshire, Ill.: Hewitt Associates, 1992.

Hicks, L. L., and Glenn, J. K. "Too Many Physicians in the Wrong Places and Specialties? Populations and Physicians from a Market Perspective." *Journal of Health Care Marketing,* 1989, *9,* 18–26.

Hillman, A. L. "Managing the Physician: Rules v. Incentives." *Health Affairs,* 1991, *10*(4), 138–146.

Hillman, A. L., Pauly, M. V., and Kerstein, J. "How Do Financial Incentives Affect Physicians' Clinical Decisions and the Financial Performance of Health Maintenance Organizations?" *New England Journal of Medicine,* 1989, *321,* 86–92.

Holahan, J., Dor, A., and Zuckerman, S. "Understanding the Recent Growth in Medicare Physician Expenditures." *Journal of the American Medical Association,* 1990, *263,* 1658–1661.

Holahan, J., and Scanlon, W. *Physician Pricing in California: Price Controls, Physician Fees, and Physician Incomes from Medicare.* Publication no. 03006. Rockville, Md.: Healthcare Financing Administration, 1979.

Holahan, J., and Zedlusky, S. "Who Pays for Health Care in the United States? Implications for Health Systems Reform." *Inquiry,* 1992, *29,* 231–248.

Hurt, W. "Drugs and Biotechnology." In B. H. Franklin, T. J. Hauser, and J. D. Jameson (eds.), *U.S. Industrial Outlook 1993.* Washington, D.C.: International Trade Administration, U.S. Department of Commerce, 1993.

Iglehart, J. K. "Japan's Medical Care System." *New England Journal of Medicine,* 1988a, *319,* 807–812.

Iglehart, J. K. "Japan's Medical Care System." *New England Journal of Medicine,* 1988b, *319,* 1166–1172.

Iglehart, J. K. "The American Health Care System — Introduction." *New England Journal of Medicine,* 1992a, *326,* 962–967.

Iglehart, J. K. "The American Health Care System — Managed Care." *New England Journal of Medicine,* 1992b, *327,* 742–747.

Iglehart, J. K. "The American Health Care System — Medicaid." *New England Journal of Medicine,* 1992c, *328*(12), 896–900.

Iglehart, J. K. "The American Health Care System — Medicare." *New England Journal of Medicine,* 1992d, *327.*

Iglehart, J. K. "The American Health Care System — Private Insurance." *New England Journal of Medicine,* 1992e, *326,* 1715–1720.

Iglehart, J. K. "The American Health Care System — Managed Competition." *New England Journal of Medicine,* 1993, *328,* 1208–1212.

Ikegami, N. "Japanese Health Care: Low Cost Through Regulated Fees." *Health Affairs,* 1991, *10,* 87–109.

Immerwhar, K., Johnson, J., and Kernan-Chloss, A. *Faulty Diagnosis: Public Misconceptions About Health Care Reform.* Public Agenda Foundation, Gallup Organization, and the Employee Benefits Research Institute, 1992.

Institute of Medicine. *The Automated Computerized Medical Record.* Washington, D.C.: Institute of Medicine/National Academy of Sciences, 1991.

International Survey Research Corporation. *Survey of Employment Benefits.* New York: International Survey Research Corporation, 1991.

"It's Time to Operate." *Fortune,* 1970, *81,* 79–83.

Jennings, F., and Robins, E. D. "The Swan Ganz Catheter: Overuse and Abuse of Pulmonary Arterial Wedge Catheters." *Annals of Internal Medicine,* 1985, *103,* 445–448.

Johnsson, J., and Meyer, F. "Who's Afraid of Vertical Integration?" *American Medical News,* Mar. 15, 1993, pp. 3, 31–32.

Juran, J. M. *Quality Control Handbook.* (4th ed.) New York: McGraw-Hill, 1988.

Kahn, K. L., and others. "The Use and Misuse of Upper Gastrointestinal Endoscopy." *Internal Medicine,* 1988, *109,* 664–670.

Kano, N., Seraku, N., and Tsuji, S. "Attractive Quality and Must Be Quality." *Proceedings of Nippon Gakka 12th Annual Meeting.* Tokyo: Nippon Gakka, 1982, 1–12.

Kanouse, D. E., Winkler, J. D., and Kosekoff, J. L. "Changing Medical Practice Through Technology Assessment." In D. E. Kanouse and J. L. Kosekoff (eds.), *Evaluation of the NIH Consensus Development Program.* Ann Arbor, Mich.: Health Administration Press, 1989.

Keenan, R. L., and Boyan, C. P. "Cardiac Arrest Due to Anesthesia." *Journal of the American Medical Association,* 1985, *253,* 2373–2377.

Kellie, S. E., and Kelly, J. T. "Medical Peer Review Organization Pre Procedure Review Criteria: An Analysis of Criteria for Three Procedures." *Journal of the American Medical Association,* 1991, *265,* 1265–1270.

Kenkel, P. J. "Taking the Direct Approach." *Modern Healthcare,* 1992, *22*(3), 45–49.

Kenkel, P. J. "Delivering Corporate Health Care Services." *Modern Healthcare,* 1993a, *23,* 24–27.

Kenkel, P. J. "While a Reform Plan Is Still Down the Road, Some Managed Care Firms Are Set to Compete." *Modern Healthcare,* June 7, 1993b, pp. 14–15.

Kerr, C. E. "Strategies for Improving the Value of Medical Services for the Consumer and the Payer." In J. S. Harris, H. D. Belk, and L. W. Wood (eds.), *Managing Employee Health Care Costs: Assuring Quality and Value.* Beverly, Mass.: OEM Press, 1992.

Kinosian, B. D., and Eisenberg, J. M. "Cutting into Cholesterol: Cost-Effective Alternatives for Treating Hypercholesterolemia." *Journal of the American Medical Association,* 1988, *259,* 2249–2254.

Kohut, A., Toth, R. C., and Bowman, C. *The Public, Their Doctors, and Health Care Reform.* Washington, D.C.: Times Mirror Center for People and the Press, 1993.

Kottke, T. E., Batista, R. M., and DeFriese, G. H. "Attributes of Successful Smoking Cessation and Prevention in Clinical Practice." *Journal of the American Medical Association,* 1988, *259,* 2882–2889.

Kottler, P. *Social Marketing.* New York: McGraw-Hill, 1988.

Kretz, S. E. "Quality-Focused Contracting for Specialized Managed Care Services." *American Association of Preferred Provider Organizations Journal,* 1991, 15–21.

Kristein, M. M. "How Much Can Business Expect to Profit from Smoking Cessation?" *Preventive Medicine,* 1983, *12,* 358–381.

Kronick, R., Goodman, D. C., Wennberg, J., and Wagner, E. "The Market Place and Health Care Reform: The Demographic Limitations of Managed Competition." *New England Journal of Medicine,* 1993, *328,* 148–152.

Laffel, G., and Blumenthal, D. "The Case for Using Industrial Quality Management in Health Care Organizations." *Journal of the American Medical Association,* 1989, *262,* 2869–2873.

Lalonde, M. *A New Perspective on the Health of Canadians: A Working Document.* Ottawa, Canada: Ministry of Supply and Services, 1978.

Lawrence, R. (ed.). *Guide to Clinical Preventive Services: An Assessment of the Effectiveness of 169 Interventions. Report of the U.S. Preventive Services Task Force.* Baltimore, Md.: Williams & Wilkins, 1989.

Leaf, A. "Preventive Medicine for Our Ailing Health Care System." *Journal of the American Medical Association,* 1993, *269,* 616–618.

Leape, L., and others. "Does Inappropriate Use Explain Small Variations in the Use of Health Services?" *Journal of the American Medical Association,* 1990, *263,* 669–672.

Lee, R. H., and Waldman, D. M. "The Diffusion of Innovation in Hospitals." *Journal of Health Economics,* 1986, *4,* 103–120.

Leibowitz, A., Manning, W. G., and Newhouse, J. P. "The Demand for Prescription Drugs Is a Function of Cost Sharing." *Social Science and Medicine,* 1985, *21,* 1063–1070.

Leibowitz, A., and others. "Effect of Cost Sharing on the Use of Health Services by Children: Interim Results from a Randomized Controlled Trial." *Pediatrics,* 1985, *75,* 942–951.

Levit, K. R., and Cowan, C. "Business, Households and Government: Health Care Costs." *Healthcare Financing Review,* 1991, *13*(2), 83–93.

Levit, K. R., Lasenby, H. C., Cowan, C. A., and Letsch, S. W. "National Health Care Expenditures, 1990." *Health Care Financing Review,* 1991, *13,* 29–54.

Levit, K. R., Lasenby, H. C., Letsch, S. W., and Cowan, C. A. "National Health Care Spending 1989." *Health Affairs,* 1991, *10*(1), 117–130.

Lichtenstein, R., and others. "The National Health Care Cost Containment Crisis: How School of Public Health Experts View It." *Findings,* 1993, 2–11.

Lipid Research Clinic Program. "The Lipid Research Clinic's Coronary Primary Prevention Trials. I: Reduction in Incidence of Coronary Heart Disease." *Journal of the American Medical Association,* 1984, *251,* 351–364.

Loftin, C., MacDowell, D., Wiersema, B., and Cottey, T. J. "Effects of Restrictive Licensing of Handguns on Homicide and Suicide in the District of Columbia." *New England Journal of Medicine,* 1991, *325,* 1615–1620.

Logsdon, D. N., Lazaro, C. M., and Meier, R. V. "The Feasibility of Behavioral Risk Reduction in Primary Medical Care." *American Journal of Preventive Medicine,* 1989, *5,* 245–256.

Logsdon, D. N., and Rosen, M. A. "The Cost of Preventive Health Services in Primary Medical Care and Implications for Health Insurance Coverage." *Journal of Ambulatory Care Management,* 1984, *7,* 46–55.

Lohr, K. N., and others. "Use of Medical Care in the RAND Health Insurance Experiment: Diagnosis Can Serve for Specific Analyses in a Randomized Controlled Trial." *Medical Care,* 1986, *24* (suppl. 1–87).

Long, M. J., Cummings, K. M., and Frisoff, K. B. "The Role of Perceived Price and Physicians' Demand for Diagnostic Tests." *Medical Care,* 1983, *21,* 243–250.

Long, S. B., and Rogers, W. H. *The Effects of Being Uninsured on Health Care Service Use: Estimates from a Survey of Public Program Participation.* Santa Monica, Calif.: RAND Corporation, Dec. 1989.

Long, S. L., Settle, R. F., and Wrightson, C. W., Jr. "Employee Premiums, Availability of Alternative Plans, and HMO Disenrollment." *Medical Care,* 1988, *26,* 927–938.

Lorig, K. R., Kraines, R. G., Brown, B. W., Jr., and Richardson, N. "A Workplace Health Education Program That Reduces Outpatient Visits." *Medical Care,* 1985, *23,* 1044–1054.

Lorig, K. R., Mazonson, P. D., and Holman, H. R. "Evidence Suggesting That Health Education for Self-Management in Patients with Chronic Arthritis Has Sustained Health Benefits While Reducing Health Care Costs." *Arthritis and Rheumatism,* 1993, *36,* 439–446.

Louis Harris and Associates. *Survey of Health Care Consumers.* New York: Louis Harris and Associates, Feb. 1990.

Louis Harris and Associates. *Poll: The Public Perspective.* Storrs, Conn.: Roper Center for Public Opinion Research, May/June 1992.

Luft, H. S. *Health Maintenance Organizations: Dimensions of Performance.* New York: Wiley, 1981.

Lundberg, G. D. "National Health Care Reform: The Aura of Inevitability Intensifies." *Journal of the American Medical Association,* 1992, *267*(18), 2521–2524.

Lundberg, G. D. "American Health Care System Management Objectives: The Aura of Inevitability Becomes Incarnate." *Journal of the American Medical Association,* 1993, *269*(19), 2554–2555.

Lynch, W. D., Teitelbaum, H. S., and Main, D. S. "Comparing Medical Costs by Analyzing High-Cost Cases." *American Journal of Health Promotion,* 1992, *6*(3), 206–213.

Lynch, W. D., and others. "Impact of a Facility Based Corporate Fitness Program on the Number of Absences from Work Due to Illness." *Journal of Occupational Medicine,* 1990, *32,* 9–12.

McEachern, J. E., Hallum, A., and Schiff, L. "The C Section Experience." In J. S. Harris, H. D. Belk, and L. W. Wood (eds.), *Managing Employee Health Care Costs: Assuring Quality and Value.* Beverly, Mass.: OEM Press, 1992.

McEachern, J. E., Makens, P. K., Buchanan, E. D., and Schiff, L. "Quality Improvement: An Imperative for Medical Care." In J. S. Harris, H. D. Belk, and L. W. Wood (eds.), *Managing Employee Health Care Costs: Assuring Quality and Value.* Beverly, Mass.: OEM Press, 1992.

McGurgan, P. L. "Potential Hazard to Cardiovascular Patients." *Medical Instrumentation,* 1984, *18*(4), 237–238.

MacKay, J., and Davis, R. M. "Assessing Community Interventions and Reduction of Tobacco Use." *International Journal of Technology Assessment in Health Care,* 1991, *7,* 345–353.

McNeil, B. J., Weichselbaum, R., and Pauker, S. G. "Fallacy of the Five Year Survival in Lung Cancer." *New England Journal of Medicine,* 1978, *299,* 1397–1401.

McNeil, B. J., Weichselbaum, R., and Pauker, S. G. "Speech and Survival: Tradeoffs Between Quality and Quantity of Life in Laryngeal Cancer." *New England Journal of Medicine,* 1981, *305,* 982–987.

McPherson, K., Strong, P. M., Epstein, A., and Jones, L. "Regional Variations in the Use of Common Surgical Procedures Within and Between England, Wales, Canada, and the United States of America." *Social Science and Medicine,* 1981, *15A,* 273–288.

Makens, P. K., and McEachern, J. R. "Applications of Industrial Quality Improvement in Health Care." In J. S. Harris, H. D. Belk, and L. W. Wood (eds.), *Managing Employee Health Care Costs: Assuring Quality and Value.* Beverly, Mass.: OEM Press, 1992.

Manning, W. G., Wells, K. B., and Benjamin, B. "How Cost Sharing Affects the Use of Ambulatory Mental Health Services." *Journal of the American Medical Association,* 1986, *256,* 1930–1934.

Manning, W. G., and others. "A Controlled Trial of the Effects of a Prepaid Group Practice on Use of Services." *New England Journal of Medicine,* 1984, *310,* 1505–1510.

Manning, W. G., and others. "Health Insurance and the Demand for Medical Care: Evidence from a Random Experiment." *American Economic Review,* 1987, *77*(3), 251–277.

Mason, E. "An Approach to Mental Health Services." In J. S. Harris, H. D. Belk, and L. W. Wood (eds.), *Managing Employee Health Care Costs: Assuring Quality and Value.* Beverly, Mass.: OEM Press, 1992.

Milkovich, G. T., and Glueck, W. F. *Personnel/Human Resource Management: A Diagnostic Approach.* Plano, Tex.: Business Publications, 1985.

Mirvis, D. M. "Physicians' Autonomy — The Relation Between Public and Professional Expectations." *New England Journal of Medicine,* 1993, *328,* 1346–1349.

Moran, D., and Sheils, J. *Report on Employer Cost-Shifting Expenditures.* Washington, D.C.: Lewin/ICF and the National Association of Manufacturers, 1991.

Morrisey, M. "Health Care Reform: A Review of Five Generic Proposals." In *Winners and Losers in Reforming the U.S. Health Care System.* Washington, D.C.: Employee Benefits Research Institute, 1991.

Mosbacher, R. A., and others. *U.S. Industrial Outlook 1991.* Washington, D.C.: International Trade Administration, U.S. Department of Commerce, 1991.

Mulhausen, R., and McGee, J. "Physician Need: An Alternative Projection from a Study of Large, Prepaid Group Practices." *Journal of the American Medical Association,* 1989, *261,* 1930–1934.

Mullen, P. D., Green, L. W., and Persing, R. G. "Clinical Trials of Patient Education for Chronic Conditions: A Comparative Analysis of Intervention Types." *Preventive Medicine,* 1985, *14,* 753–781.

Mulley, A. G., Jr. "Supporting the Patient's Role in Decision Making." In J. S. Harris, H. D. Belk, and L. W. Wood (eds.), *Managing Employee Health Care Costs: Assuring Quality and Value.* Beverly, Mass.: OEM Press, 1992.

Multiple Risk Factor Intervention Trial Research Group. "Mortality Rates After 10.5 Years for Participants in the Multiple Risk Factor Intervention Trial: Findings Related to *a Priori* Hypotheses in the Trial." *Journal of the American Medical Association,* 1990, *263,* 1795–1801.

Myers, S. A., and Gleicher, N. "A Successful Program to Lower Caesarean Section Rates." *New England Journal of Medicine,* 1988, *319,* 1511–1516.

National Cholesterol Education Program, National Heart, Lung, and Blood Institute. *Report of the Expert Panel on Population Strategies for Blood Cholesterol Reduction.* Washington, D.C.: U.S. Department of Health and Human Services, 1990.

National High Blood Pressure Education Program, National

Heart, Lung, and Blood Institute. "Hypertension Prevalence and the Status of Awareness, Treatment, and Control in the US: Final Report of the Subcommittee on Definition and Prevalence of the 1984 Joint National Committee." *Hypertension,* 1985, *7*(3), 457–468.

National Institutes of Health. *Caesarean Childbirth: Report of a Consensus Development Conference.* DHHS publication no. (NIH) 82-2067. Bethesda, Md.: Department of Health and Human Services, 1981.

Nelson, E. C., Caldwell, C., Quinn, D., and Rose, R. "Gaining Customer Knowledge: Obtaining and Using Customer Judgments for Hospitalwide Quality Improvement." *Topics in Health Record Management,* 1991, *11,* 13–26.

Nelson, E. C., and Larson, C. O. "Patients' Good and Bad Surprises: How Do They Relate to Overall Patient Satisfaction?" *Quality Review Bulletin,* Mar. 1993, pp. 89–94.

Nelson, E. C., and others. "The Physician and Employee Judgment System: Reliability and Validity of a Hospital Quality Measurement Method." *Quality Review Bulletin,* Sept. 1992, pp. 284–292.

Neutra, R. "Indications for the Surgical Treatment of Suspected Appendicitis: Cost Effectiveness of Watchful Waiting." In J. P. Bunker, B. A. Barnes, and F. Mosteller (eds.), *Costs, Risks, and Benefits of Surgery.* New York: Oxford University Press, 1977.

Newhouse, J. P. *The Health Insurance Study: Summary.* Santa Monica, Calif.: RAND Corporation, 1985.

Newhouse, J. P. "Controlled Experimentation as Research Policy." In E. Ginzberg (ed.), *Health Services Research.* Cambridge, Mass.: Harvard University Press, 1991.

Newhouse, J. P., Anderson, Q., and Roos, L. L. "Hospital Spending in the United States and Canada." *Health Affairs,* Winter 1988, 6–16.

Newhouse, J. P., and others. "Some Interim Results from a Controlled Trial of Cost Sharing and Health Insurance." *New England Journal of Medicine,* 1981, *305,* 150–157.

O'Donnell, M. P., and Harris, J. S. (eds.). *Health Promotion in the Workplace.* (2nd ed.) Albany, N.Y.: Delmar, 1993.

O'Driscoll, K., and Foley, M. "Correlation of Decrease in Perinatal Morbidity and Increase in Caesarean Section Rates." *Obstetrics and Gynecology,* 1983, *61,* 1–5.

Office of Technology Assessment, U.S. Congress. *Forecast of Physician Supply and Requirements.* Washington, D.C.: U.S. Government Printing Office, 1980.

O'Grady, K. F., Manning, W. G., Newhouse, J. P., and Brook, R. H. "The Impact of Cost Sharing on Emergency Department Use." *New England Journal of Medicine,* 1985, *313,* 484–490.

O'Reilly, B. "Drugmakers Under Attack." *Fortune,* July 29, 1991, pp. 48–63.

Page, L. "Reform Ripple: Retraining Specialists for Primary Care." *American Medical News,* May 3, 1993, pp. 1, 32–33.

Parsons, P. E., and others. *Costs of Illness (United States, 1980).* National Medical Care Utilization and Expenditure Survey, series C, Analytical Report no. 3. U.S. Department of Health and Human Services. Publication no. 86-20403. Washington, D.C.: U.S. Government Printing Office, 1986.

Pauly, M., Danzon, P., and Feldstein, P. "A Plan for Responsible National Health Insurance." *Health Affairs,* spring 1991, pp. 6–25.

Peel, E. S. *The American Hospital in the 1990s.* New York: Louis Harris and Associates, Aug. 1988.

Pelletier, K. R., Joss, J. E., and Locke, S. E. "Personal Efficacy: A Research Data Base for the Clinical Application of Self-Efficacy in Mental Health." In K. R. Pelletier (ed.), *In Pursuit of Wellness.* Vol. 7. Sacramento: California Department of Mental Health, 1992.

Peter D. Hart Research Associates, Inc., and Mildred and Claude Pepper Association. *Financing National Health Care: A Nationwide Survey of Voter Opinions.* Washington, D.C.: Peter D. Hart Research Associates, Inc., and Mildred and Claude Pepper Association, May 1992.

Phelps, C. E., and Newhouse, J. P. "Effects of Coinsurance: A Multi-Variate Analysis." *Social Security Bulletin,* 1972, *35,* 20–29.

Piacentini, J. S., and Anzick, M. A. "Employee Benefits and Total Compensation." *EBRI Issues Brief,* 1991, *111,* 1–25.

Piacentini, J. S., and Foley, J. D. *EBRI Data Book on Employee Benefits.* Washington, D.C.: Employee Benefits Research Institute, 1992.

Pierce, E. C., Jr. "Anesthesiology." *Journal of the American Medical Association,* 1985, *254,* 2317–2318.

PPO Letter. "Pharmaceutical Network Price Discounts Deepening, P.P.L. Finds." *PPO Letter,* 1993, *3*(4), 4.

Puska, R., and others. "The Community-Based Strategy to Prevent Coronary Heart Disease: Conclusions From 10 Years of the North Karelia Project." *Annual Review of Public Health,* 1985, *6,* 147–193.

Rakel, R. E. "The Family Physician." In R. E. Rakel (ed.), *Textbook of Family Practice.* (4th ed.) Philadelphia: Saunders, 1993.

Reiser, S. J. "Consumer Competence and the Reform of American Health Care." *Journal of the American Medical Association,* 1992, *267,* 1511–1515.

Riley, G. J., and others. "Changes in Distribution of Medicare Expenditures Among Aged Enrollees." *Health Care Financing Review,* 1986, *8,* 53–63.

Roback, G., Randolph, L., and Seidman, B. *Physician Characteristics and Distribution in the U.S., 1992.* Chicago: American Medical Association, 1992.

Rodgers, J. F. *Trends in U.S. Health Care, 1992.* Chicago: American Medical Association, 1992.

Rodrigues, A. R. "Pay Review Program: Trends and Claims Processing." *Business and Health,* 1984, *1,* 21–25.

Rogal, D. L., and Helms, W. D. "State Models: Tracking States' Efforts to Reform Their Health Systems." *Health Affairs,* 1993, *12,* 27–30.

Roman, P. M., and Blum, T. C. "Formal Intervention in Employee Health: Comparisons of the Nature and Structure of Employee Assistance Programs and Health Promotion Programs." *Social Science and Medicine,* 1988, *26,* 503–514.

Roper, W. L. "Financing Health Care: A View from the White House." *Health Affairs,* Winter 1989, 97–102.

Roper Center for Public Opinion Research. *ABC/Washington Post Poll.* Storrs, Conn.: Roper Center for Public Opinion Research, Dec. 11, 1991.

Rositter, L., Langwell, K., Want, T. H., and Rivnyak, M. "Patient Satisfaction Among Elderly Enrollees and Disenrollees in Medicare Health Maintenance Organizations: Results from the National Medicare Competition Evaluation." *Journal of the American Medical Association,* 1989, *26,* 57–63.

Rubie, D. "Medical Technology in Canada, Germany, and the U.S." *Health Affairs,* 1989, *8,* 178–181.

Russell, L. B., and Manning, C. L. "The Effect of Prospective Payment on Medicare Expenditures." *New England Journal of Medicine,* 1989, *320,* 439–444.

Saftlas, H. B. *Prescriptions for Sick Health Care System: Standard and Poor Industry Survey,* New York: Standard and Poor, 1991.

Schaffner, W., Ray, R. A., and Federspiel, C. F. "Persistence of Improvement in Antibiotic Prescribing in Office Practice." *Journal of the American Medical Association,* 1983, *250,* 1774–1776.

Schieber, G. J., Poullier, J. P., and Greenwald, L. M. "U.S. Health Expenditure Performance: An International Comparison and Data Update." *Health Care Financing Review,* 1992, *13,* 1–15.

Schieber, G. J., Poullier, J. P., and Greenwald, L. M. "Health Spending, Delivery, and Outcomes in OECD Countries." *Health Affairs,* 1993, *12*(2), 120–129.

Schlesinger, H. J., and others. "Mental Health Treatment in Medical Care and a Fee for Service System." *American Journal of Public Health,* 1986, *73,* 422–429.

Schmitz, M., and Courtright, G. W. "Case Study: The Corporate Physician in a Managed Care Environment." In J. S. Harris, H. D. Belk, and L. W. Wood (eds.), *Managing Employee Health Care Costs: Assuring Quality and Value.* Beverly, Mass.: OEM Press, 1992.

Schneider, M., and others. "Health Care in the EC Member States." *Health Policy,* 1992, *20,* 1–251.

Schneider, W. J. "The Corporate Medical Department's Role in Medical Benefits." In J. S. Harris, H. D. Belk, and L. W. Wood (eds.), *Managing Employee Health Care Costs: Assuring Quality and Value.* Beverly, Mass.: OEM Press, 1992.

Schoenbaum, S. C. "Practice guidelines — Why Not?" *HMO Practice,* 1991, *5*(3), 106–108.

Scholtes, P. R. *The TEAMS Handbook*. Madison, Wis.: Joiner Associates, 1988.

Schuster, C. R., and Kilbey, M. M. "Prevention of Drug Abuse." In J. E. Last and R. B. Wallace (eds.), *Maxey-Rosenau-Last Public Health and Preventive Medicine*. East Norwalk, Conn.: Appleton & Lange, 1992.

Schwartz, W. B., and Mendelson, D. N. "Hospital Cost Containment in the 1980s: Hard Lessons Learned and Prospects for the 1990s." *New England Journal of Medicine*, 1991, *324*, 1037–1042.

Scitovsky, A. A., and Snyder, N. M. "Effect of Coinsurance on Use of Physician Services." *Social Security Bulletin*, 1972, *35*, 3–19.

Service Employees International Union. "Out of Control, into Decline: The Devastating 12 Year Impact of Healthcare Costs on Worker Wages, Corporate Profits, and Government Budgets." *Medical Benefits*, 1992, *9*(23), 1–2.

Shaller, D. V., and Ballard, D. J. "Using Olmstead County Benchmarks to Assess Corporate Health Care Utilization and Expenditures." In J. S. Harris, H. D. Belk, and L. W. Wood (eds.), *Managing Employee Health Care Costs: Assuring Quality and Value*. Beverly, Mass.: OEM Press, 1992.

Shea, S., and Basch, C. E. "A Review of Five Major Community Based Cardiovascular Disease Prevention Programs. II: Intervention Strategies, Evaluation Methods, and Results." *American Journal of Health Promotion*, 1990, *4*, 279–287.

Siu, A. I., and others. "Inappropriate Use of Hospitals in a Randomized Trial of Health Insurance Plans." *New England Journal of Medicine*, 1986, *315*, 1259–1286.

"$60 Billion Crisis in Health Care." *Business Week*, Nov. 17, 1970, pp. 50–64.

Slora, E. J., and Gonzales, M. L. "Medical Professional and Liability Claims and Premiums, 1985–1989." *Socioeconomic Characteristics in Medical Practice, 1990–1991*. Chicago: American Medical Association, 1991.

SMG Marketing Group, Inc. *Freestanding Outpatient Surgery Centers: Report and Directory*. Chicago: SMG Marketing Group, Inc., 1991.

Snee, R. E. "Statistical Thinking and Its Contribution to Total Quality." *American Statistician,* 1990, *44,* 116–121.

Solis, D. "To Avoid Cost of U.S. Prescription Drugs, More Americans Shop South of the Border." *Wall Street Journal,* June 29, 1993, pp. B-1, B-4.

Somers, H., and Somers, A. *Doctors, Patients, and Health Insurance.* Washington, D.C.: Brookings Institution, 1972.

Sonnefeld, S. T., Waldo, D. R., Lemieux, J. A., and McKusick, D. R. "Projections of National Health Expenditures Through the Year 2000." *Healthcare Financing Review,* 1991, *13*(1), 1–27.

Soumerai, S. B., and Avorn, J. "Principles of Educational Outreach to Improve Clinical Decisionmaking." *Journal of the American Medical Association,* 1990, *263,* 549–556.

Sperling, K. L. "Flexible Benefits and Managed Care: Making It Work." In *Driving Down Health Care Costs: Strategies and Solutions.* New York: Panel Publishers, 1993.

Stafford, R. S. "Alternative Strategies for Controlling Rising Cesarean Section Rates." *Journal of the American Medical Association,* 1990, *263,* 683–687.

Standard and Poor. *Industry Surveys,* Dec. 5, 1991a, pp. I1–I25.

Standard and Poor. "Reports for Healthcare." *Health Industry Survey,* Aug. 23, 1991b, p. H36.

Standard and Poor. "Drugmakers Face More Challenging Environment." *Industry Surveys,* Oct. 1992, p. H18.

Starr, P. *The Social Transformation of American Medicine.* New York: Basic Books, 1982.

Starr, P. *The Logic of Health Care Reform.* Knoxville, Tenn.: Whittle Direct Books, 1992.

"Strategies in Section 125: Plan Design Discussed." *Employee Benefits Plan Review,* Dec. 1991, pp. 15–16.

Tanouye, E., Waldholz, M., and Anders, G. "Stunning Departure of Merck Head Signals Turmoil Inside and Out." *Wall Street Journal,* July 16, 1993, pp. A1, A4.

Taylor, H. *Universal Acute Health Care Insurance Preferred to Insurance for Long-Term Care or Children's Coverage.* Harris Poll no. 39. New York: Louis Harris and Associates, July 7, 1992.

Taylor, H., and Kagay, M. "The HMO Report Card: A Closer Look." *Health Affairs,* 1986, *5,* 81–89.

Taylor, H., and Leitman, R. *Corporate Health Plans: Past, Present, and Future.* New York: Louis Harris and Associates, Apr. 1989.

Taylor, H., and Leitman, R. *The American Physician: How Changes in the Health Care System Affect Their Behavior.* New York: Louis Harris and Associates, 1990.

Taylor, H., and Leitman, R. *The Changing Concerns and Priorities of the American Public.* New York: Louis Harris and Associates, 1991a.

Taylor, H., and Leitman, R. *Tradeoffs and Choices: Health Policy Options for the '90s.* New York: Louis Harris and Associates, 1991b.

Tolsma, D. D., and Coplin, J. P. "Health Behaviors and Health Promotion." In J. E. Last and R. B. Wallace (eds.), *Maxey-Rosenau-Last Public Health and Preventive Medicine.* Norwalk, Conn.: Appleton & Lange, 1992.

Tomsho, R., and Milbank, D. "Frustrated Firms Open Their Own Clinics to Try to Control Workers' Medical Costs." *Wall Street Journal,* Mar. 23, 1993, pp. B8, B9.

Traska, M. R. "Corporate Execs Can Make a Difference." *Business and Health,* 1990, *8,* 43–46.

Tsai, S. P., Reedy, S. M., Bernacki, E. J., and Lee, E. S. "Effects of Curtailed Insurance Benefits on the Use of Mental Health Care." *Medical Care,* 1988, *26,* 430–440.

U.S. Department of Health and Human Services. *Detailed Diagnoses and Procedures for Patients Discharged from Short Stay Hospitals, 1979.* Washington, D.C.: U.S. Government Printing Office, 1980a.

U.S. Department of Health and Human Services. *Summary Report of the Graduate Medical Education National Advisory Committee.* Vol. 1. Washington, D.C.: U.S. Government Printing Office, 1980b.

U.S. Department of Health and Human Services. *Detailed Diagnoses and Procedures for Patients Discharged from Short Stay Hospitals, 1989.* Washington, D.C.: U.S. Government Printing Office, 1990.

U.S. Surgeon General. *Smoking and Health.* Washington, D.C.: U.S. Government Printing Office, 1964.

U.S. Surgeon General. *Healthy People: The Surgeon General's Report on Health Promotion and Disease Prevention.* Publication no. DHEW (PHS) 79-55071. Washington, D.C.: U.S. Government Printing Office, 1979.

U.S. Surgeon General. *The Health Benefits of Smoking Cessation: A Report of the Surgeon General.* Centers for Disease Control, Public Health Service, U.S. Department of Health and Human Services. Publication no. (CDC) 90-8416. Washington, D.C.: U.S. Government Printing Office, 1990.

U.S. Surgeon General. *Healthy People 2000: National Health Promotion and Disease Prevention Objectives.* Washington, D.C.: U.S. Government Printing Office, 1991. DHHS Publication no. (PHS) 91–50212

Vartiainen, E., Heath, G., and Ford, E. "Assessing Population-Based Programs to Reduce Blood Cholesterol Level and Saturated Fats." *International Journal of Technology Assessment in Health Care,* 1991, *7,* 315–326.

Vickery, D. M. "Medical Self Care." In M. P. O'Donnell and J. S. Harris (eds.), *Health Promotion in the Work Place.* (2nd ed.) Albany, N.Y.: Delmar, 1993.

Vickery, D. M. "Self-Care in the Age of Demand Reduction." Paper presented at the National Health Management Conference, San Francisco, 1991.

Vickery, D. M., and Fries, J. F. *Take Care of Yourself.* (5th ed.) Reading, Mass.: Addison-Wesley, 1993.

Vickery, D. M., Golaszewski, T. J., Wright, E. C., and Kalmer, H. "The Effect of Self-Care Interventions on the Use of Medical Services Within a Medicare Population." *Medical Care,* 1988, *26,* 580–588.

Vickery, D. M., and others. "Effect of a Self-Care Education Program on Medical Visits." *Journal of the American Medical Association,* 1983, *250,* 2952–2956.

Wallston, K. A. "Theoretically Based Strategies for Health Behavior Change." In M. P. O'Donnell and J. S. Harris (eds.), *Health Promotion at the Workplace.* (2nd ed.) Albany, N.Y.: Delmar, 1993.

Walton, M. *Deming Management at Work.* New York: Putnam, 1990.

Warner, K. E. "Effective Hospital Cost Containment and the Development and Use of Medical Technology." *Millbank Memorial Fund Quarterly/Health and Society,* 1978, *56,* 187–211.

Weber, J., and Bhargara, S. W. "Drugmakers Get a Taste of Their Own Medicine." *Business Week,* Apr. 26, 1993, pp. 104–106.

Weller, C. D. "'Free Choice' as a Restraint of Trade in American Health Care Delivery and Insurance." *Iowa Law Review,* 1986, *69,* 1351–1392.

Wells, K. D., Goldberg, G., and Brook, R. H. "Management of Patients with Psychotropic Drugs in Primary Care Clinics." *Medical Care,* 1988, *26,* 645–657.

Wennberg, J. E. "Patient Need, Equity, Supplier Induced Demand, and the Need to Assess the Outcome of Common Medical Practices." *Medical Care,* 1985, *23,* 512–520.

Wennberg, J. E. "Unwanted Variations in the Rules of Practice." *Journal of the American Medical Association,* 1991, *265,* 1306–1307.

Wennberg, J. E., Barnes, E. A., and Zubkoff, M. "Professional Uncertainty and the Problems of Supplier Induced Demand." *Science and Medicine,* 1982, *16,* 811–824.

Wennberg, J. E., Blowers, L., Parker, R., and Gittelsohn, A. M. "Changes in Tonsillectomy Rates Associated with Feedback and Review." *Pediatrics,* 1977, *59,* 821–826.

Wennberg, J. E., Freeman, J. L., Shelton, R. M., and Bubolz, T. A. "Hospital Use and Mortality Among Medicare Beneficiaries in Boston and New Haven." *New England Journal of Medicine,* 1989, *321,* 1168–1173.

Wennberg, J. E., and Gittelsohn, A. "Small Variations in Health Care Delivery." *Science,* 1973, 182, 1102–1108.

Wennberg, J. E., Goodman, D. C., Nease, R. F., and Keller, R. B. "Finding Equilibrium in U.S. Physician Supply." *Health Affairs,* 1993, *12*(2), 89–103.

Wennberg, J. E., McPherson, K., and Caper, P. "Payment Based on Diagnostic Related Groups to Control Hospital Costs." *New England Journal of Medicine,* 1984, *311,* 295–300.

Whittington, H. G. "Assuring Value in Mental Health and Substance Abuse Services." In J. S. Harris, H. D. Belk, and L. W. Wood (eds.), *Managing Employee Health Care Costs: Assuring Quality and Value.* Beverly, Mass.: OEM Press, 1992.

Wickizer, T. M., Wheeler, J.R.C., and Feldstein, P. J. "Does Utilization Review Reduce Unnecessary Hospital Care and Contain Costs?" *Medical Care,* 1989, *27,* 632–647.

Winslow, R. "Desktop Doctors." *Wall Street Journal,* Apr. 9, 1992, p. 1 (special suppl.: "Technology").

Winslow, R. "Corporate Health Cost Rise Is Called Lowest in 5 Years; Role of HMOs Cited." *Wall Street Journal,* Mar. 2, 1993, p. B1.

Woolhandler, S., and Himmelstein, D. U. "The Deteriorating Administrative Efficiency of the U.S. Health Care System." *New England Journal of Medicine,* 1991, *324,* 1253–1258.

Woolhandler, S., Himmelstein, D. U., and Lewontin, J. P. "Administrative Costs in U.S. Hospitals." *New England Journal of Medicine,* 1993, *329,* 400–403.

Wray, M. P., and Freedlander, J. A. "Detection and Correction of House Staff Error in Physical Diagnosis." *Journal of the American Medical Association,* 1986, *249,* 1035–1037.

Yang, C., and Anderson, S. "The AMA Is Looking a Bit Anemic." *Business Week,* April 12, 1993, pp. 70–72.

Zarling, F., Sexton, H., and Milnor, P., Jr. "Failure to Diagnose Acute Myocardial Infarction," *Journal of the American Medical Association,* 1983, *250,* 1177–1181.

Name Index

Subject Index

373